THE REVOLUTION
STARTS AT HOME
CONFRONTING INTIMATE VIOLENCE WITHIN ACTIVIST COMMUNITIES

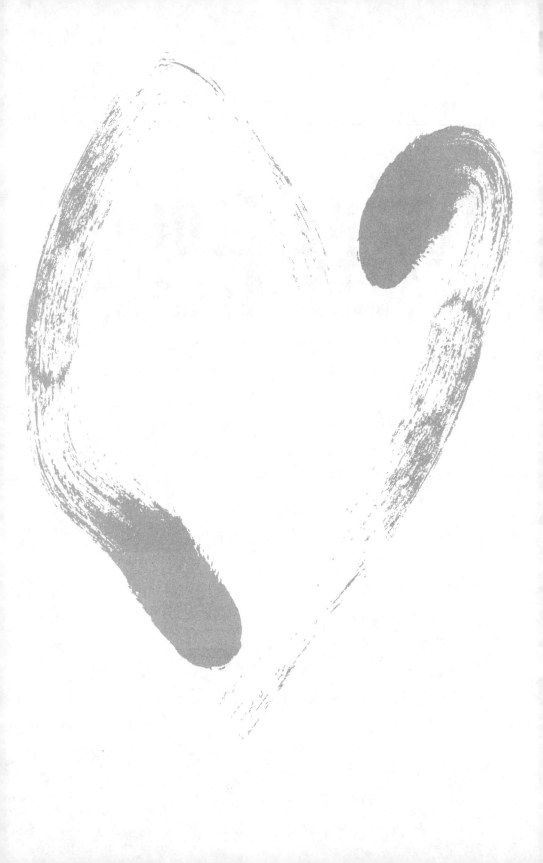

THE REVOLUTION STARTS AT HOME

CONFRONTING INTIMATE VIOLENCE WITHIN ACTIVIST COMMUNITIES

EDITED BY CHING-IN CHEN, JAI DULANI, & LEAH LAKSHMI PIEPZNA-SAMARASINHA

PREFACE BY ANDREA SMITH

The Revolution Starts at Home: Confronting Intimate Violence within Activist Communities

Edited by Ching-In Chen, Jai Dulani, and Leah Lakshmi Piepzna-Samarasinha
Introduction © 2011 Andrea Smith
All essays © 2011 by the individual authors
This edition © 2016 AK Press (Chico, Oakland, Edinburgh, Baltimore)

ISBN: 978-1-84935-262-8
Library of Congress Control Number: 2016941997

AK Press   AK Press
370 Ryan Ave. #100   33 Tower St.
Chico, CA 95973   Edinburgh EH6 7BN
USA   Scotland
www.akpress.org   www.akuk.com
akpress@akpress.org   ak@akedin.demon.co.uk

The above addresses would be delighted to provide you with the latest AK Press distribution catalog, which features books, pamphlets, zines, and stylish apparel published and/or distributed by AK Press. Alternatively, visit our websites for the complete catalog, latest news, and secure ordering.

Cover illustration by Cristy C. Road | croadcore.org
Interior design by Jocelyn Burrell/South End Press Collective
Printed in the USA

This edition is a facsimile reprint of the original published by South End Press (RIP) in 2011.

contents

ix   Preface to the Second Edition

Ching-In Chen, Jai Dulani & Leah Lakshmi Piepzna-Samarasinha

xiii   Preface

Andrea Smith

xix   Introduction

Ching-In Chen, Jai Dulani & Leah Lakshmi Piepzna-Samarasinha

PART ONE

safety at the intersections of intimate, community & state violence

5   Reclaiming Queer & Trans Safety

Morgan Bassichis

25   Ending Oppression. Building Solidarity. Creating Community Solutions.

Meiver De la Cruz & Carol Gomez

MATAHARI: EYE OF THE DAY

57   It Takes Ass to Whip Ass

Understanding & Confronting Violence Against Sex Workers

a roundtable discussion with

Miss Major & Mariko Passion

INTRODUCED & EDITED BY JULIET NOVEMBER

79   I Am Because We Are
Believing Survivors & Facing Down the Barrel of the Gun
Alexis Pauline Gumbs (UBUNTU)
INTERVIEWED BY LEAH LAKSHMI PIEPZNA-SAMARASINHA

PART TWO

on survivorship

93   Homewrecker
Gina de Vries

101   The Secret Joy of Accountability
Self-accountability as a Building Block for Change
Shannon Perez-Darby

115   Seeking Asylum
On Intimate Partner Violence & Disability
Peggy Munson

137   There Is Another Way
Ana-Maurine Lara

PART THREE

(re)claiming body, (re)claiming space

153   Manifesto
Vanessa Huang

155   Without My Consent
Bran Fenner

163   A Sliding Stance
N.

169   when your parents made you
Leah Lakshmi Piepzna-Samarasinha

175   Freedom & Strategy / Trauma & Resistance
Timothy Colm

PART FOUR

we are ready now

189   Beautiful, Difficult, Powerful
Ending Sexual Assault
Through Transformative Justice
The Chrysalis Collective

207   Making Our Stories Matter
The StoryTelling & Organizing Project (STOP)
Rachel Herzing & Isaac Ontiveros

217   What Does It Feel Like
When Change Finally Comes?
Male Supremacy, Accountability & Transformative Justice
Gaurav Jashnani, RJ Maccani & Alan Greig
THE CHALLENGING MALE SUPREMACY PROJECT (CMS)

237   Movement Building Starts with Healthy Relationships
Transforming Silence Into Action (TSIA) in
Asian Pacific Islander LBQT Communities
Orchid Pusey & gita mehrotra

265   Think. Re-think.
Accountable Communities
Connie Burk

RESOURCES

281   Community Accountability Within
People of Color Progressive Movements
Selections from the 2004 Report
by INCITE! Women of Color Against Violence

291   INCITE! Community Accountability Fact Sheet

293   Biographies

303   Acknowledgments

307   Index

Preface to the Second Edition

When this book first came out in 2011, I was convinced that by now we'd have transformative justice centers centering Black and brown queer and trans feminism all over. Reality is more complicated, and real. Since 2011, I've witnessed not the cooptation of transformative justice we feared would happen (because it turns out it's really hard to co-opt practices whose core premise is that the state is bullshit). Instead, some of what I've witnessed worries me just as much: white, anarchist activists erasing the labor of queer women and femmes of color in birthing transformative justice; the erasure of the work of feminists-of-color collectives from the early 2000s—collectives like Generation 5, Creative Interventions, CARA, and Sista2Sista. I've seen people's hearts break and people—particularly queer femmes of color, who I've seen work the hardest on TJ issues—get deeply burnt out from doing some of the most triggering work one can do.

Two or three things I know for sure, and one of them is that the only thing you can count on is the thing you never expected. As a disabled femme of color, I started working on this project over a decade ago in almost total isolation from any sick and disabled queer community. Due to the whiteness of the mainstream disability rights movement and my own internalized ableism, it was part of the reason that only one article in *The Revolution Starts at Home* talked about the intersections of ableism and intimate violence. Today, I feel really lucky to be part of a disability justice movement created and centered by sick, disabled, neurodivergent, Mad, and Deaf Black and brown queer and trans people, where disabled brilliance in surviving and resisting violence is what we talk about all the time. When *The Revolution Starts at Home* began, the term "healing justice" hadn't been invented. Today, I see movements asserting that healing, resilience, and spiritual strategies are not a sideline to the work, they *are* the work. I see altars and herbs bolstering bold actions to create justice, healing justice practice-spaces in the middle of conferences and encampments, spells for grief and amulets to heal trauma. The QTPOC witch revolution is at the core of our brilliance! I see the blossoming of trans women of color creating bold actions and sharing old and new strategies to survive transmisogyny. I see First Nations communities continuing to build on and remix anticolonial strategies to heal harm.

As I re-read this book, I see our mistakes, failures, and gaps, the marginalization of trans women, First Nations people, and sick and disabled people's brilliant strategies for surviving violence. I hold this book as something imperfect that still holds value to examine, critique, use, remix, and build on. I am excited for future volumes, for the blooming of safety teams, for millions of blog posts, community conversations, and toolkits, for everyone who tried a process, even if it was a mess or took a million years, for heartbreak and unexpected healing prayers.

I end with four assertions longtime organizers Shannon Perez-Darby and Kiyomi Fujikawa laid out at a panel held by API Chaya, an Asian/Pacific Islander antiviolence community organization, held to discuss successes, challenges, gaps, and visions for Transformative Justice/Community Accountability, in Seattle on March 13, 2014:

1. We can and must end violence.
2. Healing is possible.
3. Mass incarceration and policing cannot, will not make us safer.
4. This is hard work, but we have the capacity to figure it out.

This work is hard and lifesaving, and we are the exact right ones to do it.

—Leah Lakshmi Piepzna-Samarasinha

Sharing my story a decade ago through the zine that this book was born out of was terrifying. I am grateful for the stories in this book that chipped away at the self-hate that often comes with the act of enduring and surviving. In pain, body and psyche violated, the world of survivors of sexual and intimate partner violence systematically becomes smaller. Being believed and having access to community is absolutely life-saving. At an Audre Lorde Project healing gathering in the aftermath of the Orlando massacre, healer, educator and artist Adaku Utah, said of our society, "We are trained to disassociate." Work that is survivor-centered confronts a community's ability to challenge the various systems of oppression that isolate and disconnect us, to hold layers of ache, grief, betrayal in community. Our collective work of mourning and resistance is a constant demand. I believe our work, now more than ever, is to love and believe ourselves. There is nothing more powerful than sharing our stories for this prayer to manifest. May the values of believing survivors, of being present to and for each other with compassion, continue to be uplifted; may the skills of setting, communicating, and upholding boundaries, safety planning, harm reduction, and confronting harm be widespread; may access to healing be a right we are all entitled to; and may our stories continue to be written, spoken, and shared.

—Jai Dulani

I started working on this project (first zine, then anthology, and then the organizing that followed) because of the scared and stuck seventeen year old I was, jumping from a moving car, trying to escape sexual violence. Years later, the same scared and stuck feeling would often return, especially as I tried to support others who also were trying to escape harm. Returning to *The Revolution Starts at Home*—though a limited and imperfect gathering of voices and strategies—has often felt to me like a late-night strategy salon of my own, where I am surrounded by the brilliance of our communities, not letting me be isolated, holding space open for a collective vision of a future in which we don't have to rely on police or jails to keep ourselves safe and free. I am grateful for the second printing of this book, for those who have asked us for our last remaining copies of the previous printing, for those who will keep writing and telling these stories and sharing new strategies to end intimate partner violence and sexual assault.

—Ching-In Chen

PREFACE

Andrea Smith

The Revolution Starts at Home is an amazing book that signals how much analysis and praxis have changed within the anti-violence movement. Twenty years ago when I first became involved in the movement, even prior to the 1994 passage of the Violence Against Women Act (VAWA), it was almost impossible to question the movement's reliance on the criminal legal system. In fact, it was difficult to even see the anti-violence movement as a movement. Most programs were almost entirely funded by the state. We had become a network of social service providers and legal system advocates. We had become so single-issue oriented that it did not even occur to most anti-violence coalitions to organize against police brutality, anti-immigration legislation, or military violence. Instead, many anti-violence programs support the police state and militarism as solutions to gender violence. The assumption that the criminal legal system was friend to the anti-violence movement went unquestioned. When the few critics there were would ask why we were supporting a system that was increasingly incarcerating poor communities and communities of color, we were silenced before we could even finish our sentences.

Of course there were many organized women of color anti-violence organizations and caucuses. Yet we did not question the larger logics of the anti-violence movement. We strove to provide more inclusive services, but we did not question the actual services themselves. We created bilingual hotlines, "culturally sensitive" training programs, and ethnicity-specific shelter services. But we never asked ourselves if this approach was the best way to end violence against women of color. We organized for inclusion in the anti-violence movement but did not question what we were trying to be included in.

In 1999, Critical Resistance: Beyond the Prison Industrial Complex organized its first conference. Critical Resistance helped popularize the principles of prison abolition. It provided a framework for many of us who had been involved in the anti-violence movement and were skeptical of its reliance on the criminal legal system. We could do more than simply share concerns about criminalization: we now had an analysis of why the prison industrial complex was not the solution to anything, including gender violence. This framework then provided a foundation for the development, in 2000, of INCITE! Women of Color Against Violence. INCITE! aspired to do more than call attention to racism in the anti-violence movement. Instead, it wanted the movement to become a movement. Rather than focus on social services delivery or court advocacy, it posited that gender violence must be understood within larger systems of capitalism, settler colonialism, white supremacy, and heteropatriarchy. Social services are important, but if that is all we work for we are simply enabling people to survive an unjust system. Instead, we actually wanted to change these systems. But to do so, we had to build mass movements of peoples who were no longer willing to live under structures of violence. Our focus would have to be on political mobilization and base-building.

Of course, as this book points out, one of the major contradictions in political mobilization is that we often replicate the same hierarchical systems we claim to be dismantling. Gender violence is as prevalent within progressive movements as it is in society at large. As the editors of this volume remind us, the revolution does indeed start at home. This phrase should not be interpreted as a depoliticized call to focus on personal self-development instead of building movements to dismantle white supremacy, capitalism, and imperialism. Rather, this phrase reminds us that for our movements to be successful they must prefigure the societies we seek to build. In addition, as I have argued elsewhere, movements must dispense with the idea that we can worry about gender violence "after the revolution," because gender violence is a primary strategy for white supremacy, colonialism, and capitalism. Heteropatriarchy is the logic by which all other forms of social hierarchy become naturalized. The same logic underlying the belief that men should dominate women on the basis of biology (a logic that also presupposes a gender binary system) underlies the belief that the elites of a society naturally dominate everyone else. Those who have an interest in dismantling settler colonialism, white supremacy, and capitalism must by necessity have a stake in dismantling heteropatriarchy.

Thus, INCITE! and other organizations with similar philosophies realized that we must develop strategies that address state violence and interpersonal violence simultaneously. In doing so, we realized that we had to question our reliance on the criminal legal system as the solution to ending gender violence, and instead recognize the state as both perpetrator and beneficiary of gender violence. The question then arises: *If the criminal legal system is not the solution, what is?* Unfortunately, many of the alternatives to incarceration that are promoted under the "restorative justice model" have not developed sufficient safety mechanisms for survivors of domestic/sexual violence. "Restorative justice" is an umbrella term that describes a wide range of programs that attempt to address crime from a restorative and reconciliatory rather than punitive framework, such as that of the US criminal legal system, which focuses solely on punishing the perpetrator and removing that person from society through incarceration. Restorative justice attempts to involve all parties (perpetrators, victims, and community members) in determining the appropriate response to a crime in an effort to restore the community to wholeness. These models are often much more successful than punitive justice models. However, the problem with these models in addressing sexual/domestic violence is that they work only when the community unites in holding perpetrators accountable. In cases of sexual and domestic violence, the community often sides with the perpetrator rather than the victim. Thus, developing community-based responses to violence cannot rely on a romanticized notion of "community" that is not sexist, homophobic, or otherwise problematic. We cannot assume that there is even an intact community to begin with. Our political task then becomes to *create* communities of accountability.

What we see in this book is the work of many groups doing precisely that. They do not seek a band-aid, quick fix approach to ending gender violence. Instead they seek to end *structures* of violence. Their models are experimentations in trying to do more than just crisis intervention, and are actually structured around creating the society we would like to live in. Such work is necessarily provisional; the strategies we come up with will have their limitations and will have to change as our social conditions change. Yet they are important because they force us out of a crisis-based reaction mode into a creative space of envisioning new possibilities.

At the same time, these writers remind us that we cannot ignore present-day emergencies as we build new futures. We cannot expect to engage in "pure" strategies untainted by the current system. Thus, it is important to remember that prison abolition as well as community accountability are positive rather than negative projects. The goal is not to tell survivors that they can never call the police or engage the criminal legal system. The question is not whether a survivor should call the police, but rather why we have given survivors no other option but to call the police.

As Native feminists in particular have noted, in creating alternatives to the criminal legal system we necessarily confront the need to create alternatives to the settler-state. If we focus only on community accountability without a larger critique of the state, we risk framing community accountability as simply an add-on to the criminal legal system. Because anti-violence work has focused on advocacy, we have not developed strategies for "due process," leaving that to the state. When our political imaginaries are captured by the state, we can then presume that the state should be left to administer "justice" while communities serve as supplement to this regime, supporting it and the fundamental injustice of a settler state founded on slavery, genocide, and the exploitation of immigrant labor. Further, in so doing we do not allow ourselves to imagine new visions for liberatory nationhood that are not structured on logics of hierarchy, violence, and domination. Fortunately, indigenous peoples are rearticulating conceptions of nationhood and self-determination that are liberatory not only for indigenous peoples but all others as well.

In the end, the "revolution at home" that is needed is indeed a real revolution. It requires a dismantling of capitalism, white supremacy, and the settler state. Community accountability is not a "model program" that can easily be funded through the nonprofit industrial complex because it is a strategy for radical social transformation. It's a long road, but *The Revolution Starts at Home* provides an excellent starting point for developing a movement to end violence in all its forms.

INTRODUCTION

Ching-In Chen, Jai Dulani &
Leah Lakshmi Piepzna-Samarasinha

HOW AND WHY WE CAME TO THIS PROJECT

cbing-in...When I was seventeen years old, I began a relationship with a co-worker at the movie theater where I worked, and my family freaked out—he was a Brazilian immigrant without what they considered a "good job" or "good educational background." For the first time in my life, I lied to my family and snuck out of the house in the middle of the night to meet him. Eventually, my mother told me to sign a contract that I would break off my relationship with him or not be allowed out of the house to go to college, and I signed. I emerged from that experience resolved not to let anyone else control or decide for me whom I was involved with, or what kind of relationship(s) I chose to have. But I also became very protective and stubborn about my intimate relationships. It became hard for me to open up and let others know what was going on in those spaces of my life.

Four years later, after moving to a city where I knew no one and while in another relationship I knew my family wouldn't approve of, I turned my back on my family and friends. We were stressed out about immigration status and making the rent. In the late afternoons and evenings, I canvassed for a rape crisis center with a group of women who were largely rape and sexual assault survivors, and my partner was driving a cab on the night shift.

When our relationship became volatile, I had no one to turn to and no support system. At the time, I didn't feel part of any community. Part of my relationship experience was the feeling of being isolated—no friends, no place to go to outside of our apartment, no organization where I felt I belonged or that knew me and my history.

Years later, when I started building a circle of activists who shared similar commitments to social justice, community had come to mean not having to feel alone and isolated, being hopeful that there were ways to figure out how to feel safe in whatever, whichever ways we needed to be. It meant being able to count on someone outside of myself, which was very hard for me to do. When a friend whom I had met through community work needed to escape from an abusive husband, we worked out a system that she would call me when she was ready and I would drive over and get her out of there. And it worked!

But I soon learned that not everything was that easy or simple or clear cut. A good friend confided in me about her abusive relationship, but wanted me to act to the outside world like nothing was going on, and we were all part of the same organizing collective. I entered into relationships where I didn't know what to do because we were doing this kind of work together. Sometimes my friends hadn't yet figured out what could be helpful, or didn't want to talk about it. Sometimes I felt too far away to be of much use or help, or didn't realize the impact of what I was doing until much later.

This anthology is something that I would have loved, read, found useful throughout my journeys, both in the situations I found myself in and in supporting my loved ones. I hope you find it useful as well.

jai dulani...I come to this project
as a survivor and witness of intimate partner violence in activist
communities
as someone who has gotten it all wrong; misjudged a situation and
participated in someone's exile
as someone who was called out by a chosen family member for crossing a
boundary while drinking
as someone who is just beginning to fully understand and take
responsibility for my healing and the impact of my trauma on other people
as someone who believes in the power of sharing our stories.

Leah...In 1996, I am twenty-one. I am fucking my lover in a field outside a hippie music festival where we've both gotten in for free by staffing
the Anti-Racist Action table. I am falling in love with my mixed-race, queer
of color, survivor, separated-at-birth brother, totally sure that this is the
amazing, transformative relationship I have been waiting for my whole life.
It absolutely was. And it also became a relationship full of long fights that
went nowhere, screaming matches in the street, and choke holds I couldn't
talk about during the meeting of the prison justice newspaper we both
attended the next day.

When this violence happened in our relationship, I didn't ever think about
going to the cops as an option that would keep me safe. My partner was a
queer man of color who had already done time for "resisting arrest" after being beaten by the police. He was stopped every day by a cop who wanted to
make extra sure he had lights and a bell on his bike, who wanted to know
where he was going, who wanted to know if he was selling weed. Organizers
with a prison justice newspaper, involved in people of color anti-police brutality organizations and many other coalitions, our phone stayed connected
even when we didn't pay the bill for months; once, CSIS (Canadian Security
Intelligence Service) agents showed up at our door. When neighbors in our
broke-ass apartment building, tired of our screaming, called the cops on us,
the first thing the police did was ask about my immigration status and my

partner's probation; not what I needed to feel safe. I had no faith that any prison would lift the weight of oppression, trauma, and rage off my lover—who had, incidentally, said that if I sent him to prison, he would take me to the nearest cop shop, shoot as many cops as he could, and kill me and himself, before he let himself be locked up again.

The problem was, we didn't really know what to do instead. I believed, with my whole heart, in the power of human beings to change, in the power of self-transformation. My lover believed in it, too. After he body slammed me into the sidewalk and I ran onto the bus, I told him we would never be lovers again, but we were still, essentially, partnered. He dropped out of the batterer intervention program, saying those men were nothing like him or who he wanted to be. He went to two elders in our community for guidance. But two years later, with no change in the frightening parts of his behavior, I left. A year later, I took a job at a second wave, feminist of color–led anti-violence crisis line. The workers there believed that it was a mistake to think, or even suggest, that abusers could ever change—they just promised they would to keep their partners trapped in the cycle of violence. We knew the cops were terrible, that restraining orders didn't work, that First Nations people, immigrants, and cis and trans people of color who called us were more likely to be harmed than served by the criminal legal system. But what else could we do?

This book is an attempt to answer that question.

why this book? political context—historically & here and now

This book began with our individual stories—stories of surviving relationships that were beautiful and dangerous; of trying to move toward safety, justice, and healing without using the cops or the courts; of bushwhacking our way through alleyways, back roads, starlit fields without maps—and it is our individual stories that remain at this book's core. But our stories are so much bigger than our individual experiences—gathered together, they are the stories of everyone searching for, and finding, fresh-cut ways of keeping ourselves, our fam and our communities safe. As Alisa Bierra, cofounder of Communities

Against Rape and Abuse (CARA) in Seattle, puts it, we go on "epic adventures and conversations into community accountability." And we don't know where or when it will all end. What we *do* know is that the criminal legal system does not help us survive. And we have a fierce commitment to surviving and thriving, to figuring out the nitty-gritty details of how we will liberate ourselves from the violence of prisons and other so-called justice systems, without abandoning anyone who has survived violence.

What we call "community accountability" (some call it transformative justice, others call it as many names as there are people) has existed for as long as we hold collective memory. A simple definition of community accountability: any strategy to address violence, abuse or harm that creates safety, justice, reparations, and healing, without relying on police, prisons, childhood protective services, or any other state systems. Instead of police and prisons, community accountability strategies depend on something both potentially more accessible and more complicated: the communities surrounding the person who was harmed and the person who caused harm.

Many people are also working with the term "transformative justice." The organization generationFIVE defines transformative justice as "an approach to respond to and prevent child sexual abuse and other forms of violence that puts transformation and liberation at the heart of the change. It is an approach that looks at the experiences of both the individuals and communities involved, and the larger social conditions at work; an approach that seeks to integrate both personal and social transformation."[1]

"Restorative justice" is a term that many people might find more familiar. In restorative justice frameworks, those who have been harmed take an active role in addressing that harm and/or violence (whether it be gender violence, petty theft, or assault), and those who have caused harm are expected to take responsibility for their actions, to repair the harm they've done—for example, by apologizing, returning stolen money, or doing community service. The focus is on restoring, as much as possible, the situation to the conditions as they were before the harm. However, critics of restorative justice argue that there are serious limits to restoring the situation to what it was before the harm—what if the situation was shitty in the first place? And, as Native feminist and INCITE! cofounder Andrea Smith has pointed out, restorative justice has often failed women, especially women of color, facing intimate or stranger/state violence:

> For the community to hold somebody accountable they have to actually think that what happened was wrong. So therefore you can't rely on a romanticized notion of community or even assume that community actually exists. For a community-based response to be effective requires a political organizing component to it that actually creates communities that offer accountability.[2]

The Revolution Starts at Home: Confronting Intimate Violence Within Activist Communities is documentation of ongoing, dynamic movement history/ies, histories that even now are evolving and growing, of people struggling over "family business" and various forms of violence while seeking solutions that really create the kind of change that can crack everything open. Spanning past, present, and future, there has been and continues to be conversation and disagreement about what works, and what fails, when we refuse to accept intimate violence as an inevitability and reject its characterization as secondary to "the struggle." In the early stages of our work on this project, we wanted the anthology to document the lessons and stories that grew out of ten years of concentrated work on community accountability. For many of us, a key moment where we saw possibilities of how we might truly transform our communities came in 2000, when radical women of color organized "The Color of Violence: Violence Against Women of Color" conference at University of California, Santa Cruz,[3] to strategize around ending *all* forms of violence against women of color, the institutional and the interpersonal. Out of that first gathering, INCITE! Women of Color Against Violence was formed, and, in 2003, they created "Community Accountability Working Document: Principles/Concerns/Strategies/Models." Offering 70 different strategies that people of color could use to intervene into violence against women and trans people of color without relying on the state, this watershed document frankly addressed many of the concerns and questions we were dreaming on—the importance of not forgetting to center survivor safety and needs while saying "fuck the police"; the allure of, and problems with, public shaming of abusers as a tactic; and, perhaps most difficult of all, our real questions about whether community members who behaved in violent, manipulative ways could really ever transform, and ultimately end, those patterns. INCITE! followed this work, in 2004, with their report "Community Accountability Within People of Color Progressive Movements," spelling out in detail the particular ways perpetrators of harm within people of color movements find to minimize and excuse acts of abuse and violence, and to derail attempts to create justice for those acts of harm.[4] INCITE!'s work has inspired many of us working within feminist of color–led movements and communities to begin thinking through exactly how these "epic adventures" would work, and provided needed tools for the journey.

Across North America, other movement organizations, such as Critical Resistance, Northwest Network, and Sista II Sista, began fumbling steps toward the development of anti-violence projects for creating safety in our communities without using the state, cops, or courts. Early initiatives—like Sista II Sista's Sistas Liberated Ground, Critical Resistance's Harm Free Zone, and Northwest Network's Friends Are Reaching Out—asked delicious questions:[5] *What if we said a section of Bushwick, Brooklyn, was a no-go zone for rape and partner abuse? What if we sat on the stoop, talked to folks on the block where our office was, and began weaving a web of folks who agreed to try something other than calling the police when it came to violence? What if, as queer and trans folks, we reached out to our friends who were in "love jail"—fallen off the face of the earth into a new partner's arms—and made sure we kept our friend fam connections strong, so that when and if the relationship began to tilt into unhealthy/crazy/abusive land, that friend wasn't so isolated and knew their friends had their back?* All over, folks began to sign on to this work: small and big collectives (ones with names like CARA, Philly's Pissed/Philly Stands Up, Kindred, Northwest Network, Creative Interventions, Audre Lorde Project's Safe Outside the System Collective, Community United Against Violence, and generationFIVE—many of whose efforts are documented within this book), as well as individuals and small groups of friends who cared about their loved ones facing violence.

It wasn't easy. No one knew the right answers. We have stumbled, made mistakes, learned from them, gotten back up from our failures and train wrecks. We have every imperfect, deeply needed story in between. But after ten years, some things we know for sure. We dream and breathe and whisper and shout, at a time when the dominant paradigm for dealing with violence in our communities is at a crossroads. Over a decade since INCITE! was founded, feminist of color analyses of violence and how to transform it are everywhere—in movements that were just a glint in our eye. Maybe not as ubiquitous as direct TV or cell phones, but spreading from Philadelphia to Tucson, Oakland to Detroit—study groups, big and small; an entire track of the national Allied Media Conference; the Philly Stands Up People's Movement Assembly at the 2010 United States Social Forum, which filled a huge conference room with approximately 300 people from all over North America—some were new and curious about community accountability, but a majority of the activists had already talked about, thought through, and experimented with community accountability/transformative justice frameworks. A spirit of excited exchange—and transformation—was definitely in the air.

the revolution starts at home: from resource to transformation

In 2003, we began work on a zine with a focus on partner abuse and sexual assault in activist communities that would later become the basis for this anthology. We came together after sharing conversations and strategies in community spaces, struggling with how to do work that confronted these forms of violence that were "dirty little secrets" within our progressive movements and communities.

The vast majority of feminist or self-help literature addressing partner abuse offers few stories that looked and sounded like ours. Importantly, second wave white feminism addressed cisgender men's violence against women as a system of oppression and not as a personal issue. However, paralleling the second wave feminist movement's shortcomings in addressing the realities of women of color, queer women, and gender nonconforming people, these feminist manifestos failed to embrace an intersectional analysis of power that recognizes the multiple and complex identities we each hold in relation to privilege and oppression. Their critiques of gender violence also failed to address the disturbing paradox of prevalent intimate violence within activist communities, and the degree of collusion, refusal, and/or incapacity to address this urgent issue demonstrated even by anti-violence movement "experts." Crucially, this analysis ignored a stark reality: Anyone can choose to abuse; anyone can be abused. In contrast, as feminists of color, we knew that our stories were much more complex—that race, class, gender, ability, sexuality, immigration status, and more contributed to our choices and our relationships. Although we believed in the power of breaking silence that many earlier feminists espoused, the reality of intimate violence within our activist communities was messier and much more complex. For many of us, the exit strategies and options that might be available to white, middle-class feminists usually did not work well for us. We wanted to find a way to stay within our communities and not have to leave. We hoped that the specific truth of our stories would be enough, as famously prophesied by the poet Muriel Rukeyser, to split open the world.[6]

Our original 2003 call for submissions asked for "road maps and concrete stories." We used the word *concrete* over and over again: while we had seen groundbreaking and wonderful ideas, such as the INCITE! community accountability principles, circulating in our communities, we wanted and needed to know how they worked in practice. We wanted stories of how it could be done!

Our original flyer featured two clip-art images—a group of silhouetted protesters on one side and, on the other, an image of two individuals facing each other, signs in hand but isolated from the rest. We had tasted that isolation and choked on it. We wanted to purge it, understand it, trace it back to everyone who saw it and everyone who didn't, and figure out why. So, we asked:

Was your abusive girlfriend's best friend working on the DV hotline? Were you able to successfully kick an abuser out of your group? Were you able to find a solution where accountability didn't mean isolation for either of you? Was your abusive partner a high-profile activist? Did your anti-police brutality group fear retaliation if you went to the cops? Was the "healing circle" a bunch of bullshit? Was the trans community so small that you didn't want you or your partner to lose it? We want to hear about what worked and what didn't, what you learned, what you wish folks had done, what you never want to have happen again. We want to hear about folks' experiences confronting abusers, both by using the cops & courts and by methods outside the criminal justice system.

These were our questions. At no point during the six years that we worked on this project did the Revolution Starts at Home collective members live in the same city. Six years is a long time to communicate over email and conference calls. Each of us going through our own transitions: shifting homes, jobs, relationships; navigating loss, health challenges, and triggers. There was a lot that shook the earth beneath us. But what called us back to each other, time and time again, were our questions. Our hunger for answers, solutions. The sustenance we received from the stories. The stories our friends confessed they were too fearful to write. The stories written but retracted as boundaries and safety were negotiated and renegotiated.

Though we desired this to be a safe and supportive experience, and a useful tool for those who were confronting these situations, this was not always an easy process. We quickly realized that blasting our call for submissions out to listservs was not enough. We were asking folks to reveal truths their bodies remembered yet their communities didn't hold; to unwrap their broken hearts because we believed them and promised we were listening. We worked with writers to make their safety plans and think through "what the book could hold"—how and how much of their stories they could share without jeopardizing their safety. Some writers we love withdrew their stories. Some ex-partners of writers came forward with their own versions of the story told.

As more and more submissions arrived, we struggled through a long distance collective submission review and editing process. We worked to be compassionate toward each other as we juggled multiple commitments, busy lives, and our own healing processes. As Cherríe Moraga writes in the foreword to the second edition of *This Bridge Called My Back: Writings by Radical Women of Color:*

> If we are interested in building a movement that will not constantly be subverted by internal differences, then we must build from the inside out, not the other way around. Coming to terms with the suffering of others has never meant looking away from our own.[7]

When we began this project, just getting the stories was enough for us. But by the time the zine was printed in 2008 and downloaded hundreds of times from the INCITE! website for free, distributed to hungry hands at the tenth-anniversary conference celebrating Critical Resistance (an organization working to abolish the prison industrial complex), cited on numerous websites and blogs, used as a resource for countless groups, reviewed by *Bitch* magazine and *Feminist Review,* and solicited for publication by a certain editor at South End Press, our focus had shifted a bit. We still believed that collecting and distributing the stories was powerful. Copying a huge-ass zine, however, is expensive and time-consuming. So when we received an offer to work on it as a book—with the caveat *Could you expand it, please?*—we knew we also wanted the book to document the past ten years of community accountability work, and invited many of the collectives who have been putting this work into practice to share their stories. This is not at all meant to suggest that organizations are at the end point of their growth in confronting partner abuse. On the contrary, we recognize that many organizations—both funded nonprofits and organizing collectives—have been building, studying, struggling, fucking, and getting better ever since. We wanted to witness and capture that collective work and movement building.

In editing and expanding the original zine for release in book format, five years after our original call for submissions, we realized that a lot had changed. From isolated stories and collectives figuring out how to better put these ideas into practice, the work—and some of the formations created to do the work—had grown, ended, expanded, and been utterly transformed. By the time our zine appeared, some collectives had been working together for close to ten years, while others were just forming, building on the hard-won movement experience of that past decade. The book you hold in your hands still contains first-person stories, but it also contains movement stories—stories of groups sharing what they learned along the way as they built a fragile, yet powerfully strong network.

we are here because you were there

While the concepts "community accountability," "transformative justice," and "restorative justice" have sparked dialogue, organizing, and hope, we know that this work builds on decades of feminist activism in our communities. We realize that the struggles to make our movements for justice safe and our communities free from state violence have long been intertwined. As we study our collective memories and learn from and pass on community knowledge, we can borrow pieces of what has worked and leave behind what hasn't.

In January 2010, the Revolution Starts at Home collective joined Creative Interventions, the Safe Outside the System Collective of the Audre Lorde Project, and the Young Women's Empowerment Project to organize a national gathering of organizations using community-based strategies to address violence. This gathering brought together women of color and lesbian, gay, bisexual, two-spirit, trans, and gender nonconforming (LGBTSTGNC) people of color from around the country. Participants created a timeline documenting key moments in our movement histories that shaped our understanding of, and commitment to, community accountability. Clearly, as we began to see, the work we had gathered to document wasn't limited to the past decade:

— One participant spoke of her elders recalling their memories of the Jim Crow South. Since African American communities could not rely on racist, murderous police, "the big guys" of the community would step up and intervene in domestic violence situations.

— We remembered too the watershed publication of *This Bridge Called My Back: Writings by Radical Women of Color*, edited by Cherríe Moraga and Gloria E. Anzaldúa in the 1980s, which included so many of us within its pages. *This Bridge*'s courageous analysis of intersectional oppression and intramovement marginalization paved the way for this collection. It is poignant to note that the closing sentence of Anzaldúa and Moraga's introduction is, "The revolution begins at home."[8] In addition, we believe it vital that our movements remember and honor the sheer struggle and victory of publishing such fiercely sharp and radical voices. The publisher's note to the second edition (1983) of *This Bridge* states:

> When Persephone Press, Inc., a white women's press of Watertown, Massachusetts, and the original publishers of *Bridge*, ceased operation in the Spring of 1983, this book had already gone out of print. After many months of negotiations, the co-editors were finally able to retrieve control of their book, whereupon Kitchen Table: Women of Color Press of New York agreed to republish it. The following, then, is the second edition of *This Bridge Called My Back*, conceived of and produced entirely by women of color.[9]

— In 1974, the Combahee River Collective, a collective of Black feminists, released the "Combahee River Collective Statement," declaring "we are actively committed to struggling against racial, sexual, heterosexual, and class oppression, and see as our particular task the development of integrated analysis and practice based upon the fact that the major systems of oppression are interlocking. The synthesis of these oppressions creates the conditions of our lives."[10]

— In Jaffna, Sri Lanka, in the late 1970s, Poorani ("the whole woman") House[ll] existed as a transformative shelter for women facing abuse. It operated outside of the state and in defiance of repression by both the Sinhalese government and the Liberation Tigers of Tamil Eelam.

— In revolutionary organizations of color in the US associated with male-centered leadership, such as the Black Panthers and Young Lords, radical visionaries like Elaine Brown and Iris Morales organized from within to center their experiences and challenges to male dominance within the core values of their organizations. For instance, women in the Young Lords Party successfully demanded that the point "Machismo must be revolutionary...not oppressive" be part of the Party's primary governing document, "The 13 Point Program and Platform for the Young Lords Party."

We stand with our ancestors at our back, holding us up.

overview of critical themes & questions

We've organized this book into four sections. The first section, "Safety at the Intersections of Intimate, Community, and State Violence," looks at creating safety while living and organizing at the intersections of intimate and state violence. What happens when your abusive partner is a cop? When you are criminalized on the daily for being a sex worker? What happens when the court doesn't provide translators and your abuser speaks fluent English? What happens when you're pushed out of the labor movement because of rampant sexual assault by a leader? When sexual violence is deemed less important than the organizing campaign?

Morgan Bassichis traces how Community United Against Violence (CUAV) grappled with critical questions of leadership, sustainability, and their relationship to the state as an anti-violence organization transforming from a traditional social services–model to a collective with a membership base. Juliet November interviews three sex worker activists—Stonewall veteran and TGI Justice Project founder Miss Major, artist and activist Mariko

Passion—in a roundtable discussion about what creating safety from intimate violence means for sex workers, who are especially vulnerable to police abuse. Queer Black feminist writer and UBUNTU member Alexis Pauline Gumbs, in an interview with Leah Lakshmi Piepzna-Samarasinha spanning two years, describes UBUNTU's queer, Black, survivor-led work creating safety in Durham, NC—from organizing after the 2006 Duke University rape case to work intervening in partner abuse within their community. Meiver De la Cruz and Carol Gomez explore MataHari's work creating justice and safety within immigrant communities in Boston and beyond, and the complexities of dealing with law enforcement when undocumented.

The second section, "On Survivorship," challenges us to take a hard look at the politics of survival and what it means to our communities. For Gina de Vries, being a homewrecker was the only way she could survive and get out of her abusive queer relationship. Shannon Perez-Darby pushes us to honor the full humanity of the survivor beyond the innocent victim/evil abuser dichotomy, posing this difficult question: *How can survivors take responsibility for the range of choices they make?* Peggy Munson complicates survivorship by revealing how abusive partners are often lifelines for survivors with disabilities because intimate partner violence (IPV) organizations and our larger movement are frequently unable or unwilling, because of structural ableism, to meet or even perceive the needs of survivors with disabilities. Ana-Maurine Lara writes about the "rights and responsibilities" of survivorship, and reminds us what is possible, and what is at stake, when it comes to trauma and healing within activist communities.

The third section, "(Re)claiming Body, (Re)claiming Space," connects individual stories and experiences, and imagines what it would look like for survivors to claim agency and access their own power. Vanessa Huang's poem, "Manifesto," articulates a hope for a home where we can all be liberated. Bran Fenner thinks about consent, reflecting on the importance of establishing and respecting boundaries in an intimate relationship. Timothy Colm, a member of Philly's Pissed, shares how he was able to set boundaries with his abuser and go through a community accountability process with him. N. reveals some of the complex realities involved in using the legal system and going to court with a queer masculine partner. Leah Lakshmi Piepzna-Samarasinha's poem, "when your parents made you," bears witness to her choosing to tell her own story despite threats from her former partner.

The fourth section, "We Are Ready Now," looks at how community can come together to hold perpetrators accountable, taking theory into breathing practice. The Challenging Male Supremacy Project (CMS) shares their process of cisgender men creating accountability circles and what that experience looked like. The Chrysalis Collective holds a perpetrator of sexual violence accountable and walks us through the nitty-gritty details of an actual community accountability process: how to anticipate and prepare for backlash, how to create a culture of trust and respect while holding another activist accountable, how to evaluate process. Orchid Pusey and gita mehrotra of the Transforming Silence Into Action (TSIA) project and Connie Burk of The Northwest Network remind us how imperative it is to look at the values of our process—and how we must learn to understand violence in its context to recognize when unhealthy behavior is a pattern of control and when it is in response to abuse.

"Are you sure, sweetheart, that you want to be well?... Just so's you're sure, sweetheart, and ready to be healed, cause wholeness is no trifling matter. A lot of weight when you're well."
—Toni Cade Bambara, *The Salt Eaters*

"Are you willing to let the work transform you?"
—Adrienne Maree Brown

We are clear that we don't own these ideas, and that they are by no means the only ideas in the world about transformative justice. We want this book to be a community builder, an educational resource, a toolkit, a prayer, and documentation of a collective effort to document where we are with this work.

We dream of how this book—going even further than the zine—is going to be picked up, used, argued with, and transcended. We can't wait to edit *The Revolution Starts at Home: The Next Generation* in ten or twenty years. We can't wait to live and breathe in the world we are going to create.

Toni Cade Bambara's classic work *The Salt Eaters* opens with the healer asking Velma, a Black feminist organizer facing a spiritual and physical crisis due to burnout and betrayal by the movements she's worked for, if she is really sure she wants to be well—and emphasizes that healing is "no trifling matter." These joyful, perilous adventures of transformative justice that we undertake with no map but our breath are also no trifling matter. In embarking on them, we set off on journeys without a map—but knowing that our feminist of color heras, like Harriet Tubman, made the same lifesaving, liberating journeys without maps, guided by our dreams, grassroots genius and longing for liberation. In doing this work, we are doing the radical work of healing—our hearts, our bodies, our families and communities. After abuse and violence, with justice, comes healing. We are making the way, and surrendering to be transformed.

notes

1   From http://www.generationfive.org/tj.php (accessed 1/30/2011).

2   "An Interview with Andrea Smith, author of *Conquest: Sexual Violence and American Indian Genocide,* about the book and her work with INCITE! Women of Color Against Violence and the Boarding School Healing Project." *The Abolitionist.* Date unknown. http://www.criticalresistance.org/radicaldesigns.org/downloads/AndreaSmith.pdf (accessed 9/8/2010).

3   For additional documentation of this groundbreaking conference and subsequent INCITE! conferences, see *Color of Violence: The INCITE! Anthology,* ed. INCITE! Women of Color Against Violence (Cambridge, MA: South End Press, 2006).

4   See the Resources section of this book for selections from "Community Accountability Within People of Color Progressive Movements: Report from INCITE! Women of Color Against Violence," Ad-Hoc Community Accountability Working

Group Meeting (February 7-8, 2004, Seattle, WA). Sponsored by INCITE! Women of Color Against Violence, co-sponsored by Communities Against Rape and Abuse (CARA). Also available in its entirety at http://www.incite-national.org/media/docs/2406_cmty-acc-poc.pdf. For more information about Sista II Sista's decision to deincorporate and return to a grassroots, membership-based structure, see Nicole Burrowes, Morgan Cousins, Paula X. Rojas, and Ije Ude, "On Our Own Terms: Ten Years of Radical Community Building with Sista II Sista," in *The Revolution Will Not Be Funded: Beyond the Non-Profit Industrial Complex,* ed. INCITE! Women of Color Against Violence (Cambridge, MA: South End Press, 2007).

5   For more information about these projects, see http://www.criticalresistance.org, http://www.sistaIIsista.org, and http://www.nwnw.org.

6   Muriel Rukeyser, "Käthe Kollwitz," in *Out of Silence: Selected Poems,* ed. Kate Daniels (Evanston, IL: TriQuarterly Books, 1992), 129.

7   Cherríe Moraga, "Refugees of a World on Fire: Foreword to the Second Edition," in *This Bridge Called My Back: Writings by Radical Women of Color,* eds. Cherríe Moraga and Gloria E. Anzaldúa (New York: Kitchen Table: Women of Color Press, 1983), unnumbered folio.

8   "Introduction," in *This Bridge Called My Back,* xxvi.

9   Sadly, *This Bridge* is no longer in print. For more information about the evolving publishing history of this cornerstone feminist document: http://en.wikipedia.org/wiki/This_Bridge_Called_My_Back.

10 "The Combahee River Collective Statement," in *Home Girls: A Black Feminist Anthology,* ed. Barbara Smith (New York: Kitchen Table: Women of Color Press, 1983).

11 Nimanthi Perera-Rajasingham, "Poorani: A Women's Shelter in Jaffna," *The Sunday Leader* (9/20/2009), http://www.thesundayleader.lk/archive/20090920/review.htm.

I am not proposing that sexual violence and domestic violence will no longer exist. I am proposing that we create a world where so many people are walking around with the skills and knowledge to support one another that there is no longer the need for anonymous hotlines.

I am proposing that we break through the shame of survivors (a result of rape culture) and the victim-blaming ideology shared by all of us (also a result of rape culture) so that survivors can gain support from the people already in their lives. I am proposing that we create a society where community members care enough to hold an abuser accountable so that a survivor does not have to flee their home. I am proposing that all of the folks that have been disappointed by systems work together to create alternative systems.

I am proposing that we organize.

—REBECCA FARR
COMMUNITIES AGAINST RAPE AND ABUSE (CARA)

the revolution starts at home

part one

safety at the intersections of intimate,
community & state violence

RECLAIMING QUEER & TRANS SAFETY

Morgan Bassichis

On October 29, 2009, President Obama signed into law the first-ever gender identity and sexual orientation-inclusive federal hate crimes bill.[1] Just a few weeks later, two young queer people of color were brutally murdered—Jorge Steven Lopez Mercado in Cayey, Puerto Rico, and Jason Mattison, Jr. in Baltimore, Maryland. On December 8, 2009, two groups of mostly young transgender and queer people of color gathered in Brooklyn and San Francisco to mark both the federal policy and the murders as profound losses.[2] The Audre Lorde Project's Safe OUTside the System (SOS) Collective—an LGBTSTGNC (lesbian, gay, bisexual, Two Spirit, transgender, gender nonconforming) people of color organizing project working to end police and hate violence in Central Brooklyn—and Community United Against Violence (CUAV)—a 30-year-old LGBTQQ (lesbian, gay, bisexual, transgender, queer, questioning) anti-violence organization working to create safety in the San Francisco Bay Area—teamed up to convene a series of public conversations under the banner "Reclaiming Safety" to voice dissent against the idea that more policing, imprisonment, and prosecution will solve the devastating rates of murder and violence in our communities. We gathered out of a belief that safety comes through stronger relationships, more healing, and increased support, not more prisoners or police or longer prison sentences. We did not want deaths in our communities to be used as a call for more violence. We feared and suspected this would be the case in the deaths of both Mercado and Mattison, whose respective home communities of Puerto Rico and Baltimore are already primary targets of criminalization and persecution by the US government.

On the San Francisco side, CUAV launched our first "Safety Lab," a project where people come together to imagine and practice grounded community responses to violence that do not rely on the prison industrial complex (PIC) or its tactics of shame, punishment, and isolation. In this first Lab, participants developed creative responses to murder such as using art to reclaim public space, involving parents of people who have been murdered, engaging in compassionate, direct conversation with people who have been harmful, and creating a rapid-response violence prevention network among friends. On the Brooklyn side, SOS convened activists, attorneys, and community members to discuss how "victims' rights" rhetoric and hate crimes legislation have strengthened prison and police systems, and the need for community-based approaches to violence.

For CUAV, those early December conversations were the culmination of two-and-a-half years of brewing organizational change from being a traditional progressive social service agency toward being a radical membership-based organization working to transform both incidences of violence and the political, economic, and social conditions that create violence. This journey was made possible by the sustained struggles for PIC abolition and radical anti-violence organizations—such as Critical Resistance, generation-FIVE, and INCITE! Women of Color Against Violence, among others—who have worked for more than a decade to reveal criminalization as an ineffective, false, and violent "solution" to interpersonal violence, and to emphasize the need for transformative community approaches to harm. "Reclaiming Safety" was a powerful example of above-ground dissent at a time when many considered a pro-prison bill to be an LGBT victory, despite the increased captivity and policing it would mean for poor people of color, including poor LGBT people of color. The gathering gave voice to the often marginalized and underground efforts of those of us who are not represented by the dominant LGBT national political agenda—particularly queer and trans people of color, and poor people from these communities—and know all too well the devastating impact of "law and order" policies used to address interpersonal violence.[3] Given the escalating US-backed wars and military interventions in Afghanistan, the US Gulf Coast, Haiti, Iraq, Palestine, and elsewhere being waged in the name of "aid" and "security," the exploding number of people behind bars in the name of "safety" and "justice," and the continued ecological and economic exploitation of our communities in the name of "development," the need for alternative visions of safety and sustainability couldn't be more urgent. "Reclaiming Safety" was a small but important step in that long process.

telling stories

How do you tell a story that is still unfolding? How do you tell a story that feels both premature and long overdue? Everyday, queer and trans people are terrorized by violence, traumatized by abuse, and betrayed by those meant to protect us. And everyday we survive and tell each other stories of our struggles for love and justice. Stories are important. They help us make sense of who we are, where we come from, and where we are going. They can also hinder us in doing so. For instance, the story that "LGBT safety" will come through increased prosecution and criminalization is not a new one—it comes out of a much older story that says (implicitly white, middle and owning class) safety will come when "dangerous" (implicitly black, brown, and poor) people are disappeared by death or detention. This is the story that the United States is founded on, and it has been used by European imperialists, enslavers, border patrol, law enforcement, prison guards, corporate executives, political leaders, media conglomerates, and religious institutions, among others, to justify unthinkable levels of violence—from the displacement and physical and cultural genocide of Native peoples and the enslavement of African peoples, to the exploitation of working-class people and the lockdown of communities of color and poor communities in prisons, jails, juvenile detention facilities, and detention centers, to the sexual and reproductive attacks on women and transgender people of color, to the mass detention and deportation of Arab, African, Caribbean, Asian, and Latin@ immigrants—and to seduce marginalized people such as white people who are Jewish, queer, women, and/or working class into complicity with oppression.[4] It is a pervasive story passed down through families, culture, and institutions, with painful consequences on our ability to create liberating communities and movements.

But this is not the only story. History is filled with the powerful stories of people on all sides of oppression unwilling to sell each other out, people committed to a vision of a just, safe world for everyone. This essay about CUAV's journey is meant to lift up these diverse and infinite stories of resistance typically crowded out by state-sanctioned stories—often parading as "common sense" or "truth"—backed up by a long history of media, financial, and military might. In an era when the national LGBT agenda is focused on privatization, criminalization, and militarization—epitomized by the priorities of marriage, hate crimes legislation, and military inclusion—and the PIC is increasingly proclaiming itself as a bastion of LGBT rights (e.g., police marching in Pride parades, LGBT-focused district attorney units, transgender-specific correctional policy), there is a growing chorus of queer and trans voices refusing to accept the state's violent distortions of "safety," "security," and "democracy."

In what follows I attempt to share more of CUAV's story—even as it is very much still being written—in the hope that it can support individuals, organizations, and networks organizing at the intersections of intimate, community, and state violence. I begin with brief highlights from CUAV's history to draw out some key forces and moments that have shaped the organization's path. In the next section, I outline the specific steps that the organization has taken during its transformation process. The final sections lay out the concrete activities the organization has put into motion to accomplish its renewed vision and strategy, as well as the political and practical questions with which it continues to grapple. Ultimately, this essay is an invitation to amplify and engage with the underground stories of resistance that are helping to expand what is possible in our moment in history.

complicated rebellions

CUAV was founded in 1979 during a period of powerful and interconnected movements for liberation from imperialism, white supremacy, patriarchy, heterosexism, and capitalism in the US and around the world, alongside devastating government backlash.[5] A decade after the Compton's Cafeteria Riot in San Francisco's Tenderloin district and the Stonewall Rebellions in New York City's West Village, the 1978 assassination of beloved San Francisco Supervisor Harvey Milk and the ensuing police raids on the Castro sparked the legendary White Night Riots, a powerful demonstration of LGBT refusal to accept the status quo of violence from both police and the larger public. Protesters were outraged at both long-standing patterns of police attacks on their community as well as the reduced manslaughter charges brought against Milk's killer, Dan White, and fought back by taking to the streets, torching police cars, and defending themselves against police pushback. A complex melding of forces and politics, the Riots (and the future struggles that emerged) advanced a core question that haunts CUAV and the rest of the LGBT anti-violence movement to this day: Is the state primarily a perpetrator of violence against our communities, or the protector it claims to be?

As a visible political force in the Castro, modeled after earlier community organizing against rape and sexual assault, CUAV's first few years were focused on peer support for violence survivors (first anti-queer violence, and later intimate violence), distributing whistles, and raising awareness about queer people's lives in schools through its Speakers Bureau. In the decade that followed, CUAV adopted the dominant social service approach to violence prevention and response, including a focus on promoting cultural competence in schools and criminal legal institutions. During this period, CUAV became an original member of the National Coalition of Anti-Violence Programs, which would help shape national conversation and strategy in a growing gay and lesbian anti-violence movement.

The 1990s brought a renewed culture of resistance to the Bay Area through campaigns against neoliberal globalization, prison and police expansion, racist educational politics, and widespread displacement resulting from the first "dot-com" boom. This growing radicalization among social justice activists and organizations created the context for a number of critical departures in CUAV's history. CUAV staff of color and white allies made strategic internal demands to strengthen racial justice practices within the organization and increase accessibility for LGBT people of color in the work, including the adoption of the organization's first anti-oppression framework. A growing progressive impulse within the organization and relocation to new offices close to the Tenderloin and Mission (home, at that time, to more poor and working-class people, immigrants, people of color, and transgender people than the Castro) supported this shift. In 1998, CUAV partnered with the Ella Baker Center for Human Rights to launch TransAction, a groundbreaking organizing project to expose and resist widespread police abuse of transgender and gender nonconforming people, specifically low-income transgender women of color.[6] These efforts challenged traditional (and narrow) conceptions of "anti-gay violence," and helped to expose the state as a violent force in the lives of many, including LGBT, communities—a major departure from dominant gay and lesbian anti-violence agendas that relied on the state's definition of both the problem and the solution, and subsequently focused their organizing work on activities that increased state and police powers, such as sentence-enhancing hate crimes legislation.[7]

Throughout CUAV's history, the larger context shaping its evolution has been, on the one hand, a mounting, multi-decade effort on the part of the US government to criminalize communities of color while gutting an already faltering welfare state, and, on the other, a long-term attempt to dismantle and co-opt radical and revolutionary movements for justice. To aid the first strategy, the federal War on Drugs funneled unprecedented numbers of poor and Black people (particularly poor Black women) and other poor people of color into the country's rapidly expanding PIC. Domestic imprisonment, policing, and surveillance were offered by the federal government as economic and political solutions to growing unemployment, urban divestment, rural deindustrialization, and as complements to US military intervention in the Middle East and elsewhere. The subsequent War on Terror has expanded the focus of this criminalizing project within the US with the profiling and detaining of Arab and Muslim people, and the authorization of mass detentions and deportations of Latin@ people. Importantly, all of these expansions of the prison-police state have been done in the name of "public safety" or "homeland security," and have been accompanied by means of media propaganda fanning the flames of an anti-black, anti-brown, and anti-poor culture of fear.

Meanwhile, the attempted obliteration of radical and revolutionary movements by the US government (through tactics such as imprisonment, infiltration, and assassination exemplified by the FBI's COINTELPRO) and the broader global ascent of neoliberalism and its promotion of "individual rights" and "free-market democracy" over deep social change facilitated the rise of the nonprofit model as the dominant vehicle for large-scale social change work. This trend contributed to a growing conservatism among many parts of previously progressive and Left social movements, and has been particularly evident in the most well-resourced arms of the mainstream national LGBT movement, which has prioritized reformist demands and strategies that strengthen, rather than undermine, the reigning systems of profit, privatization, and punishment.[8] This neoliberal LGBT agenda emerged from multiple, intersecting, often oppositional political forces, including: right-wing culture wars, the promotion of the "gay market" as a sizable consumer bloc, hard-fought struggles by frontline activists committed to LGBT liberation, the production of the "good white gay and lesbian" as an acceptable figure for white and middle-class America, and, importantly, the accumulated trauma of communities that have been devastated by HIV/AIDS, demonized by community and family, and excluded from basic safety nets time and again.

At the same time, these conditions of escalating co-optation and targeting coexisted with (and likely helped ignite) an unparalleled surge of radical resistance among queer and trans communities of color and white anti-racist queer and trans communities. Organizations and collectives have flourished throughout the US and around the world, signaling a resurgence of racial and economic justice-focused queer politics articulating intersectional, visionary agendas at the crossroads of personal and collective liberation.[9] Looking back at this ongoing history through the lens of CUAV's story, it is clear that our communities and movements have suffered many losses, enjoyed multiple victories, and now face critical opportunities ahead.

shaping a new approach

This basic contradiction between who the state is set up to protect and who it is set up to harm forms the backdrop for CUAV's most recent phase of organizational transformation. CUAV staff and board gathered in May 2007 in San Francisco's historic Women's Building to begin a process of strategic planning out of a shared recognition that the organization lacked effectiveness and cohesion.[10] The generally agreed-upon goal of the process was organizational improvement, not transformation. Aided by an outside facilitator, we mapped the organization's history and evolving approach, articulated a broad, guiding, shared vision for a just world based on mutuality and safety, and plotted next steps of what we believed would be a contained project of organizational evaluation and updating. Little did we know that the process would lead—and perhaps require—us to "fall apart," to reconsider some of the most basic assumptions underlying our work and our roles in it.

Over the next year we attempted to proceed with the strategic planning process we had mapped out. Despite immense individual commitment, our efforts were impeded by political tensions and a profound lack of strategic unity (common to the anti-violence movement more broadly). Were we striving for organizational change or transformation? How deeply did we need to go? What basic level of shared analysis and approach did we need along the way? How could we engage in a deep reflection process while continuing to uphold our programmatic and funding commitments? We had no road-map, and few examples of community organizations available to us that had successfully transitioned and transformed from a social service model after nearly three decades.

To help us engage together in the process, we organized a week-long, externally facilitated retreat which did illuminate some shared ground. First, we created our first-ever collective decision-making tool, with five "gradients of agreement": the number one indicated enthusiastic endorsement; two, endorsement with some concerns; three, a neutral stance; four, support with significant concerns; and five, a block. A proposal would pass if 75 percent of staff voted a one or two, and no one voted below a three. Second, we realized we had never officially defined our constituency. LGBTIQQ communities are extremely broad and diverse (and in the Bay Area, large), encompassing hugely divergent needs. We committed to ensuring that those who face multiple forms of violence and those with the fewest institutional resources be at the center of our work, particularly LGBTIQQ people who are people of color, low-income, young, and/or immigrants. Holding the most targeted and vulnerable people at the center of our work and analysis would give us the greatest chance to transform the root causes of violence and oppression, not simply their symptoms. Third, we generated a broad brainstorm of various strategies we believed could reduce violence, including cultural work, healing, education, and organizing.

Although this work helped generate several important strategies, it also revealed the lack of a shared long-term strategy to end violence. Using the "gradients of agreement" decision-making tool, participatory facilitation strategies, and some growing shared commitment, we moved forward with our next goal, one of deepening our political unity as a basis for developing a programmatic vision. After years of working around issues of violence in our communities, we returned to some very basic and still unanswered questions: What is the concrete relationship between institutional oppression and interpersonal violence? Why do people hurt one another? How can we simultaneously reduce and end incidents of interpersonal violence while confronting and eliminating institutional oppression? We agreed that capitalism, white supremacy, heteropatriarchy, and other systems of oppression promote having power over one another, and that those systems have hidden and discredited ways of dealing with harm and healing from trauma long practiced by communities, particularly communities of color. We also agreed that ensuring that people's basic survival needs are met (such as housing, health care, and employment, among others) would greatly reduce incidents of violence. And while we agreed that harm is an unavoidable reality among human beings, we recognized that what we do to prevent and respond to harm contains the immense power and promise of creative transformation. Lastly, we recognized that state systems set up to address violence in fact exacerbate violence by traumatizing people who have been harmed, people who have been harmful, and their communities, and by extracting vital resources that could otherwise strengthen communities.

Guided by this analysis, we developed a strategy for creating viable alternatives to state intervention by creating, practicing, and popularizing social justice-guided, community-based approaches to intimate, community, and state violence. We developed a renewed mission "to build the power of LGBTQQ communities to transform violence into safety"—one based on an affirmative vision of the world we long for. Prompted by the devastating cycles of violence in our communities that entrap so many of us into abuse, prisons, poverty, and isolation, we envisioned building "cycles of safety, power, and liberation" that could expand our collective capacity to transform greater and greater levels of violence over time. We knew we had to start small, but that the possibility for powerful, resilient communities was profound. To carry out our mission, we established three core strategies: supporting the wellness of individuals experiencing violence through peer support and healing; developing the leadership of survivors and our allies to create a vibrant culture of safety and liberation; and organizing our communities into campaigns and alliances that challenge and transform power relations, including how resources and decision-making are distributed. In our view, these long-term strategies could transcend the false division drawn between "individual work" (associated with one-on-one healing and transformation) and "conditions work" (associated with organizing and movement-building) within social justice movements. Although we did not have all the necessary tools or details yet to do so, we knew that transforming society, our communities, and ourselves go hand in hand. Recognizing this, we realized that our own organizational structure and culture must embody the values we desired for our communities, including shared leadership and sustainability. To accomplish this, we agreed to transition into a collective leadership structure and committed to deeply integrating sustainability practices throughout our work—decisions we hoped could challenge both widespread oppressive power dynamics and burn-out culture common to nearly all community organizations, including our own.

During this time, a dramatic economic downturn in both California and the broader US (a crisis with global implications) resulted in significant cuts in government funding to the nonprofit sector (while funding for prisons and police continued to rise). CUAV's funding, for instance, was cut nearly in half. Dominance by the marriage equality debates and anti-Proposition 8 (the statewide ban on gay marriage) organizing in national media and on the priority lists of many powerful LGBT and LGBT-friendly foundations and individual donors created additional challenges: more and more resources were being concentrated in larger, legal equality–focused organizations, and drained from smaller social justice organizations. This rapid downsizing from a $1 million annual budget to a $500,000 annual budget forced us to reduce our staff from 12 to 6 through a grueling internal process. The significant turnover in staff presented both challenges—including potential loss of confidence from organizational allies and funders—as well as opportunities to deeply shift our organizational activities and underlying assumptions.

Rebounding from these dramatic shifts, we engaged a number of community and movement stakeholders—peer organizations with significant experience in anti-violence, community organizing, and membership-driven work—to give us feedback on our current work. Specifically, we asked them (through oral interviews and written surveys) what, in their view, were the key needs and organizing opportunities in our communities. This process of "stakeholder engagement" was significant, given our long-term insulation from organizational and movement allies, and even our own constituents—a convention that we inherited from the larger anti-domestic violence movement, which has largely and understandably, although not without costs, prioritized confidentiality over community engagement.[11] While often challenging, through this process CUAV was able to move toward clearer lines of communication and deeper relationships with allies beyond the organization.

After integrating suggestions and feedback from external stakeholders into our vision and strategy plan, we presented the results to them for another round of feedback in February 2009 at a gathering in the Women's Building, nearly two years after our first meeting there. We culminated this intensive process and released our strategic plan at our thirtieth anniversary celebration in March 2009. A powerful example of one organization navigating the intersection of government-induced crisis, accumulated community trauma, and fomenting political possibility, CUAV closed out the first decade of the new century more undone and more determined than ever.

building queer and trans power to create safety

At the writing of this essay, CUAV is completing implementation of the first year of our new strategic plan—a relatively short time given our long history, and also a period of significant and deep growth. Below are some of the strides forward that we have taken during this period of organizational transition and transformation.

1. **LIBERATION IS A COLLECTIVE PROCESS!**[12] To embody our values of mutuality and shared power, we shifted into a non-hierarchical collective staff structure with six full-time staff members delegated to various programmatic, development, operations, and organizational development

responsibilities paid on a flat salary structure. This was a significant departure from our previous traditional hierarchy, common among most LGBT and anti-violence nonprofits.

2. **I'VE GOT YOUR BACK!** We began developing and piloting a "Support & Accountability" structure in which each staff member works with a staff buddy to set and reach their personal, political, and professional development goals and to ensure the successful implementation of their work plans. This buddy system is supported by two rotating Support & Accountability coordinators, who also coordinate our biannual planning and evaluation staff retreats.

3. **MANY STRUGGLES, ONE MOVEMENT!** To help build a strong LGBTQ voice in the movement to abolish state violence and win racial, economic, and social justice, we deepened our participation in key local and national alliances, specifically with the San Francisco Immigrant Rights Coalition, StoryTelling & Organizing Project (STOP), Transforming Justice Coalition, and Bay Area Transformative Justice Collaborative.

4. **WE ARE (STILL) HERE TO RECRUIT YOU!** We began building CUAV's base through our first new member orientation in September 2009, training members in a core set of skills and frameworks for responding to, healing from, and preventing violence. Our members are predominately queer and trans people of color and young people. We are currently evolving our membership structure and developing workgroups to create effective ways for members to take leadership and ownership of CUAV's wellness, cultural, and organizing efforts. Our new member orientation included: CUAV's vision and strategy; practice in key peer support skills such as active listening, healthy boundaries, and direct communication; sharing our stories of survival and resilience; analyzing the connections among hate violence, intimate violence, state violence, and structural oppression; understanding the PIC and the critical need for scalable and transformative alternative models of addressing violence; assessing relationship dynamics and patterns; and practicing non-shaming, non-minimizing responses to harm.

5. **PRACTICE MAKES FABULOUS!** There is little space for our communities

to both imagine and practice non–law-enforcement-driven responses to violence. The PIC teaches us that we do not have the tools or intelligence to deal with violence ourselves. And unfortunately we are often dealing with so much crisis that we don't have time to reflect on our habitual responses. This is why we created our Safety Labs series, to imagine and practice community-based, non-PIC responses to violence. We have held a number of Safety Labs in conjunction with ally organizations as opportunities to "build our muscle" in grounded, non-shaming strategies for addressing harm. Each Safety Lab begins with a review of the common (often experienced as automatic, or "knee-jerk") reactions to challenging or harmful situations: minimization on one end (which can look like denial, silence, victim-blaming), and retaliation on the other (which can look like punishment, isolation, shaming, vigilantism). We talk about how these are often survival strategies that can take care of us in the moment, but have long-term costs (such as damaged relationships, further harm, unchallenged community norms). We then discuss the "middle path," that centered, grounded place we can call accountability, which is a practice of taking responsibility for our actions. Participants then use scenarios from their lives to practice each response, feeling in their bodies the difference between a shaming and non-shaming way of relating to others who have harmed us or whom we have harmed.

6. **YOU'RE QUEER, WE'RE (STILL) HERE!** Because of the high rates of intimate, community, and state violence that LGBTQ people face and the barriers that violence can create to our full participation in social movements, we have maintained our commitment to providing life-affirming support to individuals impacted by violence. This has included creating opportunities for participants to transition into members, and for members to get support as participants, as well as for bringing friends and family into the support process when called for by survivors.

7. **CULTURE IS A WEAPON!** Art is a big part of queer culture, political movements, and community healing. We've drawn on the power of creativity to ignite change by teaming up with a local printmaking collective to

train CUAV's youth members in political printmaking and by launching our first annual festival, Safetyfest. Our inaugural Safetyfest was a ten-day free celebration of queer and trans power with creative skill-shares in everything from erotic writing to healthy boundaries, film screenings, and more. The idea behind these projects is to reclaim public messages about "safety" and infuse them with values of collective liberation and self-determination.

8. **WE ARE OUR OWN SAFETY NET!** In the context of escalating budget cuts and a widely-felt economic crunch, it's clear that we need to build a strong grassroots donor base that can keep our work advancing for the long haul. A grassroots funding base also helps us remain accountable to our constituents, rather than to changing government and foundation agendas. This shift in our funding strategy has included a significant push for monthly donors (ranging from $5–$100 per month), increased cultivation of volunteers, members, staff, and board members as both donors and fundraisers, and a deeper focus on creatively integrating fundraising with our programmatic work.

loving our enemies

As one might expect, each step forward helps us to unravel significant practical and political questions in our effort to transition CUAV from social services provider to power-building organization, and more broadly in our shared journey from PIC–dependence to collective self-determination. While seeking answers to these questions, CUAV has continued to navigate the tenuous complexities and contradictions of government and foundation funding, and, more broadly, of the nonprofit structure. We still have much to learn as we pursue our goal of supporting personal transformation along-side collective transformation: How can organizations such as CUAV help advance a liberatory approach to ending violence? How can we simultaneously address the urgent need for healing in our communities and the need for confronting the systemic conditions that create violence? How can we effectively push back on the state systems of punishment and violence given their scale and speed? How will we negotiate backlash and painful mistakes that will challenge our credibility and capacity? How can we practice deeply the values of sustainability and accountability organizationally that we are working toward in our communities?

And, importantly, our movements are still in the early stages of building the relationships, skills, principles, practices, and infrastructure—the capacity—necessary to transform how our communities deal with violence. We still have a long way to go to both popularize the notion that our communities will be better off without the police and to build responsible alternatives that will make the state's monopoly on responding to violence obsolete. Because of how deeply we have embodied the police-prison state in how we are with one another and with ourselves (even when there are no police around!), we must ask ourselves: How can we ensure that our notions of community safety, accountability, and justice are not misused as justifications for shame, exile, or punishment (as they are by the current system)? How can we practice challenging violence without replicating state power, the PIC, or the many forms of oppression and abuse we are working so hard to eliminate? What internal accountability do we need to cultivate for community accountability to be authentically transformative rather than retributive?[13]

In his 1957 sermon, "Loving Your Enemies," written while in jail following the Montgomery Bus Boycott, Martin Luther King, Jr. spoke to the task ahead of us: "Have we not come to such an impasse in the modern world that we must love our enemies—or else? The chain reaction of evil—hate begetting hate, wars producing more wars—must be broken, or else we shall be plunged into the dark abyss of annihilation."[14] King's proposition is a deep one that requires us to consider how the very systems we are working to dismantle live inside of us. What stories and practices would we need to give up to love and grieve that deeply? Which ones would we need to learn, or remember? One among millions, CUAV's story is about everyday people reclaiming safety. We share our stories with a groundswell of hope, knowing that true liberation comes when we embrace the parts of ourselves that have been broken.

notes

This essay is dedicated to CUAV staff members during this transformative and windy time in our history: Connie Champagne, Tamara Costa, Tina D'Elia, Pablo Espinoza, Prentis Hemphill, Javy Luu, Liu Hoi-Man, Magdalene Martinez, M. Carolina Morales, Jovida Ross, Yaya Ruiz, Alex Safron, Oscar Trujillo, Vanissar Tarakali, Stacy Umezu, and Shawna Virago, as well as the many board members and volunteers who supported and stuck with us along the way, particularly Blyth Barnow, Celeste Chan, Tara Flanagan, Liz Haas, Nick Hodges, Mariah Sparks, Ardel Thomas, Janet Upadhe, and Fresh! White. Deep appreciation to Tamara Costa, Ejeris Dixon, Christina Hanhardt, Vanessa Huang, Alex Lee, M. Carolina Morales, Dean Spade, Mari Spira, Emily Thuma, and Stacy Umezu for their invaluable feedback on this essay and comradeship along the way, and to our numerous allies—particularly everyone at the Audre Lorde Project/SOS Collective, Creative Interventions, Critical Resistance, generationFIVE, Generative Somatics, POWER, Sylvia Rivera Law Project, and TGI Justice Project—for providing leadership on the path that CUAV is traveling. Gratitude to Leah Lakshmi Piepzna-Samarasinha and Jocelyn Burrell for their generous and sharp editorial support.

1   The Matthew Shepard and James Byrd, Jr. Hate Crimes Prevention Act was passed by Congress on October 22, 2009, and signed into law by President Barack Obama on October 28, 2009, as a rider to the National Defense Authorization Act for 2010 (H.R. 2647). This measure expands the 1969 US federal hate-crime law to include crimes motivated by a victim's actual or perceived gender, sexual orientation, gender identity, or disability, and allocates significant financial and institutional resources to federal and local law enforcement in the investigation and prosecution of hate-motivated incidents.

2   Community vigils in Oakland, New York, and other cities were held on November 23, 2009, to commemorate both deaths and support noncriminalizing solutions to anti-LGBTQ violence.

3   For in-depth looks at state targeting of low-income queer and trans people of color, particularly low-income transgender women of color, see Amnesty International's 2005 report, "Stonewalled: Police Abuse and Misconduct Against Lesbian, Gay, Bisexual and Transgender People in the US," and the Sylvia Rivera

Law Project's 2007 report "'It's War in Here': A Report on the Treatment of Transgender and Intersex People in New York State Men's Prisons," http://srlp.org/files/warinhere.pdf. Also see the following anthologies: Joey L. Mogul, Andrea J. Ritchie, and Kay Whitlock, eds., *Queer (In)Justice: The Criminalization of LGBT People in the United States* (Boston, MA: Beacon Press, 2011), and Nat Smith and Eric Stanley, eds., *Captive Genders: Trans Embodiment and the Prison Industrial Complex,* (Oakland, CA: AK Press, forthcoming).

4   For an expanded discussion on the seductions offered by US empire to "wedge" populations, see Anna Agathangelou, Morgan Bassichis, and Tamara Spira, "Intimate Investments: Homonormativity, Global Lockdown, and the Seductions of Empire," *Radical History Review,* Issue 100 (2008).

5   See Christina Hanhardt, "Butterflies, Whistles, and Fists: Gay Safe Streets Patrols and the New Gay Ghetto, 1976-1981," *Radical History Review,* Issue 100 (2008) for a look at the political and economic context in which CUAV was born.

6   During this time CUAV documented that over 50 percent of reported verbal and physical hate incidents against transgender women were committed at the hands of the San Francisco Police Department ("Walking While Trans," on file with author).

7   Other organizations, like The Northwest Network of Bi, Trans, Lesbian and Gay Survivors of Abuse in Seattle and The Network/La Red in Boston, were also using more liberation-guided anti-violence strategies. A June 1999 article by journalist Richard Kim in *The Nation* critiqued the mainstream LGBT movement's singular focus on sentence-enhancing hate crimes laws in the wake of Matthew Shepard's murder, and featured CUAV's efforts as an example of alternatives: "Undoubtedly, lesbian, gay, bisexual and [transgender] communities suffer fear and intimidation from violent assaults, but hate crimes laws are aimed at lengthening prison sentences, not creating safer community spaces.... Investing in local organizing, on the other hand, not only enables activists to connect the struggle against anti-gay and lesbian violence to such issues as job protection and the repeal of sodomy laws, it also builds gay and lesbian communities and creates safer social spaces—while at the same time reaching out to other communities to combat the problem of violence together. That's something no hate-crimes law will ever do."

8 Dean Spade and Craig Willse, "Freedom in a Regulatory State?: Lawrence, Marriage and Biopolitics," 11 *Widener Law Review,* 309 (2005).

9 These organizations, as well as the more radical impulses within current anti-violence work, were deeply influenced by the political analysis produced by INCITE! Women of Color Against Violence and the publication of the anthologies *Color of Violence* (South End Press, 2006) and *The Revolution Will Not Be Funded* (South End Press, 2007), which focused unprecedented critical attention on the ways many nonprofit and foundation structures replicate the racist, classist, ageist, and other hierarchies of corporate capitalism in both structure and strategy.

10 CUAV's full strategic plan is available online at http://www.cuav.org.

11 There are notable exceptions to this, including the Asian Women's Shelter in San Francisco (http://www.sfaws.org) and The Northwest Network for Bi, Trans, Lesbian and Gay Survivors of Abuse (http://www.nwnetwork.org).

12 This inspiring phrase has been recently popularized by the Sylvia Rivera Law Project, a law collective in New York City serving low-income transgender and gender nonconforming people of color (http://www.srlp.org).

13 Special thanks to Connie Burk and everyone at The Northwest Network for their inspiring and groundbreaking leadership in this arena.

14 Martin Luther King, Jr., "Loving Your Enemies," 1957.

ENDING OPPRESSION. BUILDING SOLIDARITY. CREATING COMMUNITY SOLUTIONS.

Meiver De la Cruz & Carol Gomez

MATAHARI: EYE OF THE DAY

VIGNETTE NO. 1

"He's still a big activist somewhere…"

2004: When I finally found out the real story, I said to him it was sexist what he was doing to us. How could he reconcile these lies, the manipulation, and emotional abuse with his big activist image, the image he had used to rope the two of us into this sick game? She is an activist too. I bet she thought the same thing I did from the start: "In this relationship I won't be dealing with this type of shit because I am dating a "conscious" man. Things will be clear. No lies, no abuse. This guy won't break down the door to my house, or turn out to be married—like the other guys." But it wasn't that different. He had lied to both of us and to himself with such vehemence that I think he actually believed some of his own stories. He enjoyed so much having the attention of two smart, young, attractive, activist women that he compromised every political principle to keep us in his game. She and I suffered a lot. I know that. We had the information he gave us; he had full control. This game made him feel like he was not the loser that he actually was. He wouldn't admit it, but he thoroughly enjoyed brewing a sick feeling of competition between us. The sad part is now I think if I met her in a different context, I would have liked to have been her friend. Either way, to challenge him never worked. It only egged him on to say things to put me down. How dare I question his politics! He was more "conscious" and more of an activist than I could ever hope to be. Look at how much people respected him. Everyone asked him for advice. He was much older and wiser than I. But now the three of us know it was sexist and wrong what he was doing to us. And it doesn't really matter. He's still a "big activist" somewhere, I'm sure.

Our activist friends were really mostly his activist friends. The circle was closed off to me in the break up. None of these friends wanted to know he was abusive. Maybe it was too unbelievable, or maybe it would have taken too deep a self-revision and too much personal change for any of them to call him on his shit.

Certain things are unique about interpersonal violence, and in particular sexual and partner violence, in activist circles. Generally the communities we call home are small, and without access to them we have a hard time "being activists." Activism is not an activity we can do in isolation. However, isolation can be a necessary part of the process of breaking up or escaping from an abusive relationship. When we move on from these partners we may also have to give up our home communities, or have to renounce certain spaces to preserve our sanity or our safety. This is not simply "splitting your friends," as with any break up. These are fissures in our movements and in the advancement of social justice. It's time we acknowledge the absence of voices, resulting from abuse, as significant political losses. These absences matter; our movements suffer as we do. Yes, we are expected to suck it up, sacrifice personal comfort and safety for the sake of supporting the work. But sometimes the wounds are too deep, and we simply can't give up anymore of ourselves. We have to run away.

MataHari: Eye of the Day[1] is a social justice organization that strengthens the leadership capacity of immigrants and communities of color, including those who are survivors[2] of domestic and sexual violence,[3] labor exploitation, trafficking, racism, heterosexism and all other forms of oppression. MataHari provides training and skills-building support to communities and organizations nationally in the form of popular education workshops and individualized short or long term consultations. We recognize that when the issues of domestic violence,[4] rape, and sexual harassment surface among family members, co-workers, and friendship circles, even the most seasoned activists[5] among us come up short on how to approach the issue.

tackling the tough questions

In the United States, one in three women in straight and queer relationships reports experiencing domestic abuse in her lifetime.[6] MataHari believes this rate to be much closer to one in two,[7] as most abuse situations remain unnamed and go unreported. As activists, we frequently make idealized assumptions that domestic and sexual violence can't possibly exist within our own circles, that we are "above" all that. Sadly, however, this is not (nor has it ever been) our reality: domestic and sexual violence is a prevalent cancer, weakening, limiting, and threatening to destroy our social justice movements. We know anecdotally that when it becomes known that intimate violence has been perpetrated by our activist comrades and committed within our activist communities, silence, denial, and organizational and community self-protection often rise to the forefront. How we as activists deal with our personal and public response when such a crisis occurs is a real test of our mettle. As activists of color, we often feel an additional responsibility to "represent" and "protect" our racial/ethnic communities. We may feel conflicting allegiances and pressure to stand in solidarity with the "cause," rather than take a unified stand against the violence perpetrated by our comrade and recognize its significant impact on our communities.

This is where our movement breaks down and community accountability fails. Our silence and inaction give permission for violence to continue. We must then turn the mirror on ourselves and take a hard look at our own internalized oppressions that act as barriers to responding to domestic and sexual violence, and ask ourselves the tough questions: *What is our collective responsibility to tackle this private and public conundrum? How do we hold ourselves and offenders in our circle accountable for abusive behavior? How do we unravel the emotional entanglements and ties that can either cloud or enhance our judgment? How do we take a stand? How can communities prioritize domestic and sexual violence as an integral part of the social justice struggle? How do we move intimate violence from the private sphere and into the public light without feeling as if we are "betraying the cause" or exposing our communities of color to dangerous public scrutiny and further oppression?*

home and the movement, one and the same

In activism, our homes are extended into our communities; our comrades are part of our family. The trauma we experience in private (whether at home or work) spills over into our community work, and often it either drives us or paralyzes us—in either instance, trauma shapes our activism. The political is personal too. In our experiences working within women of color–led activist groups in the US, we see the astounding extent to which the epidemic of sexual violence has impacted the political lenses of women of color. So much of our activism and other political work has been tainted by, driven by, paralyzed by, and/or involves fighting against sexual and partner violence. In addition, our experience of simultaneous oppressions makes it impossible to separate and respond to sexual violence, domestic violence, sexism, racism, homophobia, ableism, and classism as isolated entities. At some point it's even difficult to separate the "organizer" from the "survivor." The complexities we must navigate daily to remain committed to movements populated by our abusers, by people we feel have betrayed our trust, by movements that have failed to protect us or centralize our experiences, compounds our work and fatigues us spiritually and emotionally. Among ourselves, we kid around that our meetings of women of color activist groups are sometimes more group therapy than anything else, but there is really nothing funny about this. Claiming the complex identity "activist of color" while simultaneously identifying as survivors of abuse, racism, and heterosexism, we publicly fight oppression while nursing painful wounds. Yes, we heal as we fight back. However, the necessary process of healing can be thwarted when, in our fighting back, we remain unsafe, alone, and ignored, and those wounds are inflicted again—this time by communities that are indifferent to, or complicit with, abusers whose behavior goes unchecked.

The attitudes and silences that prevail in the experiences of many of the survivors in the vignettes[8] we share here extend to issues of partner violence, racism, sexism, xenophobia, heterosexism, and other forms of violence and repression. It is at these crucial *intersecting* oppression points that MataHari's work finds its power. Through this essay, we hope to contribute usable suggestions for creating safety and support for and with survivors. We offer suggestions to help survivors come forward with greater support from allies and to allies on how to provide that support.

our stories

The four vignettes shared are situations that MataHari members have been directly involved in. Some are personal reflections of survivors. Others are reflections by organizers. Each sheds light on what was and what could have been, and illuminates angles of intervention (or lack thereof), the impact of trauma, and the community strengths and breakdowns that occur. Although not all of these narratives directly address "domestic violence" (i.e., between two activists in a romantic relationship, marriage, or cohabitation situation), they do highlight a range of intersecting, interpersonal forms of violence between activists, by a public figure against his partner, and/or in responses from allies. The lessons learned and corresponding recommendations may provide useful guidance in developing sensible strategies for survivor safety and support. Bear in mind that there is no "one-size-fits-all" resolution to every situation. Each situation will require its own customized strategy based on each survivor's safety, socioeconomic, legal, immigration, linguistic, health, emotional, and psychological circumstances, among others. Similarly, each community that any survivor is a part of will have its own culture, its own strength in the ties and composition of members who may hold varying sets of values, experiences, and connections. How you, as survivor or ally in a given situation, receive and make meaning of these narratives and guidelines is *your* journey, as you envision creating community solutions to address partner and sexual violence. Use your creativity, insight, political consciousness, sensibility, and wisdom to learn, absorb, critique, and be inspired to make the change you see fit to in your life.

VIGNETTE NO. 2

How on earth did this become about something else???

Oklahoma, April 2006: Seven immigrant Spanish-speaking women workers make a distressing disclosure to two worker center interns tabling a booth at a health fair one Sunday. The women reported long-term and ongoing sexual abuse by bosses and co-workers in the factory where they worked. The women divulged that they had been raped, and some even impregnated. One of the women, a lesbian, said she was sexually violated, and her partner made to watch the assault in order to "straighten them out." Another woman said that her husband blamed her for the rapes and that things at home were tumultuous.

The factory is located in a predominantly white, rural community in Oklahoma. The 250 or so workers formed an isolated community of immigrants in that region. They were non-English speakers and were undocumented. They were terrified to report the abuse to anyone for fear of being arrested or deported. Initially there were no bilingual services or safe places to turn to closer than at least ten hours from where the women lived and worked. Now this small worker center, located an hour away from the factory, where the two bilingual/bicultural students interned, served as a safe haven. Lisa (who spoke only English) was the worker center director and only paid staff. The two young Mexican American college student interns, Melina and Jose, to whom the women disclosed the violence, were now the primary contacts for the survivors. And just as the workers felt isolated in the community, with this critical revelation, the worker center staff felt overwhelmed, unprepared, and helpless to handle a catastrophe of such magnitude without support.

MataHari was brought in by Lisa to offer brief consultation and training to the worker center staff. We provided the worker center team with basic information on understanding the traumatic impact of sexual assault and domestic violence, brainstormed strategies for survivor safety within the context of their particular region, and discussed potential immigration remedies for undocumented victims of violent crime.

May 2009: The worker center organized an emergency consultation meeting among several well-respected national social justice advocacy groups whom they believed could help offer strategy and intervention support for the workers in crisis. The invitees included a leading national legal services organization, two renowned civil rights organizations, a national workers' rights advocacy group, and a national interfaith labor advocacy group. Lisa sought MataHari's partnership in co-facilitating the meeting. We led by framing the discussion to describe the sexual violence affecting the workers daily, the critical situation that the immigrants working in this factory were facing, and the need to support the women with a safety plan that would help stop the violence while keeping them and their families safe from deportation and/ or homelessness. We were eager to get the expertise and input from these national advocacy giants on how to proceed, and felt like we were going to be supported by the most seasoned organizers from larger, more-resourced organizations. We expected this discussion to offer useful insight for building a comprehensive strategy and safety plan that we hoped could be implemented collaboratively.

However, Lisa and I were taken aback when, within five minutes of presenting the critical issue of sexual violence, the group discussion took (for us) *an unexpected turn. As a solution, the national advocates spoke energetically about building a "wage-an-hour" campaign for the workers. How on earth did this became about something else entirely?? An awkward silence fell when we pressed the group to discuss how we were going to address the issue of sexual assault and, critically, the safety needs of the women. There was no safety plan discussed, no community organizing strategy to deal with the violence. In our minds, Lisa and I knew that organizing a wage-an-hour campaign would take months, maybe even years to take off, if it were even possible. In this room the rape of undocumented women seemed to be accepted as routine, normal, collateral damage, to be dealt with only if the opportunity arose during the wage campaign. There were no ideas coming forth for an organizing or outreach strategy for women's safety.*

I guess we were a bit naïve. We realized, there and then, that even among the great "giants" in progressive organizing, so, so much was missing from the skills and analyses needed to address sexual and domestic violence. We realized we were alone in this. The women workers, too. People just don't know how. Or maybe it's just easier not to know....

In this situation, a small, under-staffed, under-resourced worker center was unable to take on the task of organizing any kind of large-scale intervention on its own, and required a much bigger support infrastructure. In addition, the center was smack in the middle of a particularly conservative, racist part of the state with no allies within hours. What the worker center was able to do was provide a space at their office to hold a weekly "Latina Workers' Potluck." A few women came to these groups. The numbers fluctuated. The group was facilitated with the support of the young Mexican American intern, who heard week after week about the domestic and sexual violence the women faced and fast became their de facto advocate and comrade. It was an overwhelming responsibility for a first-year college student who did not have any experience or training as a counselor, a trial by fire. MataHari was able to offer periodic consultation, from afar, to the worker center staff around safety and support as issues arose for them. This long-distance support was certainly less than ideal, but we were the only option available to this group in Oklahoma. We worked with them to identify sexual assault and domestic violence resources in closer proximity, but there were none within driving distance, and the relatively closer ones in the area were not familiar with working with immigrant and non-English speaking populations, or with workers. Together with the center team, we constantly brainstormed lists of other social justice allies who might assist them, such as the nearby faith community doing environmental justice work and the women's shelter staff at a homeless residential program in a neighboring town. Additionally, MataHari helped raise emergency funds to purchase plane tickets for the lesbian couple to escape the factory and town and return to their home country. The other women chose to remain at the factory, not wanting to either lose their livelihood or face deportation.

For MataHari, this was a powerful reminder that the need for anti-domestic and sexual violence organizing is huge beyond imagination, especially among unions and labor organizers in the US. The vocabulary and skills needed to deal with violence in the movement are sorely lacking. This kind of dispersed, "non-specific" response to workplace sexual violence is a "way out" from taking responsibility for and establishing coordinated legal and organizing protocols and strategies to assist survivors as a critical part of labor and immigrant organizing work. This raises a hard but important question: Are we collectively failing to be outraged enough to create systems that can respond to this type of epidemic faced by immigrants of color because undocumented brown people are seen as disposable? One thing is clear: We have a long way to go, and a lot of work to do, both inside and outside our social justice movements, within our communities, and within ourselves.

VIGNETTE NO. 3

My welcome into US activist circles...

1996: I was 17, a recent immigrant from the Spanish-speaking Caribbean. My mom, my younger brother, and I lived in the projects in an urban neighborhood of Boston which, prior to gentrification by white activists, was a low-income community of color. I was starting school and got my first work-study job at a nonprofit community organization in my neighborhood that did tenants' rights work, particularly working with the Latino community. I chose to apply there because the politics stated in their job description made me feel like I would be working with people whose politics I respected. I would be helping my neighbors, and making money for school. At the same time, I would be cheap labor to them. It was a sweet deal all around. I did not know it at the time, but that organization was (and still is) well known as part of Boston's radical leftist organizing community. I worked from the office as well as from three local community clinics. My job tasks varied, but in addition to data entry and providing direct service to mostly Spanish-speaking single mothers at the clinics, I was often assigned to do written translations for the Latino committee within this organization, and to do oral translations during board meetings and community forums.

The head of the Latino committee, "R," a permanent staff person, was an adult Puerto Rican married man. Although not officially my boss, he was often in the position of assigning me tasks and supervising my work. Soon after I started to work there, I noticed he would sneak in compliments to me in Spanish, speaking quickly, in the middle of talking about work, so that the other Spanish-speaking people in the office would not catch him. As a work-study part-time intern, I did not have a permanent desk, and this man would often direct me to sit down to work within his range of view. I noticed that even when I was working in a different room, he'd angle his chair to see me. Not too much time passed before he grew bolder, making comments about how I looked, telling me I was beautiful, and soon I realized there would not be a work day that he did not make a comment about my appearance. His delivery started to bother me. It became suggestive, his comments more aggressive, specifically talking about how that skirt made evident the curves of my body, something or other about my eyes, my lips. I would dread having to stay working in the office alone with him. He'd tell me he'd been a high school teacher in Puerto Rico, that I could trust him. Thinking back now to the im-

plications of "R" having access to a lot of young people makes me ill. I noticed that over the months I had started to change the way I dressed so as not to entice his attention. I had nightmares about him. At first, I was just not ready to make this into an issue. He was so much older than me, and the setting, the politics of the people we worked with, all of it made it so that I had a hard time realizing this man was sexually harassing me. Also, the relationship was sometimes that of a boss and employee, sometimes friendly, and sometimes weirdly inappropriate, with blurry and complicated lines, as often these situations are. But after a particular instance where he touched my knee, the fact that he was getting off on telling me these things became very clear to me, and I felt scared and repulsed. I finally reacted, told him off, and left the office.

I complained to two staff people, a woman and a man, also Latinos, who were also my superiors, and from them I received a mixture of excuses and ambivalence. "Tu sabes como es, somos Latinos." Our Latin culture's acceptance of compliments, our "warm blood" was supposed to serve as an excuse; he didn't mean anything bad, really. I was supposed to be understanding. Without explicitly stating so, they made me feel I should not be making a big deal out of it. On our second talk about the issue, the female staff person I spoke with (also mother to a teenager daughter close to my age) conceded that she had noticed his treatment of me was "a little" inappropriate. This same staff person also shared that another woman on staff had complained about him in the past, but he had not been fired. From her perspective, this is who he is, and we deal with him. End of story. (The person whose complaints were not heard quit the organization shortly after).

Paying attention to office politics more carefully, I realized that this man was the poster leftist Latin American/Caribbean person that the nonprofit's director wanted to use as a representative. He was quite talented at spewing off radical rhetoric in Spanish, à la Che, and getting the Latino constituents of the organization to show up to meetings and demonstrations. Having him on staff was a statement as to how radical a nonprofit they were. The director liked him because he made her look good. Also, the director, a white woman whose activism was connected to the largely white American left–focus during the 1980s on Central American political issues, appreciated his effective, friendly rapport with the large membership of the all-volunteer Latino committee—a central unit within this organization—a role that I suspect she felt she could not play.

But enough was enough. Our situation had developed over the better part of a whole year. I still felt that my complaints were ignored, so I talked to my mother, who had also become an active member of the Latino committee of this organization. In addition to my work, we both had become regular volunteer organizers and were present at many events organized by this nonprofit. It is strange now to recall how involved we had become, and what a big part of our lives this nonprofit had become, but it reflects how isolated and betrayed we felt as this all unfolded. Together, we decided we needed to bring this issue up at a board meeting. If the staff was unresponsive, at least the board needed to know what was happening. I want to stress that it was not a staff-led initiative that my mother and I go to that meeting. They did not show any desire to be involved. In fact, I felt after I had complained, I had created a division between staff who silently sided with me, and people who still wanted to be friendly with him at work and conduct business as usual (like some sick game of allegiances we might expect more in a corporate board room). The issue made everyone uncomfortable, but it was easier for people to ignore it.

My mother and I knew when the meeting would be because I was scheduled to translate at it, and we literally hijacked it. I spoke, and my mother was there to support me. I remember seeing fear in their faces. Quickly they brought up concerns about the legal issues, and the fact that I was a minor. Although they were apologetic and made efforts to show sympathy, I don't remember board members expressing concerns about my mental health or emotional well-being. After we spoke, the board members said they would deliberate, talk to him, and get back to us. A few days later, the director informed me that "R" had been asked to take time off work and attend therapy sessions for two months, which he refused to do because he did not want his wife to find out about this situation. Instead of accepting their conditions, he would rather quit. During the conversation where the director was telling me this, I informed her that I had decided to leave the organization. She responded, "After we do all this for you, you still are going to leave us?"—laying guilt on me for causing the loss of this staff person. Although this organization had not known how to protect or support me, and I left feeling that my safety and well-being had been ignored, I still was supposed to feel that I owed her something.

The organization's part-time accountant—whom I'd rarely ever seen, because usually he came after hours—was the only person who, in my last week of work, came up to me and said, "I heard you're leaving, and I want you to know that I know why you are leaving, and I'm angry about it. I'm sorry." I said thanks, but I don't think he knows how much that meant to me, and how grateful I was. Because he usually worked alone and after hours, he was not invested in the office politics and culture of silence that kept other staff members complicit. He was the only one to speak about this at work without whispering, and show me support.

For years, I stopped going to community events, rallies, and marches because "R" would always be at every event. There has never been an acknowledgement, an admittance, or an apology. I still avoid him.

2006: Moving forward ten years, at a May Day rally, as I march with a group of INCITE! Boston sisters in the Boston Common, "R" walks beside us and leans forward looking at me, smiles, and waves. Like old friends. I pretend not to see him.

On the same day, a comrade tells me there is going to be a forum where community leaders will be educating folks about ongoing legislative immigration debates, and asks me to translate. I know this comrade from that same community organization where the issues with "R" happened. She knows about my experience with "R." At the time, she had been a member of the board, and has always been someone I respected because she's a prominent organizer within my own ethnic community. I agree to translate. When I get to the venue, I realize to my horror that she has asked me to translate for "R." When I see him on the panel, I tell her I'll translate for her and a third speaker, but that I don't want to talk to him, and then she says, "Oh my God, I'm sorry—that's right. I forgot." This woman is known for being a soldier in our movement. I respect her work tremendously, but at this moment, I can't help but feel disappointed *on so many levels. As I stand there making an effort to translate for her and concentrate on the work, I wonder how long will his presence and the ghost of this experience continue to compromise every public space of activism that I have access to, and whether it will take every single one of us experiencing harassment before we take this issue seriously.*

Perhaps we would not be reading this story if the first complaint against "R" had been taken seriously. We can also imagine this situation being quite different if the staff had confronted the aggressor and intervened in visible ways. Instead, we read a story of avoidance where silence becomes complicity. Despite having a "policy" on the books, the staff of the organization did not know how to respond, and even when forced to respond, comes up short of addressing the safety and emotional needs of the survivor. This failure to respond by the involved community makes activist spaces unsafe for the survivor and makes her feel disconnected from her community. The neglect of the survivor's feelings that started at the office has extended to other community members over time, making her feel punished for raising the issue, isolated, or like it's not really a big deal and she should be silent.

VIGNETTE NO. 4

An extraordinary ordinary group of people...

Sun-hi is a Korean immigrant, a nurse in her home country, now working as home-maker and mother of two robust boys, living in relative isolation from dominant US culture in a suburb of New Jersey. She is married to Cho, a prominent, well-respected Korean man, an immigration attorney, community organizer, and mentor to many newcomer Koreans to the US. Sun-hi did not identify as a community activist, although she was relatively involved as a parent in her children's school.

April 4, 2007: Sun-hi was arrested on an assault and battery charge. After a loud dispute took place in the home in which the children called 911, her hus-

band's savvy and eloquent communication with the police allowed him the upper hand with the cops. He framed and flipped the story to implicate Sun-hi as the aggressor. Sun-hi's poor English language skills and misunderstanding of what the police were asking of her at the scene resulted in her making statements in broken English that were misunderstood as an admission to assaulting her husband. She was handcuffed, taken away, and held overnight in a jail cell. Her arrest was reported in the community newspaper. The next day, Cho hired an aggressive family law attorney to begin divorce proceedings, obtained a restraining order barring Sun-hi from him and the kids, and filed for sole legal custody of the children.

Sun-hi was at risk for being convicted of a criminal offense, which could trigger grave immigration consequences, specifically deportation. She was also faced with the shocking loss of custody of her children and homelessness from having a restraining order placed against her and no independent income with which to rent alternative housing, except from court-ordered temporary alimony that her husband was made to pay.

April 5, 2007: As soon as Sun-hi was released from court on bail after her arraignment, she contacted Hyun, her friend and a fellow parent at her children's school. Hyun happened to also be a MataHari volunteer advocate/organizer. In hearing what happened to Sun-hi, Hyun immediately reached out to her MataHari colleagues for solidarity advocacy and community organizing support for her sister in the community.

April 2007–June 2009: MataHari coordinated grassroots organizing and provided Sun-hi and the Solidarity Team with strategic guidance, education, and contextualized legal information grounded in the reality of institutional and interpersonal racism, and other forms of oppression. We prepared the group as best we could for the grueling, traumatic roller-coaster ride that was Sun-hi's now forever-changed life. (We discuss the mission, strategy, and work of the Solidarity Team below.) Over the next two years, there were small victories interspersed among many, many disappointments. The solidarity demonstrated by Sun-hi's support team helped soften the continual "blows" from her husband and the legal system. It helped keep Sun-hi's spirit alive, mitigate her sense of isolation, and give her strength to overcome tremendous losses and her feelings of overwhelming sadness and shame.

From the day that she was arraigned in court until the conclusion of the criminal case and divorce hearings (about 15-20 court dates later and spanning about two years), Sun-hi consistently experienced inept (and worse still) service from the criminal justice system. On the first day in court, fresh from the trauma of abuse and arrest, she was assigned a sexist, unprofessional Korean male court interpreter who chided and humiliated her throughout the hearing for being a "bad wife" instead of doing his job of interpreting the court proceedings. Over the next few months, she was assigned several other court-certified interpreters, many of whom were unable to fully understand or translate the legal language accurately. The ever-changing judges and court personnel were as oblivious to the interpreters' inadequacies as they were inattentive to Sun-hi's needs as a non-English-speaker. Court personnel often "forgot" and would communicate outside the line of interpretation, leaving Sun-hi lost in the process.

December 2007: Frustrated with the language barrier she faced, Sun-hi ended up terminating her (legally competent) English-speaking criminal defense attorney after a month and, against MataHari's and some members of the Solidarity Team's advice, ended up hiring a bilingual criminal defense attorney who marketed himself to the Korean community. This man turned out to be a complete charlatan, jeopardizing many elements of Sun-hi's case by coming to court unprepared, sending his interns to court instead of being present himself, and not following up on ensuring interpreter availability in court. Despite eventually realizing his limitations after several court dates, Sun-hi clung to him because of his ability to fully communicate with her in her language.

At the conclusion of her many legal battles (criminal, family court, and immigration), the only victory had by Sun-hi was the eventual dismissal of her criminal case, after four unsuccessful attempts at a trial (i.e., two situa-

tions where the court interpreters were not summoned; one incident where the prosecutor's office was unprepared to proceed with trial; and a fourth incident, where the police officer who was summoned as a witness for the prosecution was scheduled for vacation on the date of trial). A dismissal safeguarded her from being deported by immigration authorities.

The greatest devastation for Sun-hi was the Family Court outcome. The divorce was finalized and Sun-hi lost custody of her children and was only awarded visitation rights. Her children, now adolescent boys, had bonded with their father over the two years, and were themselves displaying aggressive and condescending behavior toward their mother even at therapist-supervised visitation sessions. The boys over time refused visits with their mother. Sun-hi's heart was broken.

building solidarity, creating community solutions

As an integral part of our anti-violence action and organizing work, and whenever possible, MataHari helps organize with and train a Solidarity Team, a group of trusted allies identified and vetted by the survivor and her trusted helpers to advocate on behalf of, support, and bear witness for the survivor. In areas where MataHari has networks, we are also able to help recruit and recommend trusted allies. So we did for Sun-hi's case, described as follows.

SOLIDARITY TEAM COMPOSITION

Besides Sun-hi herself as the integral member, Sun-hi's Solidarity Team from day one included Hyun (Korean, bilingual mom/MataHari volunteer, who acted as translator for the group and team co-coordinator), another Korean mother from the neighborhood (mostly Korean speaking), and three white Anglo-American moms (all stay-at-home moms from the school who stepped up and reached out to Sun-hi themselves after they read about the arrest in the newspapers), one MataHari staff (Malaysian, team co-coordinator), and several MataHari volunteers (new immigrant Korean, South Asian, Ukrainian, Chinese American, Filipino American, and Mexican American interns who intermittently came to various court dates). All in all, when the Solidarity Team first started out, there were seven core Solidarity Team members (who remained until the end) and about six intermittent members.

Most of the intermittent MataHari volunteers were undergraduate college-student activists, with the exception of two board members: a homemaker and a college social work professor. With the exception of the students and college professor (whose academic schedules were always in flux), this substantial group of seven remained steady and consistent in supporting Sun-hi throughout the two years. The flexible schedules of the moms and seniors, and the consistency of Hyun and the MataHari staff member, maintained the stability of the group.

SOLIDARITY TEAM MISSION

1. To ensure Sun-hi's personal safety was secured against her abusive husband.
2. To ensure Sun-hi's legal and civil rights were met within the various institutions she was now subjected to.

OBJECTIVES/STRATEGY

To provide the survivor with emotional support and minimize isolation. Both co-coordinators acted as joint counselors for Sun-hi, with Hyun taking on the majority of the counseling role since she spoke Korean. The four mothers volunteered to help Sun-hi maintain some level of normalcy on a consistent basis and over the long term. They organized a routine of meeting Sun-hi for coffee or lunch, inviting her to social gatherings, and keeping her abreast of her children's progress in school and at play dates. They raised emergency funds for Sun-hi to help defray the costs of some of her basic needs. These important gestures helped maintain Sun-hi's sanity, her feeling connected to her children, and her having a sense of not being ostracized or judged.

To offer allies a separate space in which to discuss the emotional, psychological, and traumatic impact of abuse. We also aimed to provide some basic information on the cyclical nature of domestic violence and the conflicting emotions of love, fear, and anger that the survivor might feel toward the abuser. We mostly had these discussions separate from the survivor (with her knowledge and permission). Given her own emotional, legal, and financial crises at the time, she was not in a position to be the "educator" for the group. MataHari's co-coordinator and Hyun facilitated this discussion and offered information based on our many years of experience supporting survivors.

To provide systematic and clear information about the criminal justice, probate, family and immigration legal systems. We provided the group with legal information about how the system works.[9] We also prepared Sun-hi and the team for the worst-case scenarios for each court proceeding. It takes a great deal of re-education and actual in-court witnessing to experience how flawed and broken the legal system really is. We engaged in discussion about institutional racism and xenophobia, detailing the barriers and limitations within each system. We debriefed with the group after each court session, and helped "translate" legal language into layperson's terms. This was an ongoing and experiential education process, as most people are socially conditioned to believe in the justice system as a place where justice and due process are actually served.

To watchdog the court system. With the myth of the effectiveness of the legal system continually debunked, the team learned self-reliance. We prepped Sun-hi to advocate for her rights in court. We prepped her to be unafraid to stop the proceedings if interpretation was inadequate, to question her defense counsel if she didn't fully understand his strategy. The allies monitored the legal proceedings and every attorney meeting. At least one person, in addition to Hyun, accompanied Sun-hi to those meetings, so that Hyun could play the role of interpreter and the ally could second-seat Sun-hi by listening to the information presented and by helping to ask clarifying questions of the attorneys. The allies could then debrief and strategize with Sun-hi if she had to make decisions on her case. Hyun monitored the hearings for accurate translation by the court interpreters. If there were inaccuracies, the Solidarity Team took collective action to inform Sun-hi, the counsel, and/or the judge. The team's monitoring enabled us to have the sexist interpreter permanently removed from the case and officially put the court on notice about the language access gaps. The team also played the role of security, while in court, to minimize interaction or visibility of Sun-hi by Cho, ensuring that we physically blocked Sun-hi from Cho's sight in the waiting areas and otherwise maintaining physical distance between them in public spaces. Watch-dogging the system was important in order to peacefully and respectfully bear witness for Sun-hi, provide emotional support, and monitor a flawed court system to ensure that Sun-hi's rights were not violated. Over the next 20 or so court dates spanning more than two years, groups of about 8-15 people showed up in court with Sun-hi, drawing public, positive acknowledgement from judges about the unusual and extraordinary community presence. More than anything else, this community support loudly signaled to Cho that his behavior was not condoned by the community and that all the years he isolated Sun-hi from the world had begun to be undone.

BUILDING SOLIDARITY

Shortly after Sun-hi's arrest, Hyun and MataHari connected her with two other Korean women who had survived domestic violence. These women were further along in their healing journey, and offered Sun-hi peer-to-peer support when able. As the case progressed, we also folded in Sun-hi's family law attorney, who was amenable to being part of the team when able. He allowed the core team to accompany and ask questions of him at strategy meetings with Sun-hi (at no extra financial cost to her).[10] He expressed personal benefit and appreciation for the community support.

By the final year of the case, through Sun-hi's own organizing efforts, the Solidarity Team had expanded exponentially. The numbers of supporters increased from seven to about 27! These supporters were friends Sun-hi developed after she joined a Korean Presbyterian church not long after she was banished from her home. These church members became an active and daily source of support for her in a time of need. Most of the 15 people were elderly women (probably retirees) and a few men. They were Korean-only speakers.

CENTRALIZED COORDINATION

A MataHari staff member and Hyun played the role of team co-coordinators. This role can be fulfilled by one person or two. In this case, having worked together before and having a bilingual partnership was particularly beneficial for the composition of the team. Due to the fact that both people in question had the most experience in managing domestic violence situations, the group naturally looked to them for initial leadership. The co-coordinator's role was to ensure that the entire team remained on the same page with the same information at all times. They helped Sun-hi ensure that timelines, court dates, and other necessary deadlines were not overlooked. The coordinators did not run the agenda or make any decisions for the team, but merely set a gentle structure and offered guidance about next steps to the team. Over time, different members of the core team informally rotated coordination and provided coverage when one of the official co-coordinators was out of town or couldn't make it to certain court dates. Stepping back and allowing for community members to take on leadership roles was an intentional goal for MataHari.

COMMUNICATION

Streamlining communication is a crucial aspect of community organizing. In this case, the entire group was comfortable with the use of email as a key mode of communication in addition to scheduled face-to-face preparation, debriefing meetings, and court date/lawyer's office accompaniment. The Coordinator acted as the communications hub, setting up a secure email listserv through which the group could communicate logistics, and making sure to create and distribute a list of team members' names and cell phone numbers. Timely and consistent communication (whether by email or phone) is a strong asset that keeps everyone well connected and minimizes miscommunication.

Given our teams' multilingual needs, bidirectional interpreting support was made available at all times.[11] Hyun was able to fulfill this role. When Hyun knew she would be unavailable, we scheduled one of the Korean domestic violence survivors who had been providing peer-support to Sun-hi; she would adjust her work schedule to join us in court.

CONFIDENTIALITY

Very early on, the team discussed confidentiality practices. We agreed not to discuss our interactions or work with anyone outside the team. We took several precautions to ensure that our written communications did not become "evidence" that could be subpoenaed in court and potentially used against her: We agreed not to put anything pertaining to the details of Sun-hi's case in writing, including anything that she shared or disclosed to us. When using the listserv, we agreed that only logistical information would be shared by email. No information about Sun-hi's emotional or psychological state, nor anything pertaining to the incident leading to her arrest were to be documented.

DECISION-MAKING

The survivor is central in all decisions as she knows her safety, emotional, and practical needs the best. The survivor drives the process and sets the pace for the Solidarity Team's work (although when involved in the legal system, the "wheels of justice" often drive the pace and timing of crucial matters). The Team supports the survivor and provides critical feedback, acts as a sounding board, is attentive to concrete datelines, and contributes critical thinking, ideas, and strategy for support and action as needed.

As an example, over the two years, Sun-hi sometimes expressed a desire to reconcile with her husband, despite clear rejection from Cho and, eventually, from the boys. This was difficult for the ally team to witness, although we did understand her deep desire to maintain her role as mother to her boys and preserve the family unit. The Team did its best to support her and not judge her for her intentions. It was also difficult for the team to tolerate Sun-hi's defense attorney (the charlatan). We could all clearly see his incompetence and were forthcoming in sharing our concerns about him with Sun-hi. Despite that, Sun-hi felt reluctant to let him go. The Solidarity Team members each struggled with being diplomatic toward him, some better than others. Once it was clear that Sun-hi was going to stick with this lawyer, we had to resign ourselves to accepting her decision. We discussed among ourselves that, for Sun-hi's sake, we had to help her make the best of the situation. We made sure to watch-dog him and call him out on his games. There were times when meetings were tense. There were even times that Sun-hi preferred for us not to be in the room with her and him, since he had expressed his discomfort with us. Ultimately, we had to let go of our own feelings, for Sun-hi's sake. We sucked it up and monitored each court date with dread and trepidation.

ADDRESSING CHALLENGES

Managing Conflicts of Interest. The moms on our team were also acquainted with Cho through the school. One Korean mother and her husband were more closely acquainted with Sun-hi's family. To manage her participation in the Solidarity Team, she had an agreement with her own husband about how to manage communication with the Cho family. Her husband was a casual friend of Cho's. This couple agreed between themselves to offer casual support to both parties separately, maintaining some distance in their relationship with Cho and the boys. They did not actively terminate connection with Cho, but rather kept a healthy distance. The other mothers maintained and drew clear boundaries in their ongoing interactions with Cho (at playgroups and school). They did not engage with Cho on a personal level, but maintained consistent, neutral behavior toward Sun-hi's two boys.

Community gossip. Sun-hi faced some amount of backlash from within her ethnic community. She tried to distance herself from those who were unsupportive, to minimize her stress. She connected over time with a new Korean community through a church she joined that increased her support and helped mitigate isolation.

Communicating with children. In our Solidarity Team ally-only meetings, the mothers discussed and shared how to communicate with their kids about what had happened to the Cho family. Because of the public nature of the incident and media coverage, rumors abounded in the school yard. The moms took various approaches. Some did their best to quash rumors that the children were hearing at school about their peers' parents. Others gave minimal information about the family separating, without going into details.

Language limitations. The majority of the team members' own language limitations limited our ability to communicate with Sun-hi on a deeper and more complex emotional level. We were tremendously fortunate to have Hyun, the counselor and de facto interpreter for us all there from the beginning, but this meant that the weight of the day-to-day communication and emotional support landed substantially on one person. Informally, among ourselves, we processed our own feelings of sadness and anger.

Solidarity Teams are a powerful way to mobilize and build the capacity of a community of people. Organizing ourselves and our friends around providing a safety net for the survivor proved to be an effective way to engage a group of individuals with activism and social justice work. The partnership between community members working alongside the survivor offers an opportunity to provide much needed support while creating space for deep political consciousness-raising work. Allies may gain greater empathy for the complexity of domestic and sexual violence situations. The benefits and life lessons learned can continue to bear fruit beyond the life of this one action. And, hopefully, community members may become better equipped to act on or find support with (universe-forbid) a future crisis that may emerge in their own life, and take strong(er) leadership in organizing a response.

afterword and tools for action

Many variables shape our potential responses to domestic and sexual violence. But much of our ability to respond must come from our hearts, our political conscience, and from being in an emotional, spiritual, and psychological place that is grounded and in full "conscientization."[12] What is it that we can live with at the end of the day? What can help us sleep at night, knowing that we did our best as an ally, a friend, a loving, compassionate person, to account for the violence that is taking place in our circles? Be solution-focused: We must remember that our goal as an "ally" is not to get sucked into or become a voyeur of someone's pain, but instead to be very conscious and intentional about helping and journeying with the survivor to reach a place of safety, wellness, and stability, as soon as possible. It is crucial to be intentional about not demonizing people in the process, but to be genuinely instrumental in recreating safe conditions, mending broken spirits, providing compassionate support, and finding the best available path toward social justice for all.

notes

Pronouns used in this essay are interchangeable and not intended to create or reinforce binary distinctions along the gender identity spectrum.

1   The word "matahari" is of Malay/Bahasa Indonesian origin, meaning "the sun," or, translated literally into English, "the eye of the day." (Mata—"eye"; Hari—"day"). In Sanskrit and Hindi the word "mata" means "mother" and "hari" denotes "god/son of god," thus loosely translated the word means "mother goddess."

2   In this article, we use the term "survivor" to refer to survivors of domestic and sexual assault.

3   In this article, the term "sexual violence" includes sexual harassment, rape, molestation, and incest.

4   In this article, we use the term "domestic violence" interchangeably with partner violence, intimate partner violence, and domestic abuse.

5   In this article, we use the terms "activist" and "organizer" interchangeably.

6   Lawrence A. Greenfeld, et al. *Violence by Intimates: Analysis of Data on Crimes by Current or Former Spouses, Boyfriends, and Girlfriends* (1998). The one in three rate accounts for survivors who report abuse in medical settings and to law enforcement.

7   We "guesstimated" this figure from MataHari survivor data, gathered over the last seven years. This is also an estimate based on MataHari staff's prior professional experiences of working as counselors/advocates in traditional domestic and sexual violence programs over the last 15 years. This data is also reflected in *Violence by Intimates*.

8 Identifying information, including details about location, in all vignettes has been modified to protect the confidentiality of community members involved.

9 This MataHari staff member has had three years of working as a domestic violence and crime victim advocate within the criminal justice system and close to 15 years of advocacy experience with survivors in criminal, probate, and immigration courts. Hyun had about ten years of experience advocating for survivors in probate court.

10 Always ensure that the survivor has an upfront conversation with any of their attorneys about how and what the attorneys charge their clients for. Typically the cost of a family law attorney ranges from about $150–$300/hour (in most urban settings on the East and West Coasts). Most attorneys charge by the quarter-hour (15 minutes) and a brief five-minute phone call to your attorney could cost you 25 percent of their hourly fee. So, too, with community meetings or calls that allies might make to the attorney on behalf of survivors to clarify legal information.

11 Locating interpreting resources may be easier said than done. Survivors will usually have trusted bilingual people in their circles who may be pulled in. Otherwise, safe, vetted comrades from the community who are willing to help out may be recruited (e.g., from local INCITE! chapters or other conscious activist groups). In some communities, there are volunteer activist interpreter circles (e.g., Boston Interpreters' Collective). Whatever avenue is chosen, check for conflicts of interest and be sure confidentiality agreements are made.

12 We define "conscientization" as consciousness that is understood to have the power to transform reality.

APPENDIX

CREATING COMMUNITY SOLUTIONS: A PULL-OUT GUIDE

Below is an abbreviated pull-out guide of summary points that can be used in a wide variety of supportive actions or interventions for loved ones facing intimate violence within our activist communities or otherwise.

TABLE 1

Suggested Practices for Organizing Solidarity Teams

- The survivor drives the process, with the support of her/his trusted community allies.
- The survivor selects and vets who becomes part of her/his support community, including those introduced to her/him by allies.
- The survivor is central to all decisions that are made. S/he knows her/his safety, emotional, and logistical needs the best.
- It is helpful to appoint a "coordinator" of the support team to streamline and ensure smooth and timely communication among all members. This "coordinator" is probably someone other than the survivor. The coordinator should be someone who is efficient, consistent, reliable, organized, and detail-focused who can keep track of deadlines and is good at scheduling and anticipating logistical needs while being tuned into the group's emotional and practical needs.
- A decision-making process should be discussed early on in the formation of a support team.
- Survivor (and supporter) safety should be a priority for all.
- There should be open, respectful, and healthy dialogue, strategizing, and debate pertaining to physical and emotional safety and health as well as economic, immigration and legal soundness.
- Survivors' decisions should be respected, even if the team members don't fully understand or are uncomfortable with the decision.
- If there are children or other family members/loved ones directly impacted by the violence, their needs and voices should be considered as well.

- For multilingual support teams, interpreting support needs to be made available to all members at all times, to accommodate the full participation of all.
- It must be ensured that the confidentiality of communication be sacred and maintained within the ally group. This, of course, is crucial for maintaining the safety, trust, accountability, and integrity of the process.
- Each team member should be realistic about what they can offer. Do not overcommit. It is crucial to maintain complete reliability, consistency, and accountability so as not to violate trust with survivor and comrades.
- Never assume that everyone on the support team, including the survivor, are on exactly the same page around values, ideology, and politics. Assume the need to start with a group discussion on the basics of anti-oppression work. Part of the "process" toward safety and liberation is the unpacking of issues of power, privilege, and oppression together as a team and working toward consensus-building and/or respecting differences.
- Honor the process and have patience with it. The work of relationship- and trust-building takes time and happens over time. One cannot rush the process. It has to evolve, with its high points and low points.
- Don't give up without putting forth your best effort. Stick with the process and give your all to building this process and creating communities of support.

TABLE 2

Tools for Being a Good Ally
- Listen fully, effectively, actively, and emphatically.
- Maintain the survivor's confidence and resist the urge to disclose the story to others, unless the survivor gives permission (and there is a strategic reason to disclose to a particular person, i.e., someone who can help the survivor).
- Provide non-judgmental and supportive counseling.
- For those with expertise in the law or other systems, offer helpful information in clear and simple language.

- Assess physical and psychological safety and risk at every step of intervention.
- Assist survivors in strategizing and prioritizing while in crisis and when encountering the systems or situations that may become involved as a result of the abuse (and frequently with timelines beyond her control, e.g., court dates and hearings).
- If a survivor-trusted and vetted support team is formed, ensure that the team coordinates information and facilitates communications well, and ensure that the same is done with key services that the survivor may end up interfacing with.
- Engage in community anti-violence and oppression work, prevention, and education.
- Participate in developing policy, legislative, and/or community-based support that is aware and sensitive to the experiences of those who have survived violence.
- If appropriate and relevant, and in partnership with the survivor, work proactively with the media to simultaneously publicize the prevalence of violence as a social issue (while protecting necessary individual and community privacy).
- Always remember—the SURVIVOR knows her/his safety and situation the best. Don't second guess or pressure her/him to act before her/his time or before s/he is ready.

TABLE 3

Survivor Vulnerability Factors
- Social isolation and depression.
- Loss of friends or colleagues and/or facing community backlash due to disclosure of abuse by a well-loved activist.
- Self-doubt and internalization of responsibility for the abuse.
- Blaming of oneself for "allowing" the abuse to happen, e.g., "as an activist, I should've seen the signs."
- Loss of trust in the community. Not being believed. Being judged.

- Feelings of responsibility for protecting the abuser (of color or queer, particularly) from additional scrutiny and repression by an already oppressive system.
- The couple may have children together, which makes divorce or separation much more complicated.
- Economic disadvantage or impact from abuse—loss of job, bankruptcy, ruined credit, holding a minimum wage job, paying costly attorney fees for divorce.
- Survivor may be dependent on a two-person income for affordable housing, health insurance, etc.
- Experiences of racism, homophobia, transphobia, ableism, or other forms of institutionalized oppression.
- Laws and systems that establish neither safety nor justice for survivors— e.g., limited rights for survivors/victims, inability to get time off from work to attend multiple court hearings, little/no financial compensation for days off work to attend court dates or appointments, childcare limitations.
- Survivor may be dependent on partner for immigration status—e.g., survivor may be undocumented, a dependant spouse of a US citizen abuser, or reliant on a work visa (H1B) at a job where the abuser is the employer.
- Survivor may hold an H2B visa (dependent spouse of H1B visa-holder) which doesn't offer work authorization to be able to live self sufficiently.
- Survivor may be undocumented, and therefore afraid to draw any attention to her/himself by reporting abuse for fear of being reported to immigration and deported.
- Language barriers—literacy in English and/or native language—where most resources and helping services are monolingual and frequently print-based.
- New immigrant status may result in survivor being relatively unfamiliar with US laws, social rules, culture, language, and institutional and social systems.

TABLE 4

Risk-Assessment Checklist: Information to Gather in the Wake of a Crisis

- Survivor safety: extreme depression, suicidal feelings, substance use, medical conditions, mental health crisis. Does the person need additional, professional support?

- Primary abusive partner information and history: lethality, access to weapons, criminal history, accomplices, substance use, mental health history, suicide risk, homicidal risk. Remember that in domestic violence situations, the critical point of safety risk for the survivor is often when the survivor takes a step to set boundaries against the abusive person, or leaves. This is when the stalking and homicide rates often go up.

- Safety of family and loved ones—children, parents, relatives, neighbors, colleagues: Are they at risk of being harmed by the perpetrator? Are they colluders in the abuse? Assess each group for safety, supportiveness, and/ or liability to client.

- Safety of community, e.g., friends, family, colleagues, neighbors, care providers, ethnic community, and so on: Are they at risk of being harmed by the abusive person? Are they colluders in the abuse? Assess each group for safety, supportiveness, and/or liability to client.

- Are there other perpetrators of violence in the survivor's life?

- Effectiveness and quality of care from systems and care providers: Are service agencies and institutions that the survivor may have to interface with (e.g., courts, legal services, health care facilities) trained to be and sensitized around working with trauma survivors? Are the services and environment culturally and linguistically competent to meet the survivor's needs? Are there issues of institutional or historical oppression, such as racism, classism, xenophobia, ableism, heterosexism, or sexism that the client may encounter within helping systems?

IT TAKES ASS TO WHIP ASS

Understanding & Confronting Violence Against Sex Workers

---

a roundtable discussion with
Miss Major, & Mariko Passion
INTRODUCED & EDITED BY JULIET NOVEMBER

i. introduction

Sex workers are working people. We are highly stigmatized and criminalized, but workers nevertheless. Despite the monolithic stereotypes, there is nothing intrinsically violent about providing a sexual service. For the most part, violence against sex workers is the same as violence against workers everywhere: the more privilege we have, the more likely we are able to work in the safer and better-paying parts of our industry. The less privilege we have, the more likely we are to face shitty working conditions that may also be dangerous.

While working people everywhere face a range of risks from their work—from hotel cleaners and agricultural workers who risk cancer from chemical exposure, to industrial accidents in factories, to the physical, sexual, and psychological abuse experienced by nurses, to depression and addiction in almost every form of work including parenting—what is unique about the sex industry is that often the very ways we sex workers might protect ourselves from clients or from our partners are criminalized by the state. Not accidentally, in every jurisdiction in North America, sex workers can never work together in a location under their own control or employ drivers or security. Street-based workers can't negotiate services ahead of time or in well-trafficked public areas. Sex workers can't report violence without the risk of arrest, child removal, eviction, or job loss, and we can expect the criminal legal system to minimize or outright ignore violence against us, including rape and murder, in particular if the worker is also multiply marginalized by racism, transphobia, and/or poverty. Since the state is a major source of violence, sex workers have always had to rely on alternative methods of preventing, confronting, and healing from violence.

WHAT IS VIOLENCE AGAINST A SEX WORKER?

For many of us, the first and only image of violence against a sex worker is that of a client abducting a street-based worker and leaving her body in a river. Yes, this has happened; it's why I became a sex work organizer in the first place. Stranger violence is part of the risk picture. But from what I can tell, the most common form of violence against sex workers is in the home: intimate partner violence. When I tell people I'm a sex worker, I'm often asked if I'm "being safe." No one ever asked me that when I told them I had moved in with my partner even though partnership is often at least as dangerous if not more.

Partner violence is not the only form of violence sex workers face. Colonialism, misogyny, and other types of oppression are forms of violence themselves, and from my experience, most North American sex workers are working-class women, with a disproportionate representation of Indigenous women, women of color, and trans women communities. So when someone tells me they want to end violence against sex workers or reduce harm, I ask: What violence do you mean? Against whom? Because if you're talking about violence against the sex workers I know, do you mean at the hands of our partners? Do you mean a doctor turning in a woman to "child protective services" after finding out she is a sex worker? Do you mean ending arrests and incarceration? Strip searches on mere suspicion of working, as often happens to trans women of color? Do you mean "quality of life" policing (aka targeting and harassment) that justifies frequent police contact with trans people of color no matter what the circumstances? Do you mean raids of immigrant-run massage parlors by cops with drawn guns and deportation orders? Not being able to work legally but punished for returning to sex work?

By violence, are you including the emotional, social, cultural, sexual, and spiritual violence against sex workers—something so many of us experience as having much more lasting harm? Are you thinking about the violence of being so stigmatized that you can't talk to your family for years? Of being abused by partners or unable to access public services because your boyfriend might get arrested as your "pimp" (especially if he is a man of color)? Are you thinking about rejection from a lover or a lover's family? Are you thinking of the soul-crushing damage of knowing that your friends pity you and strangers might consider your death a joke or a welcome cleaning up of a neighborhood? Do you consider how your attitudes might be part of the violence against sex workers? Over and over, sex workers tell me that these are some of the most common and harmful forms of violence we face.

These myths that violence against sex workers is exclusively physical and client-based deflects any focus on the intimate, structural, and state violence against sex workers that is just as prevalent. Instead, just about every effort to "help" sex workers justifies expanding control over us through the prison industrial complex (PIC). For example, we are told that we just need better cops (or more of them), or tougher sentencing for bad clients, or more educated judges, "rehabilitation" programs, surveillance cameras in identified street-working areas, "neighborhood watch" programs, mandatory drug treatments, more "sensitive" imprisonment and, in some places like New Orleans, the placement of sex workers under a decade-long surveillance via sex-offender registries.

Even many feminists believe sex work is violence in and of itself, and further support criminal "solutions" to the so-called problem of prostitution. I and many other whores feel enraged and betrayed by other (often white middle-class) feminists who go so far as to organize against us, drowning out our voices, analyses, and ideas. But we whores don't take shit lying down, so to speak. The following roundtable discussion was organized in large part to debunk these dangerous myths about violence against sex workers and to explore truly viable solutions for ending violence against sex workers. Together, the worldy Miss Major and Mariko Passion (each a sex worker and organizer) call on us to recognize the varieties of violence we face—in particular the emotional, cultural, sexual, and spiritual violence of sex worker oppression—as well as the fact that violence against sex workers has many sources, including the state, but also our partners, friends, communities, and families. Because systems of oppression keep us separated from one another, sometimes a sex worker will have no one to turn to. What's s/he gonna do when an abusive boy/girlfriend starts pounding on the door threatening the kids? There are times when there is no option but to call the cops for an immediate intervention. But then what? How can we prevent that shit from ever happening in the first place, and heal from it if it does happen?

ii. roundtable

What are ways you, or other sex workers you know, have found to stay safe from violence (from cops, customers, lovers and partners, child services, the medical and psych establishments, immigration, and other sources)?

MISS MAJOR: The thing about this question that you have to keep in mind is that there are different kinds of violence: spiritual, psychological, sexual, physical, and emotional.

Each one is going to have a different effect on us, and those effects impact each of us differently. For example, someone who is FTM will be different than an MTF because socialization will affect the results of the violence—how you receive or resist it. Taking that into consideration, one of the things I tell the young [trans women] is that you've got to find ways to stand up for yourself that don't incur more wrath on you. For a trans man, they're usually not over 5'7", and because of their size, I've noticed that the aggressor often takes it to an extreme. They will go beyond verbal assault to show that they are a "real man." With trans women, they're less likely to overpower us one-on-one because we're bigger than the average bear. It's more likely to be in groups or from a distance (for example, throwing shit from a car). The funny thing is, they'll attack people they think are fags because they think they're weak and effeminate but with black trans women, well, we have a reputation in black communities. You don't fuck with the sissies and queens. Going back to the 1950s, you hear them say it about trans women: "You can chase them but don't back them into a corner!"

So, with violence, you go through stages:

— You can fight back physically.

— Sometimes you can't do that, especially for girls who are prostituting, so then we'd sometimes carry two bricks in our purse. Two red bricks, and reinforce the purse straps so that it wouldn't snap off when you'd hit someone with it.

— If girls had cars, we'd get little kids' baseball bats (about a foot long), soak them in water for two weeks. This way when you use it, it won't break. Then dry it, cover it with electrical tape just the exact width of your hand. One side of tape down, one side up so that once you grabbed it, it was in your hand till you were through. We'd keep these under the front seat. Necessity is the mother of invention.

— We would go to bars, take cue balls and put them in two socks. Girl, it takes ass to whip ass—if you're gonna take a piece of mine, I'm gonna take a piece of yours. Some of the girls would match the socks to whatever they were wearing. Had to be flashy!

— We would work in neighborhoods together. If we saw a girl running, all she'd have to do was scream and we'd all wait for the boys to follow. Then we'd all run behind the boys. We'd listen for this because we knew we weren't in a safe zone. When the girl knew we were behind her, she'd usually stop. And then it was on. We don't always win, but...we've gotta protect ourselves because we can't afford to be hit in the face or in the chest and have our tits messed up. This reminds me of a scene in the movie *To Wong Foo, Thanks for Everything! Julie Newmar* where it's the transgender woman who kicks ass—not the sissy or the gay boy.

— If you can't fight, you buy a gun.

MARIKO PASSION: In my personal escort work, I hire a security person to stay awake with me during my graveyard shift and check in and out of shows [jobs]. He has a car and we've talked about emergency plans. He has copies of my driver's license to get me out of jail on my own recognizance and he has my car/house keys. I carry a stun gun, pepper spray, and am currently training in self-defense!

I try to always screen well and not be in a hurry or desperate for cash, but that doesn't always go as planned. I know that neither the police nor my security person will help me during my next incident of violence, but they will be able to help me after, or hopefully help me out. I de-escalate angry customers with logic, calm, and nonviolence. I retreat before fighting. I blog about my experiences of violence to the world. I perform pieces about it. I Facebook about incidents of violence as soon as they happen.

I had a few friends while I was with my last boyfriend who helped encourage me to get out of that relationship. It was horrible to call the cops on someone who you lived with and loved for almost two years *knowing* that they were on probation and could go to jail. When the cops came to my door, they gave me the "No Excuse for Domestic Violence" training talking points. The cops did get me to see that this relationship *needed* to end. In my relationship both of us were on probation, so any run-in with the cops would be a violation. We were very aware of domestic violence laws and even sang a song by Snoop

Dogg: "First one gets to the phone, the other one's goin' to jail..." that captured this sentiment on our romance.

My boyfriend was my driver and he helped me stay safe, although reluctantly. Although he was paying his rent by being my driver, he was not exactly thrilled that I was having sex with people that he was driving me to the front door of. I wished he would get a job and he wished I would not be a sex worker.

The sex worker and driver couple can easily become a Bonnie and Clyde duo if they want to. Except because it's illegal to employ a driver, your boyfriend is then legally defined as your "pimp," and this can be another violation of probation. We had discussed that if he or we were pulled over in a prostitution sting that we were to tell the cops that we were NOT in a relationship and that we did NOT live together and that he did not know what I did behind closed doors. Those are the things that police try to link to pimping in an arrest.

The violence of the system has it so that the systems or people that you enlist to protect you become the targets of unjust laws, discouraging us from using our own systems of protection where the police have failed.

What are ways you, or other sex workers you know, have found to deal with violence when it has happened (from cops, customers, lovers and partners, child services, the medical and psych establishments, immigration, and other sources) without using the police?

MISS MAJOR: The thing we've learned about calling the cops is that we've learned not to call them, period. Most of the time, even when we have a problem with our partner, we hope they'll take our side. They don't. So we learn how to talk ourselves out of things. Or we'll walk close to the building to protect our back when we're in a crowd that might not be safe. With police you simply ride that out. You'll hear the zipper or the belt unbuckle and you know they just want a blow job. Usually on the hood. So you just position yourself so you can back away after. You never turn your back to them because then they can say you were trying to get away and do whatever they want. Do you get a badge number and complain? No. You got no proof that he made you suck his dick.

With lovers, you really learn to deal with it yourself. You try hard not to make it adversarial, not to escalate, and when it calms down, you manipulate the situation to put yourself in a safe space. For example, send him out to the store and change the locks while he's gone. If he's acting the fool outside your door, you can get the cops to come because they won't be taking any sides. If he [your partner] is inside, you've got to handle it yourself. You learn to think on your feet. The amazing thing is how a sense of humor and sarcasm can take you right across the bridge [to safety] before they ever know what happened. You've got to read a group to see who is the real agitator. Mob mentality always has one person leading everyone else on, and they're rarely at the front. You need to make fun of that person. Then he'll need to [turn his attention to his friends and] defend himself to restore their respect.

Dealing with violence is different for everybody. Like with hooking: there's folks who do it for survival and some who do it because it's fun and exciting. Each of them will have very different experiences. I got involved with hooking because I thought it'd be exciting and it was. It wasn't horrible, frightening, miserable, or annoying. So for me, the violence was what came along with prostitution; it was the nature of the beast. Going through that, I'd rather go to the hospital, but if someone tries to hurt my spirit or wound my pride, it's those things that I never get over. Being beaten up or raped, I have found that the mind is a wonderful thing. It can get you over and out of shit you never thought possible. Your body heals, the pain subsides, the thoughts slowly, slowly, fade and the mind replaces those thoughts with other things.

When you've been hurt, friends have more than likely gone through similar things so you can learn from them how to deal with it—or hide it. It's often the same thing we did as a kid! Take time to pay attention to yourself, sort out what works for you. If you have a decent lover, who'll give you a human response, they can help you.

Agencies, psychologists, doctors—I don't think they give a damn. The longer you hold onto [the pain], the longer they can milk you. The solution isn't what's going to get them the money. For example, a cure for AIDS won't get them the money; only the drugs will. AIDS is another form of violence. Society never realized that people [with AIDS] didn't have to die. That when these people died, a part of them died too. I just kept going and did my best to help my friends. The older you get, the more you realize how true the clichés are! And so "there but for the grace of god go I." It could easily have been me. Easily. This [AIDS] was brought on us; this wasn't a natural thing. I've had two lovers die of HIV and people don't think about the guilt of the survivors. You ask yourself, "Why am I here?" A question no one can answer but you.

MARIKO PASSION: One strategy I use is posting the phone number and description of any violator—perhaps a girl will Google his phone number as part of her screening before seeing him, and my negative report will come up. I also find emotional support in other sex worker colleagues that I am very close to. This is the beautiful part of this community that has allowed me to survive and blossom. Sex workers have organized Day to End Violence Against Sex Workers on December 17 each year and we can talk about violence then. SWOP-LA [Sex Worker Outreach Project of LA] used to have a worker support circle.

When I broke up with a boyfriend and had to call the cops on him, my therapist was my only friend. I started using Facebook because it was an important part of my support network, my new friends, a way to express myself and receive immediate feedback even from folks who couldn't do anything else. When I Facebooked about calling the cops on my boyfriend, I got responses from people who had done the same thing, from sex workers who dated people in prison and who knew. Facebook helps me feel ok because it's an open journal in a clearly public forum; it's a way for me to get my words about violence out there and to let people know that this really happens.

I have a personal spiritual practice. I pray, I journal, I write. I go to the ocean when I'm having stress about work or life. I spend a lot of time alone. I smoke a lot of pot to deal with my Post-Traumatic Stress Disorder (PTSD). In fact I came into the sex worker movement through my healing relationship with marijuana as a medicine.

"These myths that violence against sex workers is exclusively physical and client-based deflects any focus on the intimate, structural, and state violence against sex workers that is just as prevalent...

Instead, just about every effort to 'help' sex workers justifies expanding control over us through the prison industrial complex (PIC)."

—Juliet November

What power can sex workers and allies leverage against people who cause harm to us? What can we do to protect ourselves, fight back, and hold abusers accountable without relying on the cops, courts, and prisons?

MISS MAJOR: You can't rely on cops or prisons.

If the prison system worked to help us feel safe, there'd be one prison in each state. Why are there so many? Because it helps control the people the state doesn't want to exist. Which is why they were so encouraged by AIDS: it was going to wipe out the junkies, queens, gay people, and speed freaks—so why cure it?

We have to rely on ourselves, community, friends, and blood or chosen family. I don't feel that accountability happens in [my] realm of existence. For example, guys who have unprotected sex when they know they're HIV positive. That's murder. So the thing is to hold yourself accountable. And to fight back emotionally and spiritually. It's a matter of keeping yourself safe and sane. It's a matter of not letting your anger and frustration over violence ruin your future, because it can mess things up permanently so you never have joy, happiness, or peace of mind, the things that make life worth living. Yes, those things are fleeting, but no one promised you a rose garden. You have to fight to keep yourself safe.

So yes, I've been robbed and so on, too, but girl, don't throw a pity party. Sorry, but go do something about your anger. Go to the movies, go punch a tree, play it out: put on some blues, get a glass of wine, break a dish, rant and rave, piss and moan and then, the next day, get up and get on with life. Because the best kind of revenge is to not let it get you down. No matter what situation you're in, you can eke out joy, sanity, fun, and happiness. I was in Sing Sing and I was not going to let that shit ruin my life. I was young with little titties, with pretty red hair—I was the cutest thing on two feet! And Sing Sing was little New York City. There were pimps, whores, and snitches, and I had so much fun. They wouldn't let us girls work, but we dated the guys who were allowed to work. I just flirted and wrote sweet notes to the guys—didn't even have to be with them physically, and we got treated to all sorts of things.

MARIKO PASSION: This is a difficult question because I don't think that we will ever be able to hold abusers accountable. I think that we can fight back when attacked, and protect ourselves and the ones we love. But if we are against prisons and death penalties, what methods can we use to punish violators? I am personally bent on using any means necessary. This, however, always works against the sex worker and it never really happens like the movie scene robberies.

I can resist and defend. I was born a defender but I have learned tools to fight back. I want to get to the point where I can present an equal threat of combat, not an easy target. I feel like I'm a soldier in a war that I didn't enlist in. I have created myself as a whore revolutionary as a way to survive.

I risk a lot of violence given the type of sex work that I choose to do. But I don't think we get to choose our class. Poverty is a kind of violence. I've always wanted to be a $2000/hour escort, but I can't get that high rate. I feel like I have to do the risky work to make the money I make. It's different than a street worker but it's an indoor street hustle, which creates an additional risk for me. I minimize my chances of being victimized by not having a pimp or using drugs (not pot) or working the street.

People want to deal with child soldiers and people dying, so how can I feel like people should be concerned about my being a sex worker who got robbed? That's something that [writer] Laura Agustín points out regarding the rescue industry. People want to rescue trafficking victims, but they don't want to help us decriminalize prostitution or organize better working conditions in massage parlors. They'd rather come in with guns drawn, dogs, and raid and rescue. That makes a better story: pictures of terrified girls, invading people's privacy—not working with them as intelligent people and as workers.

"I risk a lot of violence given the type of sex work that I choose to do. But I don't think we get to choose our class...

Poverty is a kind of violence."
—Mariko Passion

A lot of sex worker activists focus on decriminalizing sex work and, in the meantime, on trying to get crimes against sex workers prosecuted. If we decide that we're fundamentally against the prison industrial complex (PIC) and that "fixing" the cops and courts won't work—that the PIC in particular will continue to punish sex workers of color, immigrant workers, trans and gender variant workers and survivor workers—how does this change the way we organize in the sex work movement?

MISS MAJOR: I don't think that [way of organizing] works. The government isn't going to prosecute johns because most of the time they have money, position or power—and they vote! Most hookers don't vote. So to me, if they decriminalize [sex work], they're changing the rules of marriage! They're not going to open it up for women who are not married to have the privileges of married women. How many girls like me grew up wanting to get married so they could get a new caddy or fur? It's the same with prostitutes! Yet [wives and prostitutes] are still portrayed as opposites.

Some of the girls I've talked to have suggested turning sex work into a regular business. Let's have prostitutes working for a company with other girls, like they do in Nevada, with medical coverage. This would help eradicate the lines between the girls who work in the street, for agencies, who advertise in the paper, etc.

MARIKO PASSION: The one factor unifying all workers in the movement is the fight for decriminalization, not legalization. People like Robyn Few (of SWOP-LA) were able to help ignite a movement on the basis of that unity. But we disagree on a lot of other things: when to decriminalize, how to start a campaign, who should be in the conversation. And beyond that, we have patriarchy, classism, racism, etc., in our movement.

We also agree on destigmatization. For a long time I didn't believe in voting, but while I'm still very skeptical about electoral politics, I've educated myself on the electoral voting process e.g., how to create citywide legislation like Prop K [a 2009 San Francisco campaign to decriminalize "prostitution"]. Now I understand it. I believed in Prop K enough to devote my full time energy to it. I talked to as many people as possible and in the old-fashioned way—by knocking on doors. It was amazing for me because I felt that change was a possibility for the first time.

The Prop K committee was mostly white workers, working-class and middle-class, some former workers. It was not a very diverse and representative group. I was the sole person concerned with anti-Asian racism. Ironically, anti-Asian racism helped to defeat Prop K—the "No on K" people used the image of a trafficked Asian woman in a massage parlor as a red herring for keeping prostitution illegal.

I wanted to be recruiting people in jails or just out. I was arrested once and it took up 18 months of my life fighting it. I can imagine people who are being arrested multiple times a year; it's hard to get out of it. It was impossible for me to do anything but sex work, so the system traps you in the PIC, and then, once you're out, forces you to continue doing illegal things just to meet your basic needs. If you don't want me to end up in court here again for the same crime then I need more work! How can I teach, for instance, when while on probation I was suspended from being a teacher for up to five years?

The decriminalization/sex worker movement has not focused on this aspect enough—of actively recruiting people out of jail. We're getting better. Our involvement in CR10 [tenth anniversary of Critical Resistance] was positive, and I felt very included by the majority of the prison activist movement. It was transgender and sex worker inclusive. At CR10 these were issues discussed throughout the conference, not just issues talked about in one little workshop.

"People want to rescue trafficking victims, but they don't want to help us decriminalize prostitution or organize better working conditions in massage parlors. They'd rather come in with guns drawn, dogs, and raid and rescue...

That makes a better story: pictures of terrified girls, invading people's privacy- not working with them as intelligent people and as workers."

—Mariko Passion

How can we build solidarity with each other across lines that divide us (e.g., whore hierarchy, classism, racism, transphobia) so that we can have each others' backs and build whore power and self-determination?

MISS MAJOR: Sex workers are what divides sex workers. Whether they're MTF or not, there is always this thing of judgment. Rarely is it race, because there is a common bond. [Racism] does exist but those aren't the big rifts. For my girls, it's over which girls make the most money, and judging the woman who looks scruffy but who turns trick after trick after trick.

We're not going to get together and sing "Kumbaya." We don't have a common bond except for our work, which differs a lot. The trust we used to have, honor among thieves, the bond between street workers—that's gone. When girls started disappearing we'd take down the car make, license, description of the guy and call the cops. Did they care? No. That undermines your sense of camaraderie, because why be concerned if no one cares?

What builds community between sex workers is bonding and sharing your life stories, your truth. Folks don't like to do that these days. It takes heart. Folks in this country can't even ask how much money you make. People get up in arms about that and won't even tell their wives! Say hi to people around you, ask how someone is doing, and hang in for the answer. Come from your own truth and open yourself up. This generation can't do that because of the computer. People don't call to talk anymore—it's all computer, which is full of wonderful information but it means we care less about people. Go to a bar and say hi to a stranger. Open yourself up by being who you are.

MARIKO PASSION: I think that the sex worker rights movement that has taken shape in the Western hemisphere and globally is a huge indicator that solidarity exists. We communicate and keep in touch across the world, reaffirming each other's confidence in this work by sharing posts of each other's events and actions. There are lots of conferences and summits, and even a few grants. But most importantly, there are people in the movement who care and help others develop their own organizing and survival skills. To address solidarity building across race, class, and gender, many organizations and conferences, like [US-based] Desiree Alliance, have started in the last five years to focus on social justice and anti-oppression organizing.

Another challenge to our solidarity is how many of us are dealing with mental health issues, like PTSD, and are survivors or drug users, and the infighting this sometimes causes. I want to work on the mental health issues of our community and not ignore them. As survivors, it is critical that we create a space for openly talking about sexual and physical abuse, and how that violence, particularly when experienced during childhood, remains with us, affects our personality, and can seriously undermine our lives, our relationships, even our ability to make more than survival income. My next project is to really deal with PTSD among survivors, specifically drug use and the acting out we do against each other.

I want to create "The Hustler's Survival Guide for LA" to spread basic knowledge regarding current prostitution laws, including resources that people may not know—like how to get out of jail on your own recognizance, early termination, and not having to pay for a lawyer. The process of learning how to survive being arrested has been very empowering, and I have demanded it with my own determination. If I could share that knowledge with other sex workers, they could take back their lives. Even if only just a little bit more. It certainly doesn't free you entirely but it's one less shackle.

"The government isn't going to prosecute johns because most of the time they have money, position or power—and they vote! Most hookers don't vote. So to me, if they decriminalize [sex work], they're changing the rules of marriage!...

They're not going to open it up for women who are not married to have the privileges of married women. How many girls like me grew up wanting to get married so they could get a new caddy or fur? It's the same with prostitutes! Yet [wives and prostitutes] are still portrayed as opposites."

—Miss Major

I AM BECAUSE WE ARE

Believing Survivors & Facing Down the Barrel of the Gun

Alexis Pauline Gumbs (UBUNTU)

INTERVIEWED BY LEAH LAKSHMI PIEPZNA-SAMARASINHA

When I stumbled online upon the work of UBUNTU and Alexis Pauline Gumbs, I was simply blown away. Based in Durham, NC, UBUNTU is a coalition led by women and gender nonconforming people of color, queers and survivors that came together following a sexual assault,[1] perpetrated in March 2006 by members of the Duke University lacrosse team on several Black sex workers (who are also honor students, mothers, lovers, and community members), and the national attention—which largely took the form of vicious, racist/sexist backlash that unfurled against the survivors of the assault.[2]

The name UBUNTU reflects a commitment to a traditional sub-Saharan African concept which, roughly translated, means "I am because we are." According to their mission statement:

UBUNTU is a Women of Color and Survivor-led coalition of individuals and organizational representatives. We prioritize the voices, analyses, and needs of Women of Color and Survivors of sexual violence in both our internal structure and our external work. We are Women, Men, and people who do not fit into the gender binary. We are non-trans and trans. We are People of Color, Multi-racial, and White. We come from throughout the Triangle area and have roots both within and outside of the United States. We are sex workers, students and community members. We are workers. We are Lesbian, Gay, Bisexual, Two-Spirit, and Questioning. We are Queer and Straight. We are young, old, and in-between. We come from a broad range of economic, geographic, spiritual and political experiences, backgrounds, and perspectives.[3]

In response to the horrifying assault and backlash, UBUNTU organized a National Day of Truth-Telling—a march that filled the streets of Durham with hundreds from the community holding "I Believe Survivors" signs, huge painted adinkra symbols of power, and tiny signs made from magazine cutouts and popsicle sticks. Survivors and their families marched up front (including Alexis's supportive mom, participating in her very first direct action!). The march alternated between *Carnaval*-style dancing through the streets to "Survivor" by Destiny's Child and the beats of the Cackalack Thunder Drum Corp, to a moving silent walk past Duke's campus to the house where the violent lacrosse team party took place. At the lacrosse house, Alexis took to the bullhorn and, after crying her way through the silent march, read a love poem comprising 57 loving wishes for her community of survivors. Then the marchers danced all the way through downtown to the courthouse where a dance interpretation of Audre Lorde's "A Litany for Survival," and speeches from the seven coalition organizations pumped marchers up to keep marching toward North Carolina Central University and the WD Hill Community Center for a day of workshops, strategy sessions, and performances. All of the major local news outlets reported on the action, and the Day of Truth-Telling Media Team prepared survivors with talking points the coalition had aligned on while also speaking their truth on their own terms. This action, and the kind of fierce and nurturing work by and for survivors of violence UBUNTU members have fostered in their community, has filled many of us, including feminists of color, survivors, and our allies far beyond Durham, with so much heart and hope. In May 2008, I had the chance to have the following e-mail exchange with Gumbs about the approaches adopted by the coalition in confronting different forms of violence in their community. In June 2010, I had the opportunity to ask deeper questions about how UBUNTU's work has grown and evolved over the past two years—with its use of creativity as a form of healing, its expanding interventions into situations of violence faced by community members, and its involvement in Durham's Harm Free Zone project.

Alexis, in the interview we did in 2008, you mentioned that at UBUNTU you "have created a complicated community of people ready to be there for each other in times of need (including recent instances of partner violence, loss of loved ones, etc.) and to celebrate each other ("we just had an amazing fair trade chocolate extravaganza to celebrate a 35th birthday in our community"). Can you talk more about the concrete ways people in this community have found to be there for each other and intervene in situations involving partner abuse? What does this look like?

I am really proud of the fact that we have built a community that allows us to call on each other. I've told people that I really wish my mother had access to a community of support like this when I was growing up. I wish she had access to a community like this right now. When violence is something that has to be managed all alone by the person experiencing it, the cost is huge, especially when little ones are surviving the violent situation as well.

So far, our immediate responses to partner violence have included literally "being there" for an UBUNTU community member who had reason to fear physical violence from a threatening partner, and brainstorming together to make a plan that provided safety for this community member and her family on her own terms. Creating a safety plan might include offering our homes as safer places to stay; staying at the community member's home; providing child care; researching legal options and community-based alternatives; coming up with plans, back-up plans, and times and places to check in and shift the plan; and listening and listening and being ready to support.

In one instance, an UBUNTU member happened to meet a young woman of color who was walking down her street after being beaten by a former partner. She called the rest of us to see who was home and available in the immediate neighborhood, took the young woman into her home, and contacted the spiritual leader of the woman who had experienced the violence. Calls were also made to other women from her spiritual community that the young woman trusted, who also came to the home and made sure she received medical care. She also arranged for members of our UBUNTU family to have a tea session with the young woman to talk about healing and options, to share our experiences, and to embrace the young woman and let her know she wasn't alone in her healing process.

In each case these responses were invented on the spot, without a preexisting model or a logistical agreement. But they were made possible by a larger understanding that we, as a collective of people living all over the city, are committed to responding to gendered violence. This comes out of the political education and collective healing work we have done, and the building of relationships that strongly send the message, *You can call me if you need something, or if you don't. You can call me to be there for you...or someone that you need help being there for.* Since we have come to see each other as resources, we no longer think our only option is to call the state when faced with violent situations.

In that way, everything that we do to create community—childcare, community gardening (our new project!), community dinners, film screenings, political discussions, and much more—helps to clarify how, why, and how deeply we are ready to be there for each other in both times of violence and celebration.

 I know UBUNTU was instrumental in intervening in a situation of relationship violence where a member of your community was facing violence from a partner who was armed and a member of the local police force. This is a "worst-case scenario" for a lot of folks trying to figure out how to use community accountability strategies—the kind of situation where most folks feel like anything we do won't be enough. Yet your community was able to intervene to make sure that your friend and her kids were safe. Can you say more about the strategies you used, and why you think they worked?

At a very complicated time, during the midst of a complicated relationship transition, an UBUNTU member/cofounder's husband, who was also a police officer issued a gun, began threatening her and having violent outbursts.

The night after the first violent/threatening outburst, she (let's call her "June") and some folks on her behalf called other UBUNTU members and asked them to gather at her home to brainstorm. After arriving at her home, we asked her if she would rather have the conversation some place other than the home which she had been sharing up to that point with her husband. She agreed, and we moved the meeting to the home of another UBUNTU member. There the conversation started with her needs and priorities and vision for the situation. Her priorities were that she and her kids be safe, and that her kids know that they were loved by everyone (including their father, who was being violent).

From there we brainstormed possible plans of actions, including information to be obtained (for instance, the name and contact details for an important person respected by her husband who could talk to him and hopefully bring him back from the violent place he had gotten to, and the process for and consequences of obtaining a restraining order so that she could decide if she wanted or needed one). Then we assessed what resources we could assemble, including: a place for her to stay that her husband did not know about and to which he had never been; people to accompany her to meetings with him on arranging logistics regarding the kids and the separation; folks to attend the kids' dance recital that the husband would also be at; people to hang out with the kids while they did their homework etc. so that she could have difficult phone conversations with her husband that she did not want them to overhear; people to stay at the house with her and the kids so that she would not have be there alone with the threat of her husband possibly showing up.

We also wrote out plans for what would happen at every point of the day and stayed available by phone in case plans needed to change; we arranged check-in points as well as plans for June to leave town for her mother's home, where she and the kids felt safer at night. My personal involvement included spending time at June's home, watching her kids at my home, and volunteering my home as a stopping place for checking in and a workstation for handling logistical issues, like changing all of her passwords, creating her own bank account, and searching for contact information for her husband's family members who might be able to advise and convince him to act in everyone's best interest. Of course there were also many hugs, mugs of tea, and needed laughs that were not planned and yet were so very crucial to the process.

Looking back, I think the purpose that we served during this intervention was to help the survivors attain safer passage through the most difficult and potentially volatile time of their crisis. By supporting our fellow UBUNTU member, and honoring her vision for her children to have their father in their lives in a loving and safe way, we created the possibility of space and safety for everyone involved. By providing safer spaces for June, we also gave her husband (now ex-husband) space with himself to get through a time when he was verbally abusive and indicated that he would resort to physical violence—without allowing him the opportunity to inflict more verbal violence or to realize his threats of physical violence on his family/our community members.

I know that now June's vision is fulfilled in a long-term and sustainable way. She has transitioned into a different relationship with a partner who loves her children, and still has a working parenting partnership with her former husband which allows her children to have access to infinite love and the support of a family that has grown without the trauma of witnessing or experiencing the level of violence that it seems would have been likely without the support plan that she led us in creating for and with her.

This experience has taught me so much about the complexity, contingency, and power of mothering as a relationship and as a community vision. I know that at times in my life when my mother had no one to turn to, I witnessed and experienced violence that would likely have been prevented if she'd had the support she deserved to fulfill her vision for herself and for our family. Too often simple but crucial resources, like people to talk to, and space and time to deal with something hard and/or scary, are not available to most people. But when we decide to support each other, we have what we need.

 In UBUNTU's statement of principles, you say, "Although our work is long-term, it is also urgent and immediate. We see providing immediate support for individual survivors and longer-term social transformation as interrelated and mutually strengthening types of work. To resist, we must heal; to heal, we must resist." I love that you believe this and that you put this vision of sustainability in your work. How do you balance providing one-on-one support and organizing for social transformation? I

know that in a lot of groups I've been part of, even as folks talk about (and understand the importance of) self-care, it's hard to provide direct support to folks in crisis and work to organize on an ongoing basis.

This is definitely a difficult set of issues. Currently, our major strategy for balancing individual healing work and long-term community building (while addressing the need for crisis care on a broader level, including for folks who we may not know yet) relies on several key tactics, including:

— *Working in coalition.* As a coalition, UBUNTU consists of many individuals and some organizational entities. Some of the organizations, such as North Carolina Coalition Against Sexual Assault and Orange County Rape Crisis Center (with whom we often work) are direct service providers that respond to individual crises and have much of the legal and organizational information that helps us navigate situations of violence...even when those experiencing it don't want to go directly to the service provider. This coalitional relationship means that the political visioning and creative work we do likely influences the work of those organizations (whether those organizations are officially part of UBUNTU or have worked with us in coalition on projects such as the National Day of Truth-Telling). And people who end up connected with those service providers also have access to the work of UBUNTU, a survivor-led space of continued healing through the long-term process of building community.

— *Creating access to "community" in a broader sense.* UBUNTU also functions as a site of sustainability in another sense. The fact that we have built informal mechanisms to offer childcare, trade massages, do aromatherapy work, share personal fitness training, cook for each other, grow food together, help with homework, borrow cars, and offer a space to crash, means that as each of us takes seriously the work of responding to violence in our scattered community (for me this often means responding to violence that my students are experiencing and immigration violence that my family experiences), we also have a support network to help us, feed us, hug us, massage us, or create a healing oil for us when we need it. And we often do. I know I so often just need a cup of tea or a poem from my community.

On a broader scale, UBUNTU, in partnership with local coalition partners SpiritHouse and Southerners on New Ground (SONG), has started organizing community dinners at WD Hill (a local community center at which one of our members is an employee) to let people know that this work exists as a tangible resource. UBUNTU has been strongly present at important community celebrations from Kwanzaa to "community day" to the MLK celebration. I think this builds the message that since there are people in this community who will show up to provide community support for face-painting, food, and art—people who volunteer to get something done and bring their vision for ending violence into those spaces—that means there is a visible community of support on hand to help and show up when it comes to responding to violence.

We are not formally "providing services," but, from our experiences so far, I feel confident when someone in a state of emergency calls that I have a rich set of resources to offer them, be it legal help, relocation assistance, a breathing circle, a poem, medical attention, or a meal. Since we are not linked to the state, we have the potential to provide people with a more robust set of options that can respond to their needs and desires, and I think that is important...especially for women (trans and cis) and genderqueer folks of color and immigrants who have such good reasons to avoid the retraumatizing impact of the state.

Can you talk about how UBUNTU has changed, four years after its founding in 2006?

Currently, UBUNTU does not meet regularly as an organization, but does organize and provide support as a community network in some of the same ways we did during June's situation. We have gathered several times since then to support a different survivor and UBUNTU member whose partner became violent and threatening at the time of a breakup. We provided the survivor a safe place to stay, listening ears to help her process and figure out what to do next, and support as she transformed what had been a shared home into a safe space for her spirit. We have gathered to support a young survivor who was never directly involved in UBUNTU: her former partner sexually assaulted her, and also stalked and threatened her and her support network at her school. UBUNTU members provided housing, a book of love letters, many conversations, and our presence in spaces where she thought she might be confronted alone by her attacker. We have supported families whose children have been assaulted at school in designing responses that spoke to their vision for accountability and communication. UBUNTU has also continued to show visible support for the self-identified survivor of the Duke lacrosse attack, speaking out publicly when the scene of the crime was bulldozed in an effort to erase the memory of what had happened, and showing up to support her in an ongoing court battle for custody of her children. We also have shown up for each other big time for rituals of birth, rebirth, partnership, breakups, death of loved ones, and graduations. We are gathering to write love letters to survivors (one of our major tactics) for Lisa Factora-Borcher's collection of letters of support for survivors next month.

The most tangible outgrowth of the UBUNTU process, however, is the Durham Harm Free Zone, an explicitly abolitionist organization—which includes UBUNTU members and cofounders, as well as participants who were never involved in UBUNTU—dedicated to developing practices of ending interpersonal and state violence in our communities. We have held community roundtables geared toward creating a community mediation council, and currently are working, in partnership with the Ella Baker Project in Chapel Hill, with a group of public housing residents who are finding ways to create safety and accountability in their community, which right now (as in many branches of state-assisted life) polices the parenting and lives of its residents in ways that threaten their ability to manifest their visions for their families.

notes

1   Viv Bernstein and Joe Drake, "Rape Allegation Against Athletes Is Roiling Duke," *New York Times* (March 29, 2006).

2   For just a few examples of victim-blaming, racist, sexist, and whorephobic media coverage of the case, please see "Crystal Gail Mangum: Profile of the Duke Rape Accuser," *Fox News* (April 11, 2007), http://www.foxnews.com/story/0,2933,265374,00.html; "'Duke Accuser Lying,' Second Stripper Says," http://nbcsports.msnbc.com/id/15238767/; Chris Cuomo and Lara Setrakian, "Exclusive: Guard Who Saw Alleged Duke Victim Says No Sign or Mention of Rape," *ABC News* (April 17, 2006), http://abcnews.go.com/GMA/LegalCenter/story?id=1849938&page=1; "That Night at Duke," *Newsweek* (April 23, 2007), http://www.newsweek.com/id/35379 (accessed September 2, 2009).

3   http://iambecauseweare.wordpress.com (accessed November 2, 2010).

for more info, check out:

http://www.iambecauseweare.wordpress.com

http://brokenbeautiful.wordpress.com

http://www.thatlittleblackbook.blogspot.com

http://www.atthekitchentable.blogspot.com

http://www.loveproduction.wordpress.com

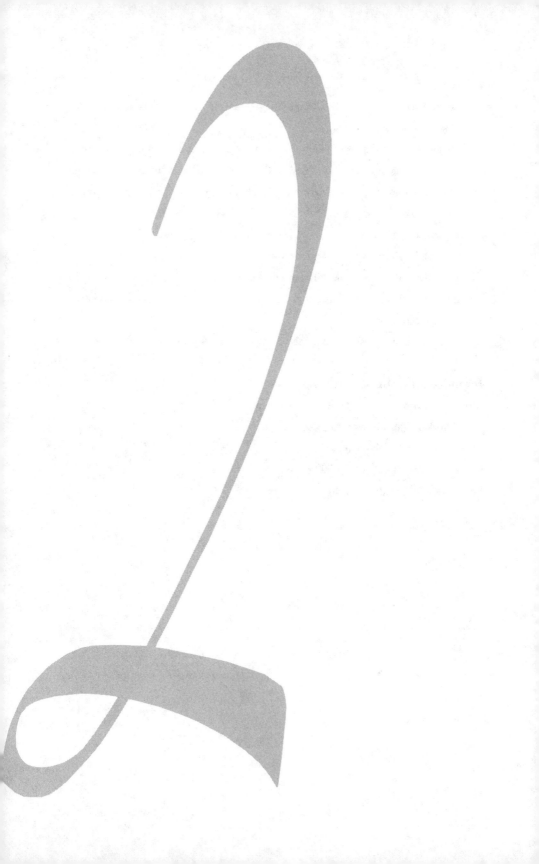

part two

on survivorship

HOMEWRECKER

Gina de Vries

1. hook

She wanted to turn me against the rest of the world, that girl. It was me and her, radical revolutionary partners-in-crime fighting the fucked-up human race. We met at a radical queer youth conference in Washington, DC. I'd flown in from San Francisco with my straight ally hippie mom; she'd flown in from Atlanta with her LGBT youth group. We danced together in the hotel ballroom that'd been rented out for the conference dance, which was like every awkward high school dance ever, only gay. Then we curled up under the phone booths right next to the ballroom, stayed up all night flirting and telling each other stories.

She was a poor white Southern kid with a story not that far from my own—abusive dad, crazy mom, little sisters she raised because the actual adults couldn't or wouldn't. She was stuck in that queer kid, poor kid, dysfunctional family, the-world-owes-me-because-I'm-a-victim frame of mind. The kind of girl who'd experienced enough drama for seven lifetimes, who was fifteen-going-on-fifty, and who didn't have a goddamn clue or reason to trust or love anyone, least of all herself. She made up for what she didn't know by being big and bitchy and loud, taking up as much space as possible. And always having the last word.

I was sixteen, and just as enraged and betrayed by the injustices of life. The problems of my world—my father's drinking, institutionalized racism, my best friend's depression, the boys at school who threatened to rape me—all felt insurmountable. But she made me feel stronger by proxy. Like maybe I could absorb some of her self-assurance, inherit her cocky attitude. I liked her strength, her confidence, her wicked sense of humor. I liked that she was trying to get her Southern accent back. She had short, spiky hair, a wiry, boyish body. She was pale and skinny, had almost no tits at all. She wore baggy jeans and tiny baby tees, one of those metal ball-chain necklaces, black Converse. The classic baby dyke, cute and vaguely punky, not even close to butch and aloof, my usual type. But her voice had that lingering hint of North Carolina drawl and she was hopping mad, and the anger and sass were enough to hook me.

We didn't even kiss, that first night. We held each other, sweetly, tentatively, while the tired and annoyed hotel night-shifters threw us shade for cuddling under the phone bank. But it turned into so much so fast, the way it does when you're sixteen and the smallest gestures take on the deepest meaning. The way it does when someone finally gets your rage and your politics. The way it does when you can will yourself in love with someone you barely know, because they like you, they really like you, a lot, and you're flattered, not used to that sort of attention.

Flirting under a hotel phone booth turned into being Instant Best Friends with big crushes; long-distance phone calls and 3:00 a.m. AOL IM conversations on my dad's ancient laptop. This turned into being long-distance girlfriends, and then came the fights. She was jealous of my exes; she was angry that I couldn't visit her because of money and distance and time; she was enraged when I said that I wanted to cool off, just be friends again. Something felt wrong, too big, too possessive. But she liked me, and she was so smart, so funny. What was my problem? We were hyper-aware of every power dynamic in everything, be it ageism or classism, heterosexism or white supremacy. We were young, revolutionary, radical queers together. We had deep bonding conversations that involved the words *problematic* and *fucked up.* How could someone like her possibly be so controlling, especially from 3,000 miles away? Was I crazy?

And she became such a good friend after we broke up, after we'd taken some time apart. She'd changed and she'd worked on her boundaries and she was so kind and supportive, and, God, she listened. She was always there. Always there. Sending me smiley faces on the computer, leaving sweet, silly messages on the family answering machine. I'd get home from school and my dad would yell "The phone's for you!" and hand me the receiver with a knowing grin on his face. And then we were both applying to colleges and ended up deciding to go to the same school and we were such good friends, we had such history, we liked each other so much, why not try dating again? That old stuff, the stuff that had happened before, that'd changed, right? We were aware, we were watching. She was different.

When I met her, I could have been any scared sixteen-year-old girl, easily ensnared by someone tall and smart and manipulative. The criticisms and demands started small, but then they were all she ever offered me. All the ways I was failing her. All the ways she needed me desperately. Me and my girl against the terrible world. It worked until I became the enemy.

2. passing/desire

According to her, my offenses were as follows: I stopped wearing my wire-rims and started wearing cat's-eye glasses. I wore my hair in pigtails and put glitter on my eyelids at inappropriate times. I didn't want to own a car. My make-up was glittery. I didn't want to be monogamous. I was turning into a hipster. I didn't like sex enough. I didn't care about passing. I was friends with people she thought were famous. I didn't believe in marriage. I thought trans women were women.

I got scared when she threw her alarm clock at my head. I got scared when she threatened to jump out the window. I got scared when she hit herself and left bruises the size of grapefruits on her thighs. When she pushed her fingers inside me after I'd already said *No,* loudly, clearly, I told her to stop. I didn't want to bottom to her anymore, because the only times she wanted to top me were after she'd thrown something. When I was anorexic, it took the attention away from her. I dressed slutty and punk. I wasn't professional enough. No one would ever take me seriously. No one would ever understand me like she did. No one would ever love me as much. I wanted to pierce my lip. She told me I'd be more beautiful without a lip ring, so I didn't. I said *No.* I was a baby. Over-sensitive, over-dramatic, making a big deal out of nothing. This wasn't abuse, she wasn't hitting me, not exactly, she wasn't raping me, it'd only happened once and she'd stopped when I said *No* the second time. She wasn't cutting herself in front of me, just hitting herself, that was different. The absence of blood and razors made it ok.

Boys were the problem, she said. Masculinity was the problem, she implied, every time my eye wandered away from her jeans and fitted tees to women who wore their clothes very differently. I didn't love her enough. The kind of sex I wanted was too perverse, too queer. The women I wanted were too tough, the men I wanted wore more make-up than I did. I wasn't really queer because I was bisexual. I was too queer because I was bisexual. Why did I have to talk about it? A hot flush of my desire was enough to enrage her for days. I wanted to suck cock and I didn't care if it was flesh or silicone; I just wanted to be on my knees and have my mouth filled by someone who wanted it as much as I did. I wanted someone to hurt me because it made them wet, made them hard, made them shiver. Not because they were angry. I wanted dangerous things. I had sex with someone she'd told me I could have sex with. People wanted to fuck me and they didn't want to fuck her. I asked her to pick up the Mountain Dew cans she'd strewn around my bedroom. I didn't eat red meat. I don't think sex should be an obligation. I didn't believe in punishment. I didn't want to process all the time. I wanted one night a week to be alone. I wanted to sleep in my own bed. I missed my friends.

But these problems were our business, our life as a couple. Talking about it would be, as she put it, "breaking her confidentiality." In our world I tried to pass us off as healthy, happy, normal; meanwhile I barely passed at all. I wanted to be held, loved, cherished like I had been before; I wanted to do right by her, I truly did.

But no matter how hard I tried, everything I was, everything I wanted, was wrong wrong wrong wrong. We had to be middle class. Married. Respectable. Respectable lesbians were not bisexual leather dykes. They were not outspoken perverts and sluts and queers. Respectable lesbians did not dress like glam rock Italian-Catholic school girls, they did not wear short skirts and keep their hair long and still never, ever get mistaken for straight. They were not the trampy, brazen, not-gay-enough, too-queer failure of a lover that I was.

3. homewrecker

When I left her the last time, she screamed at me. A clear, loud, thick sound, ricocheting off the tiny walls of her messy bedroom. I could hear our housemates discussing us timidly in the living room. They were worried. *How Dare You* she shouted, as more objects from her floor whizzed by my face, a foot, six inches, three inches away from me. Her clock, as per usual; books; pillows and blankets, too. *You're going to FUCK him tonight, AREN'T you?* The boy she'd told me I could have sex with and then demanded I cut off after we made out against a brick wall. He was dangerous because he was a boy, but really what that meant was he was dangerous because he wasn't her. I said, weakly, *This isn't about him. I just can't do this anymore. I'm tired.* I murmured, *Please, stop.* I kept waiting for her to hit me. I almost wanted her to—it would have made it all real. It didn't occur to me to just leave the room. It took me three days to break up with her, because I'd start trying to leave and she'd try to convince me it would work, *slam*, another book hurled against the wall, we had a wonderful relationship, *smack*, the sound of her hand hitting herself. We were happy, weren't we?

She said I wrecked her home by leaving. She said I was erasing her family. I was her everything—*You're taking away my life*, she said to me, *Five years of my life, all this history with you, how can you do this? How Dare You.* I don't know what made my words stick the third night. My Nana says that sometimes these things just happen in threes.

She clung to the story of how I ripped her safety out from under her, discarded the holy sanctity of our five-year lesbian partnership to fuck boys. The mantra she screamed at me as I cried and ducked and weaved and tried to walk out of her room unscathed, an entire gender shouldering the blame for my leaving. *You're leaving me to fuck boys.* The disgust in her voice was so thick. And I could feel it in the room, whizzing past my ears along with the clock and the books and the little stuffed cat she'd had since she was two. *No one will ever be this good to you, you stupid girl, and you're leaving me to fuck the enemy? You're wrecking our home for this?*

But how do you wreck a home that's already way past broken, the foundation rotten to its awful core? Even when my senses of safety and individuality had crumbled to dust I swept under the carpet, even when I'd convinced myself that everything she did was okay, that nothing was a problem, even when I lay awake at night having tense spinning conversations with myself, repeating over and over that if I just worked hard enough, if I was just good enough, she'd stop—I still had my desire. My desire was the one thing that never went away, and my desire is what finally rescued me. Fucking the enemy is what got me out of there. Yes, I wanted to suck dick, yes, I wanted to get beaten because I actually wanted it, not because it was how someone punished me for wanting freedom.

Being a homewrecker was my last and only survival strategy. Being a homewrecker was the only way I could get out. I left to make my home in myself, and that is something no one can ever take away from me.

THE SECRET JOY OF ACCOUNTABILITY

ACCOUNTABILITY

Self-accountability as a Building Block for Change

Shannon Perez-Darby

The domestic violence movement has claimed many victories. Through decades of tireless work, we've drawn increased mainstream attention to victim-blaming, and dramatically changed the way society views survivors of domestic violence. But in our ongoing quest for legitimacy and safety for survivors, the domestic violence movement has too often boiled complex concepts down to easily digestible one-liners. Many activists and other members of my communities imagine survivors of domestic violence as perfect angels who can do no wrong; we think of every action they've ever taken as noble and necessary. When tackling such a complex, difficult problem in what remains such a hostile climate, it is understandable that organizers might reach for a "simplifying" logic that states: If survivors are perfect, then people who batter are evil monsters, barely human. This binary allows us to think of batterers as people who exist somewhere else, in fantasy and stories but not in our lives, communities, and homes. Our fear of what surviving really means compels us to grossly oversimplify the experiences of both survivors and people who batter. Put on the defensive, we react to victim-blaming—like "it's all your fault" and "she was asking for it"—by drawing borders around who we think survivors are (and are not). We're careful not to let in any scary, wicked, nasty words. By creating systems that can't hold complexity, we are unable to see all the things survivors do in the context of surviving abuse. These things aren't always beautiful and noble. And we're killing each other by not talking about it.

The term "survivor" is only effective as long as it serves me. Sometimes I cling to the term because it describes the hurt and hiding. It's a tool to get to the bottom of a relationship that brought me to my knees. It's helpful because sometimes I find healing in the words of others who call themselves survivors. The word survivor means a thousand things I can't claim; it's perfectly imperfect and I want that to be ok. What I need the word *survivor* to be is a placeholder, a shortcut to say all the things I'll never get to say. It's a tool to get inside and understand all of the moments of choice that came together and brought down my world: the times I went back, over and over again, how I gave away every part of myself while chasing a story I made up about my life.

Working with LGBT survivors of domestic violence at The Northwest Network of Bi, Trans, Lesbian and Gay Survivors of Abuse (NW Network), there are times I hear someone else's story and remember what it felt like to be in the thick of it. What I don't know how to tell you is there are times when I hear a survivor's story with moments so much like the ones I remember that it takes my breath away. Sometimes when I hear myself explaining the insanity that I lived in, I immediately want to diminish what happened, pretend it was different than it was. I explain it away because I don't want to be the person who lived like that.

I'm still trying to call back the two halves of the person who loved him: the person who felt understood, cared for, and loved, and the person who feared him, who watched around every corner, feared every party, whose heart would skip a beat every time a dark German-made car came into view. What I'm scared to tell you is that I moved in with him even after the worst of it. We got back together after months of panic attacks, failed attempts at sharing space, and crazy-making negotiations. There are short, simple phrases to tell you what it was like, but the reality encompasses so many nuances that feel impossible to explain.

Relationships are made of tiny moments of intention and choice.[1] I reached my own bottom through all these tiny moments strung together until they became something bigger than me, something I was so inside of that I couldn't see. Sometimes I'll tell myself it wasn't that bad—the kind of fucked-up relationship that people are in sometimes, but not abusive. Hardest to explain is how nothing was shocking: each insane reality made sense at the time. I loved getting his 2:00 a.m. text messages; it felt normal to be available to him any time day or night. At one point I promised my friends and myself that we wouldn't get back together, but after a 3:00 a.m. phone call—with him driving drunk to my house—there we were in bed again. Every time things fell apart and I was willing to walk away, I was offered the next thing I never thought I'd get. I could never explain how it happened. It was daily chaos every time I agreed to do something I knew I couldn't, such as having sex with other people or accepting the ongoing intimacy between him and his ex. I twisted and bent myself into a person who could become someone I wasn't. I did things that weren't consistent with the person I wanted to be in the world.

The last time we were together, I went back because it felt like I could undo the pain caused by months of not speaking, tense negotiations, and uncomfortable fights over community spaces. I didn't want to fight, struggle, and brood anymore. I wanted to find a way of being together without either one of us compromising ourselves. I thought I wouldn't have to feel so bad inside if I just tried a little harder. There are still moments I want to call him, hope that we could just talk it out and make it right between us, that we could just learn how to be ok with each other. This is the trap it feels like I'll always be running from. Sometimes it feels like I can never completely let this relationship go because that's just the moment he'll come back into my life. When I finally decide to put it all behind me, just when I'm feeling like it's truly over—that's when the phone will ring, and before I know it we've exchanged hours of I'm sorry's and I love you's. And there I'll be, right back in the same pattern I was trying to escape.

It's easier to tell you what he did and harder to tell you what I did. It's harder to tell you about the times I lied to him. It's harder to tell you about the panic attacks or moments when I just couldn't fight anymore. I'm afraid that if I tell you the whole story, the extent of the devastation will, paradoxically, get lost. I'm afraid I'll tell the wrong story. I'm afraid that I can never explain just what it was like; that if I do a bad job of sharing my whole truth, then it'll be like I'm lying and all of this healing work will have been for nothing. I'm afraid my story isn't the story you want to hear. I'm afraid to say that my healing means taking responsibility for the fucked-up things I did because then I'm not the survivor everyone wants me to be.

In the years since this relationship ended I've dramatically changed the way I talk about it. I used to tell the story over and over again to anyone who would listen, the story of all of the things *he* did to *me*. This story was important but it was also devastating. Every time I told the story it was self-soothing and restimulating; it allowed me to constantly relive all of the pain and drama I experienced. This story of the horrible ex served me in so many ways: it helped me rally support, it helped me feel sorry for myself, it helped me break up with him, and it helped me move him out of my life bit by bit. But what that story never did was help me heal. The old story kept me stuck, trapped in old patterns that weren't serving me anymore. I had to change the story I told. Gradually, I took some distance from dramatic stories of the horrible things he did to me and started looking at ways I could take responsibility for my actions. This was hard at first because I had surrounded myself with people who told me that I was justified in my actions. His dramatic ups and downs served me in that I didn't have to examine the ways that I was afraid all of the time; I didn't have to look at the ways that intimacy deeply frightened me. All of the drama kept us just far enough away from each other that we never had to be truly intimate with one another. Focusing on him kept me trapped and made me feel like there was nothing different I could have done to change what happened in our relationship. When I started focusing on the things I did in the course of surviving that weren't in line with who I want to be, the part of me that was obsessed with our relationship, and closed off in that way, started to open up and I began figuring out who I was outside of this relationship.

In the course of surviving, I cried a lot. In the course of surviving, I lied, manipulated, invaded my partner's privacy. In the course of surviving, I hurt and put in harm's way my friends, my communities, my partner, myself. In the course of surviving, I hurt my family connections. In the course of surviving, I drank. In the course of surviving, I dated, kissed, and slept with people I did not treat very well.

In my process of healing, the question I keep coming back to is this: What would it look like to take responsibility for the complex choices I made in a grounded, centered, and accountable way? Where are the places I can talk about choices in a manner that contextualizes them within systems of violence? It's not enough to tell me that I had no choice. Time after time, survivors are told *you had no choice; you did what you needed to do to survive.* Survival is resiliency, and it is necessary. But survival is not without cost. We make choices within a system that's meant to turn a powerful person who can act and make choices on their own behalf into someone who becomes an object and is acted upon. People are always resisting objectification. They are fighting, pushing, screaming to be people who can act for themselves. Sometimes we fight and we scream and we push against the edges of the things that are holding us, and sometimes in the course of trying to be who we are in the world, we do things we never thought we would.

Domestic violence is a pattern of power and control that by design limits survivors' choices. But even within this pattern, survivors make a million little choices everyday. Recognizing these choices is an essential step toward creating a different life for ourselves. The solution to breaking a pattern of power and control that limits choices lies in an increased ability to act powerfully and make choices on your own behalf. In domestic violence movements we call this ability to make choices *agency*. Agency and self-determination encompass all of the beautiful ways we honor ourselves, as well as the choices we make that pull us further away from who we want to be. Choosing to go back can be one form of self-determination. And, so often for survivors, self-determination means choosing the less awful of two shitty choices.

If we can't grasp that survivors are people who make choices, then we incorrectly name some of the things they do as battering. Nothing frightens me more. We have to understand domestic violence as a pattern of power and control that governs the entire relationship. For survivors, this pattern of power and control is experienced in all the ways their world gets smaller and their choices are limited, but also in all the good times when they love their partner more than they can stand. These dynamics work in conjunction with each other, and together they keep people invested and make it that much harder to change. This pattern of power and control encompasses all of the moments of violence and love that pull together to weigh people down. There is no one behavior that can tell us who is surviving and who is battering in a particular relationship. To decide whether a relationship is abusive or not, we must look at the entire picture created by all those moments of intention and choice. Without this big picture, it's far too easy to look at one choice by one person and mistakenly believe we know what's going on.

There are few places in which this understanding of the larger context is more important than in queer and trans communities. The system of sexism privileges men's power over women, producing an environment in which, in a heterosexual context, it is overwhelmingly men who batter women. Because of homophobia, transphobia, and sexism, gender becomes a much less reliable tool in queer and trans communities for evaluating who is battering, and who is surviving in relationships. This added complexity has pushed our queer and trans communities to find other ways to suss this out. At the NW Network, people have worked over the years to develop powerful tools for holding this complexity. What we have come to learn is that a process of open questions and information-gathering does not only help queer and trans folks in abusive relationships but that it can be helpful to everyone struggling in their relationships to step back and look at larger dynamics.

When thinking about how we can respond to violence within our communities without using the institutions that are set up to mess with us, it's essential we understand the context in which people are making their choices. It's amazing to see all the ways that social justice activists are imagining to respond to violence within our communities. Where I think we need help is in the *application* of our innovative and brilliant notions. We need to build the capacity within our movements to respond to violence, and I believe that work begins with building *our own internal capacity* to look at and be responsible for our choices. Among the frameworks my queer and trans communities have used in response to violence are community accountability models. In their simplest form, community accountability models strive to address violence using community-centered responses based outside of the state's criminal legal system. Where I think our community accountability models have missed the mark is in our desire to rush into action. In our visioning, we have confused our desire to have communities with the skills and knowledge to respond to violence with the reality that most of us are walking around with a dearth of accountability skills. In other words, I think we've gotten ahead of ourselves. We've started to think of community accountability models as services the anti-violence movement might provide rather than as a set of internal skills we are all working to build with the goal of creating the conditions necessary for loving equitable relationships.

In my observation, we fall short each time we've tried to apply our beautiful notions of community accountability to our daily realities. I don't think this is because it's impossible to engage in a structured accountability process but because we haven't spent the time building our individual skill sets to help us reach this goal. Think how far forward our movements would be if everyone got just 25% better at taking responsibility for their actions. I understand the impulse to swift reaction because people are in abusive relationships right now; if we don't act immediately, we feel like we're failing the people we love. So we've often rushed to solutions while trying to find ways to hold people who batter accountable. Sometimes I think we want to swoop in and be the hero. But urgency isn't serving us in this goal. In the face of crisis we have to find the time to pause and reflect; otherwise we'll remain trapped in these same cycles of violence. In that reflection lie answers, and further clarifying questions, that will help us learn how to respond to these challenges from a more centered and emotionally-resourced place.

Community accountability models raise many challenging questions: Whom do we want to be held accountable? And what do we want them to be accountable for? Too often I've seen people ready to jump in headfirst and try holding someone who is battering accountable. Only later, they realize that the process isn't what they thought it would be. Sometimes the story shifts and changes, and suddenly what we thought we knew may make no sense at all. We have the potential to do a lot of harm with partial information. I'm cautious about using community accountability models—not because I think they're impossible but because I don't think we're there yet. We are still building the skills we need to engage in this work, and first and foremost among these skills is learning how to engage in our own process of self-accountability.

In the process of exploring community accountability models we often come to the following question: What do we do with people who perpetrate violence? To engage in a process of holding people who batter accountable, we must understand who batterers are. Something we often don't understand about batterers is that they're people. Most often they're hurt people who have almost no support in taking responsibility for their actions; they are also people often determined to avoid taking responsibility for their actions by nearly any means. People who batter are scared. People who batter often believe down to their very core that they are the ones being harmed. Many batterers believe that the world is out to get them and that no one could ever understand. People who batter are also very persuasive when it comes to convincing others that these beliefs are true. Batterers are people skilled at messing with others and exploiting vulnerabilities.

Among the most compelling things I learned while working at the NW Network was how people who batter can use their own real and perceived vulnerabilities to set up and maintain patterns of power and control. One of the myths of battering is that people who batter are all-powerful villains who both are and feel themselves to be strong and capable. Due in part to mainstream understandings of domestic violence, we typically equate battering with privilege. We've seen heterosexual men utilize male privilege to batter women, and again we've boiled down a complex set of dynamics to a simple idea: men batter women. While the idea that batterers are people with privilege is based on a type of battering that does exist, I've often seen queer and trans survivors of domestic violence struggle to reconcile this assumption with their own reality, in which the person who battered them claims one of any number of marginalized identities. Frequently we hear batterers say, "I have a disability so I can't batter," "I'm genderqueer so I can't batter," "I'm a person of color so I can't batter." There is no identity that inherently bars people from being batterers—virtually all of us are capable of setting up and maintaining a pattern of power and control.

In my work at the NW Network, I've seen this play out time and time again. For example, a batterer might tell their partner how scary the world is, that because of their trans (or other marginalized) identity the world is not safe for them, and so their partner must help shoulder the weight of this oppression. Batterers who share marginalized identities with their partners can also utilize the vulnerabilities in those shared identities to batter their partners. I've seen this manifest with batterers who exploit the isolation inherent in maintaining oppression to enforce more personal levels of isolation, saying things like "it's you and me against the world," or "no one else can understand you like I do." Perhaps even more insidiously, batterers from activist communities can skillfully yield anti-oppression language to weave an ever-tightening web where, because of the oppression inflicted by the outside world, a person who is surviving must forever do what their abusive partner says. Many survivors who are legitimately trying to be allies to their partners become caught in a trap where no amount of listening or compromising will ever offset the oppression their partner experiences. For social justice activists and people working hard to dismantle intersecting oppressions, this can be an extremely effective strategy for setting up and maintaining a pattern of power and control.

Survivors, having been taught to take more than their share of blame, often take too much responsibility for the struggles in their relationships. Survivors are hiding, lying, steeped in shame, afraid to tell their friends, families, and support networks the truth because they believe there are things they've done that are too horrible to talk about. For a person who is battering, a survivor's shame and silence is an extremely powerful tool for maintaining power and control. There should never be anything we do that's too shameful to talk about. Shame is our enemy, a ghost that keeps us trapped in all the ways we hurt ourselves and others. I can't tell you the number of survivors I've talked to who believe there is something they've done in the course of surviving for which they can never be let off the hook, something so shameful they believe they deserve to suffer and be unhappy.

What survivors need is support in their own self-determination and safety. What batterers need is support in accountability.[2] One of the many gifts of my job is talking with brilliant and skilled people about complex topics such as accountability. While doing this work I often hear people ask questions about how they can hold someone else accountable. So often, people jump to an external definition of accountability that is about other people assuming responsibility for their actions rather than imagining accountability as an internal process where each of us examines our own behaviors and choices so that we can better reconcile those choices with our own values. I define (self) accountability as a process of taking responsibility for *your* choices and the consequences of those choices.[3] I deeply believe that the skill of self-accountability is one of the fundamental principles we've overlooked in developing community accountability models. In a process of self-accountability, this reconciliation isn't dependent on another person's involvement, but instead engages with our own sense of values and what is important to us. In the work of self-accountability, we are constantly striving to align our actions and our values, knowing it's likely they will never be exactly the same. When there's a gap in that alignment we can reflect on what choices we would need to make in the future so our actions are more in line with who we want to be.

While I don't think it's possible to hold others accountable, I do think we can create environments that support people in their efforts toward self-accountability. Our work at the NW Network is largely about creating the conditions that make it possible for people to have loving, equitable relationships, built in part on self-determination, support networks, and abundance. That is some of my favorite work. What is the point of devoting so much time and energy to talking about all of the hurts if we're not equally committed to envisioning how our lives and relationships can improve?

I think about how much would have changed if I'd just believed there was enough; if I had understood that love wasn't finite but never-ending, something that is always available to me. What if I had treated sex and the ability to connect as something that's abundant and overflowing? Perceived scarcity is as much to blame for the times I've been wrecked in my life as anything else. I kept going back to this relationship that wasn't working for me in part because of my own internal sense that this was all there was. I believed there would never ever be another mixed Latino queer who would love a fat, mixed Latina femme. I didn't see a community where I was desired, where fat bodies were loved and celebrated, and I didn't know a community that loved and relished fabulous femmes in all of our beautiful, flashy brilliance. I didn't know there were others who would love me as I am. What I knew was a beautiful community that was loving and open but didn't always know how to make space for everyone in it. While working to support all of the amazing masculine queers who were fighting to be seen and to gain safety, we traded in our love for intentional, fierce femininity. We didn't know how to love femininity and femmes.

This community of beautiful, wonderful, radical queer and trans folks also didn't know how to talk about the times we messed up. While trying to be free we were *so often* cutting each other down: community norms tended toward secrecy and gossip. Today I'm able to recognize how the larger community context surrounding my relationship was as important as what happened between the two of us. There weren't people around me whose relationships

I wanted to emulate. It was hard to envision what transparency, good communication, and boundary-setting could look like in radical queer and trans communities when the romantic relationships I saw around me continued to fall very short of the radical theory we were claiming allegiance to. I watched my friends and loved ones struggle through tireless negotiations, and often when someone tried to find new ways of constructing their relationship, they either got exhausted and gave up or simply left the community entirely. I want to create more places where my fellow activists can advance practical applications for all of our visionary ideas.

Healing is like a corkscrew, spiraling forever upwards. There's no end, no final destination, just new tools and understanding as I hit those familiar bumps in the road. My healing has come in waves, and key to that process has been recognizing the choices I made and the choices I have. Beyond recognizing these choices, I am searching for communities that will lovingly support me as I take responsibility for the choices I made in the course of surviving that weren't aligned with my values.

Today my life is so different, and so are my relationships. I left the relationship, and eventually I left the state. I left a community that loves and supports me fiercely because I didn't know how to heal surrounded by the same community-wide conditions that were reinforcing the similarly broken parts of our relationships. So I made the difficult choice to leave in search of other ways of creating loving, equitable relationships in queer and trans communities. What I found in this exploration was a place where femmes are loved and where there are fat queers in every part of my life. I found a place that offered me the space and time to heal. I found a place that was eager to support me in my journey to find ways of relating and loving without the obsessive insanity that had become my second nature. I left with a deep desire to know how to do it differently next time, to talk to my communities and to figure it out.

It feels like we're such babies at this, new and fresh. We're fucking up and stumbling left and right, and that's ok. I know the stakes are high, and it feels like one slip up can be the difference between life and death. But we have to start from where we are. I want my radical queer and trans communities to understand the violence we do to each other. I want us to understand it using our own words and stories. I want us to find healing in the ways we are doing it better, and I want us to create spaces for healing all around us. I want us to not get ahead of ourselves in our quest for better community engagement models. I want us to build our capacity for complexity and to continue moving beyond the domestic violence movement catch phrases like "you did what you needed to do to survive" and "it's not your fault" that we've relied on for far too long. I want us to stay connected with each other and to practice vigilance during the times our friends fall off the map. I've yet to see a structured community accountability model that I would want to recreate in my life and communities, but at the same time I've also seen so much growth in our movements and in the people around me. I'm excited about creating the conditions for loving each other the very best way we know how—beautifully, fully, and as people who can act powerfully and make choices on our own behalf.

notes

1   The Northwest Network of Bi, Trans, Lesbian, and Gay Survivors of Abuse, *Relationship Skills Class Curriculum* (forthcoming: 2011), http://www.nwnetwork.org.

2   Connie Burk, NW Network, *Survivors' Use of Violence Training* (2009).

3   NW Network, *Class Curriculum*.

SEEKING ASYLUM
On Intimate Partner Violence & Disability

Peggy Munson

I was lying on my back, holding the container of jerk chicken my current abuser had cooked for me, when I flipped to the Logo channel and saw my *former* abuser's best friend staring back at me from the television screen, microphone in hand. There she was, interviewing queers seeking asylum from oppressive political regimes. But, from me, she had walked away when I approached her seeking my own kind of asylum from the abusive partner who was my only source of caregiving. That day, years before, she hauled his boxes to her truck, helping him move out of the building we shared. At one point when she was alone, I approached her and began to tell her about the abuse. She spun quickly on her heels, leaving me hanging in mid-sentence.

Later, when I was with another abuser, and even more disabled and homebound, I watched her interview then–US presidential candidate Barack Obama on another channel. They were talking about able-bodied issues that "transcended" race and sexuality: complete abstractions to me. At some point, she did ask him about health care reform, and he leaned forward with an engaging glint in his eye. I knew neither of them could comprehend my situation. For months, I had been trying unsuccessfully to get a telemedicine or home visit doctor to give me an echo cardiogram at home, as I was growing terrifyingly ill yet could not travel to doctors' offices. All I thought about was how on earth I would get care if my abuser left me. Watching her with Obama, I couldn't help but think about social collusion and the forces that had entrapped me.

Social collusion with intimate partner violence (IPV) can start to feel Orwellian, and in my case, this feeling was pretty literal, since my former abuser's best friend had become a prominent voice of the left and people around me referenced her to me all the time. Yet, in my own universe, built on activist ideals, with enlightened and brilliant friends, I could not find anyone to care for me most of the time except for abusive partners. The best friend, in her moment with my abuser, had been only an unwitting pawn, but she was an example of how pervasive civilian dismissal of the disabled really is, by both larger society and left movements, and how easy it is for even the most informed person to ignore violence against us.

Abusive relationships are often difficult to escape. But when inflicted upon a person living with disability, and thus buffered by social ableism and inaccessibility, abuse is often virtually or literally inescapable. In my own life, gaslighting (a term coined from the film *Gaslight* to denote psychological abuse in which false information is given to a victim to make her question her own perceptions) had become not just an abuser's tool, but literal gaslights spewing mercaptan or carbon monoxide or "illuminating gas" injured me too. With my various disabilities, including multiple chemical sensitivities (MCS), total strangers cause me injury all the time by using common products that outgas chemicals just like old gaslights, and abusers have often helped me when the world had left me for dead. (In the years I was dating him, I was already being unknowingly poisoned by actual old gaslights in my apartment, though the gas company did not identify the leak until much later. My MCS had grown worse there, and as a result I spent most days resting on a small futon in a small room.) The day the best friend dutifully hauled his boxes to her truck, my abuser stood on the other side of my window screen and blew cigarette smoke into my apartment to intentionally make me sick.

So one abuser's ally broadcast to my living room in a glowing box was not my problem: it was the masses she represented, and the pervasiveness of both social ableism and inaccessibility. Lundy Bancroft devotes a whole chapter in his book *Why Does He Do That?* to the allies of abusers, who function at all levels of society. "If you are aware of chronic or severe mistreatment and do not speak out against it, your silence communicates implicitly that you see nothing unacceptable taking place," writes Bancroft. "Abusers interpret silence as approval, or at least as forgiveness. To abused women, meanwhile, the silence means that no one will help—just what her partner wants her to believe. Anyone who chooses to quietly look the other way therefore unwittingly becomes the abuser's ally."

Abusive partners have been the same people who often saved my life and gave me caregiving for much of the last ten years, while simultaneously brutalizing me. I found myself, by my late twenties, trapped in a city where I knew almost no one, so sick I could barely leave my bed, unable to move back home due to the severity of my illness, trying to negotiate with ableist strangers over the internet and phone to get love, care, help, anything. The reality was nobody, including my family, wanted the responsibility of taking care of someone with my extreme combination of limiting disabilities, and it was nearly impossible to get anyone to become fragrance free to even meet me, or even to pay people to get fragrance free to run errands for me. I was beaten long before I ever met a batterer. Though my kind, non-abusive partner took care of me for many years before that, when she moved away I was screwed.

For years, I was offered a Hobson's choice: abuse or neglect. My disability seemed a magnet for abusers, and only got lip-service from everyone else. Weighing my options, I tried desperately to figure out which one would enable me to survive in a post-modernity that, once I left academia, began slowly killing me. The abusive partners were actually more likely to save my life than not having the care I needed would. They were rare in their willingness to offer consistent, reliable caregiving for long stretches of time, whereas other people I met and dated offered other trade-offs for my disability, such as their addictions that made them willing to hang out with someone who could only lie around. The problem was, I was too ill to even date those people without adequate outside care. I needed care from within a close relationship to even date because I got so ill from interacting with people.

Able-bodied activists tend to see my need for a partner-caregiver as a theoretical abstraction, focusing for example on notions of heteronormativity that conflate romantic (heterosexual) partnership with social well-being. However, such an analysis falls flat on the survival issues disabled people need discussed: who is going to help with bathing and toileting the way a loving partner, rather than an unknowing stranger (who might refuse the task), would do? The world of the disabled is more complex than a clean political agenda will allow. My queer disabled friends and I talk about how we get more disability-acceptance from right-wing Christians than from the queer community, for example. Dr. Judith Wallerstein found, in the largest longitudinal study of divorce, that disabled/vulnerable individuals fare worse in terms of care in divorced families (vs. "intact" married families), so that makes an argument that a partnership-obsessed society (queer or straight) might actually benefit many people with disabilities. With intimate care needs, an intimate, lifelong relationship can become a necessity: my survival, for example, often depends on someone having a comprehensive knowledge of my disabilities—something that cannot be easily trained but has to be experienced over time. It is often a chore to get my revolving-door crew of Personal Care Attendants (PCAs) to make a phone call or send a package correctly, let alone take care of the intimate tasks of caregiving, especially when the turnover rate of PCAs is so high.

A relational element seems almost intrinsic to effective care—in my experience, there is something like an oxytocin effect in which those who truly bond to me are the only ones who give care that is actually life-sustaining and helpful, rather than dangerous or not that useful. It's easy for activists to argue academically about social privileges, but I personally wouldn't choose a more impersonal form of cooperative or institutional care (even if it was relatively clean and functional) over the personal model of the Amish, where in-law suites are built into every house because it is assumed that people will take care of their elder relatives. A more socially progressive, cooperative care model could certainly borrow from the Amish, but the problem is, many severely disabled folks can't afford even an hour in a failed utopia. My queer disabled friend told me a story of how she had to lie about why she was sending her uber-religious PCA to buy vibrator batteries so that she could get off with her lover: she had no one else to do the shopping. Another friend, living in poverty and with no other options, had to rely on an offensive, bigoted man for assistance because nobody else would help her, even though she completely disagreed with and was disgusted by his politics. Our lives don't fit a simple political agenda due to the ubiquity of ableism even in the most forward-thinking circles.

I got sick right after leaving Oberlin College, known for its radical activism and coursework geared toward social change, and yet most of my friends after college could not help or care for me except in minor or temporary ways, so imagining a care system based on friendship and activist ideals is hard for me though I may wish for it. A radical revisioning of care is certainly possible, but only if the survival panic of the disabled is truly, deeply *felt*.

To understand how disability functions in Intimate Partner Violence, one has to shelve denial about how deeply inaccessible US culture can be to people with some disabilities. The Americans With Disabilities Act, after all, polarizes disabilities into the "reasonable" and "unreasonable" by using the term "reasonable accommodation" to denote just how far requisite allowances must go. Most people look at dating, or even friendship, the same way. Some disabilities cross a line, becoming—by cultural standards—too unwieldy to accommodate, resulting in a warped and deadly triage of the "reasonably" disabled who get some human rights, and the "unreasonably disabled" who don't. When the Domestic Violence and Developmental Disabilities Committee of the Wisconsin Coalition Against Domestic Violence and the Wisconsin Council on Developmental Disabilities put together an alternate "Power and Control Wheel" on domestic violence and disability, it didn't fully account for this social reality. The wheel assumes disabled people have freedom or care in society to begin with, which in my experience is a false assumption. For example, it notes that abusers may exercise "caregiver privilege" by committing acts such as "Treating person as a child, servant," "Making unilateral decisions," "Defining narrow, limiting roles and responsibilities," "Providing care in a way to accentuate the person's dependence and vulnerability," or "Ignoring, discouraging, or prohibiting the exercise of full capabilities"—all of which may occur in an abusive relationship. But in my experience, society has already stripped so many living with disability of those rights so thoroughly that abusive partners may play a contrary role of empowering us by, such as in my own experience, getting me adaptive equipment, making food for my special diet that the PCA program won't allow, or taking care of me in the long, drawn-out crashes after medical appointments when I had no other care. If this "Power and Control Wheel" was made by people with disabilities, they were likely more socially privileged than I or most of my disabled friends. The Wheel does note that abusers might "terminate relationship and leave the person unattended," which is more of the danger I have experienced, but the Wheel doesn't account for what happens next, when the disabled person no longer has a consistent partner-caregiver and society abandons its responsibility to protect vulnerable communities.

Random date prospects I met on the internet, the seemingly sane ones, would not give up their shampoo or laundry detergent to meet me. Meanwhile, abusers showed up with alarming regularity. After I broke up with abuser #1, my first date was with someone who came to my house and brought me Indian food, then admitted on the phone the next day she was enrolled in a batterers' program. When I moved to my new house in the woods, hoping to escape the memory of my past abuser, the people I had met on the internet and hoped to meet in person all had issues with my accommodation needs—except the handsome butch who told me she was interested in green building too, and had stood up to her carpentry boss about formaldehyde in building products. Before long, when she was sexually battering, terrorizing, and torturing me, she also made frantic calls to my doctor trying to get me medical care. She cooked my meals and put them in individual containers and froze them. While my PCAs worked limited hours, she came in the middle of the night in a health crisis and stayed for as long as I needed her. By the time I was fully dependent on the relationship, it was winter, and I often needed her to feed me, bathe me, and help me go to the bathroom.

Because my PCA's hours were simply not enough to keep me afloat, my family was far away, and my close friends had all scattered around the country, when I was too ill to relocate, I became an abuser's perfect victim: an isolated, helpless symbiont. When I broke up with that abuser, the first person who seemed willing to get fragrance-free and meet me admitted that her last girlfriend had a restraining order against her. I tried to find someone for a live-work exchange to live in a room in my barn so that I might have extra care, but the one interested applicant also told me she had a restraining order against her from a recent relationship. Lundy Bancroft writes, "Some abusive men seek out a woman who comes from a troubled or abusive childhood, who has health problems, or who has suffered a recent severe loss, and present themselves as rescuers." Here Bancroft is touching upon something much more socially endemic: many disabled people have come to expect abuse, and to expect social service agencies not to rescue them.

"Abusers will offer you that one thing that you need," said the domestic violence counselor, who had agreed to counsel me over the phone. "That one thing nobody else will give you." The language of her organization, like that of the disability organizations, was all about "independence"—transitional housing, independent living. But none of their services fully accommodated people with severe multiple chemical sensitivities.

How do I explain what that one thing I need is worth? How this year I lay on a bathroom floor for about ten hours a day for seven straight months, with ants tracing Mercator lines across my belly, dying in the only spot to which I could drag myself from my bed, because I was too weak to even crawl to my bedroom door to escape my room, as my father flew out from another state and then pathetically came into my bedroom for ten minutes but wouldn't do anything to help me, as I called Adult Protective Services because my mother was going to abandon me without care when I was choking for breath in some kind of severe respiratory failure, when I was unable to go to the hospital again due to MCS, when I spent months sucking on the end of a ventilator trying to save my life and could not get help. Adult Protective Services told me they could not intervene until significant harm had already been done to me by caregiver abandonment, and I had no way of medically proving how much harm had been done. My PCAs kept quitting and my friends were only able to offer brief care. At this point, I had such severe neurological and respiratory problems that I could not speak out loud, listen to any sound, endure touch or the presence of people, or reach a few feet to the end of my bed without increasing collapse. The specter of death felt terrifyingly near every minute.

In the years between those abusive relationships, I spent time engaging the world-at-large, begging everyone else for care, trying to find non-ableist allies when I could rarely leave my bed—then I returned, crestfallen, to the abusive people who were willing to offer what nobody else would provide. At some point in the interim, I would have a surge of idealism and energy for self-advocacy, trying to rally other sick friends to join with me in intentional community-building, researching a new treatment, maybe even luring my family out for a brief caregiving stint. In the end, I always ended up in the same place. Meanwhile, I had to face the social embarrassment of admitting I could not make anything else work, even though people with far more social clout have told similar stories. Pulitzer Prize–nominated writer Susan Griffin wrote about her terrifying search to find adequate care when she was very ill: "Night after night, thinking about how I would survive, as fear dissolved into anguish only to become panic again, I was afforded a vision beyond my private history into the nature of society itself. Over time these were the words that formed in my mind: They would have let me die."

So what does this mean on a social level? Lundy Bancroft writes, "Abuse is the product of a mentality that excuses and condones bullying and exploitation, that promotes superiority and disrespect, and that casts responsibility onto the oppressed," adding in a different chapter, "In short, the abusive mentality is the mentality of oppression." A person with disabilities must combat societal oppression at every turn in trying to escape an abuser, and sometimes that oppression feels more abusive, or at least more inescapable, than its intimate analogue, interpersonal abuse. Say a woman has a life-threatening heart condition that worsens if her heart rate becomes too high, and her rageaholic partner can inflict severe physical harm through prolonged yelling. Over two years, she goes from being semi-bedbound to totally bedbound from her partner's verbal abuse, yet she cannot get a restraining order because her partner never slapped or punched her. She tells an advocate that her partner did inflict bodily harm, in ways she might never recover from, but the advocate fixates on the heroic ways her partner helped her out after her last hospital stay. She talks about Munchausen syndrome by proxy (how a caregiver might harm a patient to gain positive attention for himself as the caregiver) and how her partner loved the attention, and asks if any courts in the state allow phone access, but she may as well be explaining chronic emphysema to an unmindful marathoner. The advocate finally concedes "emotional abuse" is "very real," and mentions the battered women's shelter is "working on" making one room disability accessible, but it's "not a funding priority." Her phone therapist says, "Well, you do have a degenerative condition—are you sure your partner made you sicker?" Meanwhile, she can't get up for a glass of water, and a simple phone call leaves her exhausted. She finally contacts her abuser because she needs someone to pick up a prescription. Her partner stops at the drugstore and rekindles the abuse cycle. It's not about flowers and chocolate: it's about meds that keep her alive.

IPV organizations have begun to address these realities of disability, but they rarely do more than cite statistical horrors (people with disabilities are at least twice as likely to be abused, a likely outcome in a society that consistently devalues the lives of people with disabilities) and impose an activist template that doesn't fit. Disability is treated as an afterthought, not something with dramatically different risks and needs. Many IPV organizations are in fact performing oppressive acts of neglect and exclusion that mimic those of abusers, by denying access (not providing materials in braille, not installing wheelchair ramps, not enforcing strict fragrance-free policies) that effectively shut out disabled survivors and keep them locked in violence. Afraid or unwilling to confront their own ableism, these organizations rationalize the ways that disabled people are denied help, using a tired social argument that it's too hard, too expensive, or too embarrassing to ask others for accommodation requirements so that they avoid accountability for their marginalization of people with disabilities.

People from social service agencies frequently tell me that my disability would place unreasonable demands on everyone else, another stark example of ableism. Meanwhile I do see good ideas in the world, like the architectural concept of universal design—that is, housing design that would work for both the disabled and able-bodied. But the concept of universal design is not one that is typically applied to organizational structure, to the great detriment of the same people IPV organizations ostensibly serve. IPV organizations need to start looking at each facet of policy in terms of universal design. Class has been explored as a primary reason why women don't flee abuse (because they simply can't afford the escape or the life after), and disability also needs to be seriously considered. For example, during the tragedy of Hurricane Katrina in 2005, newscasters seemed flabbergasted that some people did not flee their homes right away because they could not afford transportation. Yet nearly half of those who died were 75 or older, which seems to indicate that physical ability might have been a pressing yet overwhelmingly overlooked issue, deeply conflated with race and class. With the epidemic reality of abuse toward people with disabilities (and seniors, who often share similar concerns), a "universally designed" set of IPV guidelines should be treated as a central issue.

In a culture that shuns and penalizes human vulnerability and provides at best an inadequate and spotty caregiving net, people with disabilities often rely on their abusers for food, bathing, toileting, transportation, and other survival needs. Many caregivers—not just partners—have intimate access to the lives of people with disabilities. But leaving an abusive relationship can be imminently life-threatening because victims might lose sustaining care, and replacing this can be next to impossible unless there are non-abusive family members or friends willing to provide it. If IPV organizations don't understand the pressing need for transitional (or long-term) hands-on care, a disabled person will often not be able to leave. Most IPV literature erroneously attributes this literal dependency to "victim psychology" instead of addressing dangerous social depictions of people with disabilities as needy (and superfluous). If the only alternative to an abusive caregiver is institutionalization or worse, a disabled person may be weighing one bad option against another. Are four sterile walls better than an abuser who offers affection, money, or other perks? Not necessarily.

By and large, it is not Stockholm syndrome that holds a disabled person captive to an abusive caregiver, but material and often elaborate acts of physical deprivation and torture. When someone has a disability, these acts are easy to inflict (and obscure from the view of others): they may just be a matter of hiding someone's painkillers, or sabotaging his TTY (text telephone), or—most insidiously—becoming an indispensable aid so that he can't function without the provided care. Disabled individuals subjected to violence can't always just get up and go—an idea rooted in the ableist assumption that all people are unencumbered by physical restrictions. Whereas a safety plan for an able-bodied person may involve words like run, walk, call, or drive, these action verbs may not be possible for a quadriplegic, a heart failure patient, someone with a brain stem injury, or someone with cognitive impairment. It is naive to assume a disabled person can be ushered into a world of safety simply by leaving her abuser, when the world at large is full of physical, emotional, economic, cultural, and social barriers.

Typically, when interpersonal violence is committed against people with disabilities, it is handled administratively (that is, through social service organizations rather than through the criminal legal system). This reveals a disturbing and broadly held worldview: our society does not really view abuse of the disabled as a crime. Although many states have mandatory reporting laws for abuse against people with disabilities, and social service personnel are legally mandated to report such abuse, few IPV organizations are familiar with these laws. And the court system is quite literally inaccessible. Several years ago, a woman contacted me because she was being regularly dragged down hallways by her hair and thrown against walls by a partner. I tried to convince her to get a restraining order, but this was immeasurably hard for her due to her anxiety disorder and extreme agoraphobia. She was multiply-disabled, but it didn't matter as far as the courts were concerned. When I asked a friend of mine who was also an attorney what it would take for the courts to accommodate a homebound person, she laughed and said, "Oh, they won't come to you unless you get a doctor's letter saying you're going to die very soon."

Later, I tried to get my own restraining order against one of the partners who was terrorizing me. Bedridden and homebound, I could not even make calls to advocates, who kept refusing to talk to my PCA on my behalf, probably because they assumed she was my abuser, and they couldn't imagine a disability hindering someone's ability to make phone calls. Finally they agreed to speak to my PCA, telling her there was no way I could get a restraining order without going to the courthouse unless an attorney filed a special motion on my behalf. Not only can I not travel, but I cannot go into facilities that are not fragrance- and chemical-free. It took my PCA about fifty calls (she estimates) to find an attorney who would do this. The attorney said time was of the essence as weeks had passed since my last contact with the abuser, and then she stopped returning our calls. I gave up in a state of complete despondency. I was extremely ill and couldn't even fight for appropriate medical care, let alone coordinate the changing of my locks or legal action against my partner. My helplessness wasn't learned: it was literal. Even lifting a phone receiver or talking into it required more strength than I generally had.

The West Virginia Coalition Against Domestic Violence reports that disabled victims are more likely to be blamed for their abuse, because they are perceived as difficult to be around or care for, and "caregiver stress" is considered a legitimate excuse for bad behavior. These social myths are no different from abuser jargon that habitually accuses those harmed of provoking the abuse. Because of the subtleties involved in abusing a disabled partner, people with disabilities might not identify themselves as abused, and rarely receive support from a society that lionizes the abusive partner as self-sacrificing for dating crips. It is common for batterers to "target punch" their victims to avoid getting caught. With an able-bodied partner, this might mean hitting her torso where bruises will not show. With a blind partner, this could mean putting obstacles in her path so she will trip and fall. With a frail partner who is too neurologically impaired to deny consent, this could mean using body weight to hold her down during sex even while she tries to resist by stiffening her body and pushing weakly with her forearms, then forcing sex in a way that physically harms her. Batterers of able-bodied partners may target punch by punching a woman on her torso instead of her face, but they have still committed a crime recognized by the state; when battering disabled victims, physical harm can often easily be inflicted on a disabled partner without punching at all, and even with murderous consequences such cases are hard to prosecute. In one court case, a woman with MS was murdered by a caregiver who fed her a bagel, knowing she could not swallow on her own and would choke to death; in another case, a man with chemical sensitivities was assaulted by his former partner when she intentionally and angrily sprayed him with scented products to cause him physical injury.

Advocates working with disabled survivors must first redefine what constitutes IPV, tailoring their definition to an individual's disabilities just as the abuser has probably done. Abusers will often use the minimum amount of force required to maintain power and control, and this minimum amount of force used on a disabled person—though it may cause substantial injury—might not fit neatly into legal definitions of abuse. Coercion and threats to a disabled partner could involve threatening to withdraw basic support, an act that can be more dangerous to a person with a disability than a violent beating. Intimidation tactics might include harming or mistreating a service animal. Economic abuse might include embezzling funds from a disabled partner who can't fill out a deposit slip, or giving her lavish gifts of adaptive equipment the state won't pay for to encourage her dependence. Physical abuse might consist of rough handling when transferring someone out of a wheelchair, or over-medicating. Sexual abuse might include forced abortion, inappropriate touching during bathing or dressing, or put-downs about a disabled person's sexuality. Neglect can include withholding care, medication, or life-sustaining attention. Many forms of abuse against people with disabilities, particularly those against some of the most vulnerable groups, such as the developmentally disabled, involve discrediting a person's own voice when she tries to convey her experience. Emotional abuse might take the form of denying the person's feelings by attributing injuries to the disability itself ("You're just touch-sensitive! That didn't hurt.").

Activists need to remain alert to the creative ways abusers cover up their violent behavior and get away with it. Key to an abuser's ability to manipulate friends, therapists, social workers, and the court systems is the still underexamined reality of societal ableism. Abusers sail through life, therapy, and the court system with a "not as bad as that guy" philosophy. They routinely rationalize their behavior, and can often pass off controlling behaviors toward a disabled partner as "concern." If they can convince themselves or others that looking through a partner's garbage, monitoring his phone calls and mileage, and insisting to know what he does every waking hour is not abuse and is instead a form of worry or concern, they will. The "worry" excuse is a particularly effective tactic when used by abusers of the disabled, since frequent checking on a disabled partner (and depriving her of freedoms in the process) is so socially acceptable: plus, she may need someone to check and make sure her wheelchair ramp has been cleared of snow, or to confirm she has food in the house. For a disabled person confined mostly to a home or bed, such acts of control both mirror and amplify the inherent suffering created by the disability in the first place. Most people will believe the abuser's pleas that she was simply trying to protect her (ungrateful, in society's view) disabled partner.

At every turn, society is complicit in the abuse of disabled people. For example, an abuser will seek to isolate his partner. If that person is wheelchair-bound, and very few venues in town are wheelchair-accessible, the abuser is not the only one isolating her: society has shut her out by relinquishing responsibility for accommodation. When she comes forward with her abuse, her peers might side with the abuser because they are, through inaction, supporting and privileged by a similar agenda. When the abuser talks about all he has done for his victim, as abusers are prone to do—and the list includes bathing her, driving her to medical appointments, and hand-dispensing medication—people might view him as a hero. This too reflects the deep threads of ableism in US culture, which forwards the belief that basic, hands-on care for most disabled people is exceptional and heroic, and should not be socially mandated.

Without a social philosophy that frames care as everyone's duty, society participates in a "slow code" ethic toward the disabled. ("Slow code" is a term used among hospital workers to denote the practice of only giving futile, going-through-the-motions resuscitation to some patients whose lives are considered too impaired to be worth saving.) A society that abandons people with disabilities, giving them few care options and tacitly accepting their abuse, simply will not adequately punish the same abusive caregivers who provide the care it refuses.

While capitalism, narcissistic cultural values, and other forces create care gaps, this care problem can't be plugged into a simplistic cultural analysis. Due to what many attribute to traditional family values that demand respect for seniors, for example, Japan shows signs of outpacing the US in creating a humane and innovative care system. In some areas, active members of society can "pay in" to a collective care system called "Koreikyo" by volunteering to care for frail members of society, to get "credit" for care when they need it, and the Japanese government has heavily funded robotics scientists who are working on caregiving robots to assist the elderly and disabled with such things as transfers (from bed to a wheelchair or bath) or vital signs monitoring. Despite these innovations, there is a Japanese term, kodokushi, or "lonely deaths," as so many uncared-for seniors now die alone, leaving human-shaped stains as they decompose and often are not found for long periods of time.

This idealized, sometimes robotic (literally) approach to care is what I call a cortical (higher brain) solution to a limbic (emotional/fight-or-flight brain) problem. Academic approaches around disability can easily become too robotic, pulling activists away from the shadowy realities of physical survival that haunt most disabled folks. A robot will never combat a problem as vast as social isolation or the horror of dying alone, nor will one lone gesture from an IPV organization to provide TTY access on its hotline help a person who is trapped in a rural setting, homebound, and living with late-stage AIDS. Additionally, a caregiving system will not actually make people care, and the problem with caregiving systems in general is that they easily become sterile/neglectful, or abusive, themselves, which is evident in the horrifying statistics of abuse in nursing homes. The human response must be deeper than that. Just as Lundy Bancroft argues that the abusive mentality is the mentality of oppression, I would argue that the Darwinian response to disabled folks (abandon the weak) is in fact the mentality of oppression, and people must be constantly challenged to question this way of thinking.

In an ableist framework, people often conflate disability empowerment with taking a "just like me" attitude that presumes a disabled person wouldn't want exceptional treatment—even if that treatment is a fragrance-free accommodation or a sign language interpreter, or, more subtly, acknowledgement of physical vulnerability. The differences in human vulnerability can be huge, especially when talking about IPV dynamics that involve power and control. Ignoring this fact denies the reality of people with disabilities and reinforces a mentality that only wheelchair athletes and feel-good supercrips should be recognized. Understanding the intricate differences in people's physical power and ability enables activists to calibrate their definitions of abuse. While the abuser of an able-bodied person might bar her exit by pushing furniture in front of escape routes and pulling phone cords out of the walls, the abuser of a bedridden individual can subtly inflict the same level of terrorism by simply charging into a bedroom and screaming when she can't get up and leave. It is critical that anti-violence movements in particular understand and treat such acts as equivalent. It can be enormously invalidating for a disabled abuse victim to hear, "I would just leave if someone treated me that way!" Or even, "I would just ask the abuser to leave." Asking an abuser to leave is often not an option for someone with a disability: she might need him to take care of her after he battered her. And who is going to explain to the hospital staff the medical needs relating to her rare congenital condition? My PCAs, who rarely keep the job more than a few months, could not describe my mitochondrial damage or dysautonomia or intricate hypersensitivities to an EMT, and this could mean the difference between life and death.

What often endears a batterer to a disabled person is her investment in the disabled person's vulnerability and his acquired knowledge about her condition, which most of society insults, ignores, and doesn't respond to in an empowering way. All abusers are dependent on keeping their victims vulnerable, a fact that transcends disability. When disability is involved, abusers put this attunement to the power imbalance toward monitoring what a disabled person needs, and then how to give or withdraw what is needed to gain power and maintain control. And more often than not, other able-bodied people just stand by and don't offer help. Few people know the intricate ergonomics of a disabled person's life, even though her ability to function—and survive—depends upon this knowledge. Ironically, abusers come to intimately understand this same complex reality that most people do not notice or care about. For years I tried to explain to my family why I needed someone to be on call 24 hours a day due to my erratic medical emergencies, to bring me food and water while I was lying down unable to move, and to nurse me during the unpredictable crashes I suffered following a chemical exposure or over-exertion. In response, they offered inconsistent bursts of help and care—a week here and a few days there—assuming (or hoping) that someone "out there" would fill the long gaps in between. But there was no one, no one but an abuser carefully tuned to my vulnerabilities. While others in my life would try to create a cheerful mood and occasionally bring me take-out, my abuser would dig into the gritty realities of my disability, draping a blanket over my legs before I even said I was cold, bringing me a glass with a straw so I could drink lying down. These were the acts of kindness woven into the abuse, and without them I would not have survived. Other people were willing to show up here and there, but my abuser craved the traumatic bonding of weathering my illness up close. This isn't to excuse the abuser's heinous behavior, but to point out that until people have access to the resources that can help them live healthy, functional lives, they will remain easy prey.

The details, in other words, cannot be afterthoughts. Wheelchair ramps, phone access, and other accommodations are essential for disabled survivors to make the first move toward escape. Abusers tend to look for social cues to tell them whom they can most readily victimize. As a critical step in ending abuse, IPV organizations must prioritize educating their staff and building their policy and practices around disability, and include the voices of people with diverse disabilities in that education process. Extensive planning must go into making sure services are accessible before a person with a disability calls; when stopping abuse, time is of the essence. And no one should have to beg for access. Meanwhile, more and more IPV survivors are becoming disabled. It is not uncommon for initially able-bodied victims of IPV to become temporarily or permanently disabled by physical injuries inflicted by abusers, or to develop ongoing psychiatric disabilities caused by the abuse. A study published in the *Journal of General Internal Medicine* found that domestic violence survivors have higher health care costs than other women for three years after the abuse ends. Survivors of IPV who develop new disabilities are at risk of entering relationships with new abusers who may then use the additional disability against them, or incorporate it into abuse strategies. The underpinnings of abuse have to do with distorted notions of strength and weakness, with the essence of bullying.

IPV activists must ferret out inequities in their own organizations to take a concrete stance against the exploitation of able-bodied privilege. Disability is a central issue in ending IPV. Organizations must start with full, unapologetic access for all people with disabilities. Access should include creative solutions such as Skype or phone access for those who are homebound. Where different disabilities have contradictory needs (for example, putting in a wheelchair-accessible bathroom may involve toxic building products that could harm a chemically sensitive person, but both needs can be recognized with the help of a green building consultant who understands universal design), able-bodied activists have to think beyond the ableist notion of compromise. People with disabilities cannot compromise their disabilities, so access must be fully realized. Second, IPV activists must ask themselves in challenging and perhaps uncomfortable terms how they view "reasonable accommodation." Who are they shutting out by rationalizations of what they deem reasonable, and why is this acceptable to them? Third, a radical social revisioning of care must include the willingness to take radical action. IPV activists must ask: if an abuser is committed to offering care for the next five years, who is going to replace that? Many shelters provide childcare and even pet care, but I have not heard of one providing care for the disabled. So what I am proposing is the radical notion of doing what is needed. Oppression is what is unreasonable, and seemingly unreasonable barriers must be conquered. This truth must serve as a basic mantra for activists looking at ableism.

As activists, many of us put a cap on our benevolence that distracts us from what is sensible. One time, while waiting for a bus in Berkeley, a woman approached me. She said she was trying to leave an abusive husband and needed money for bus fare. I only had twenty dollars in my wallet but, sensing she wasn't scamming me, I offered it. She said it wasn't enough, and tried to convince me to go with her to the ATM but I refused. She handed the twenty back. "It's too late," she said despairingly. "The fare is twenty-seven dollars and my husband is getting home from work and will see I'm gone. I have to go back home." She did not reach for my money again. IPV organizations have to understand the literalness of that extra seven dollars, both in terms of poverty/class issues (which are epidemic among the disabled as well as able-bodied IPV survivors), and in how it applies to disability, and they must find ways to bridge the seven-dollar gap that often excludes so many people. The first question an IPV organization needs to ask a disabled person is, what are your needs? Then, it is important to see the difference that seven more dollars, or a ramp, or fragrance-free access, or another accommodation that goes all the way, can make.

IPV organizations and activists need to carefully examine their stereotypes about violence, and constantly work to bring disability into the conversation.

Identifying an abuse dynamic always has challenges, and with disability there are unique issues. A seemingly combative person with encephalopathy may appear angry yet still be dealing with caregiver abuse. A deaf abuser may yell with his hands. People may perceive a disabled person as being a demanding bully and an abusive caregiver as a victim simply because she is moaning piercingly in discomfort and needs assistance.

In terms of broader activism, anti-racist organizations might look at the long, troubled history of eugenics activities that have almost always targeted people based on both disability and race, and how these have advanced other forms of violence. Queer organizations should consider how much they have to learn from those whose bodies have been historically loathed for their queerness. Disability is a common cause of homelessness and poverty, and should be included in discussions about these issues. Prison reform and abolition work must include an analysis both of how disabled prisoners are treated and cared for, but also how prison conditions create disability—for example, how solitary confinement is a physically disabling form of torture, since research shows it may cause organic brain changes and psychiatric damage.

Lastly, IPV workers must all be trained on disability-sensitivity and challenged to confront their ableism by always keeping an eye for inclusion. The ability to convey the gestalt of a traumatic experience to a receptive witness, and validation that truly comprehends differences in vulnerability, is crucial in aiding IPV survivors to step out of the fury and into a safe future.

works cited

Lundy Bancroft, *Why Does He Do That? Inside the Minds of Angry and Controlling Men* (New York: Berkeley Trade, 2003).

Paul A. Fishman, Amy E. Bonomi, Melissa L. Anderson, Robert J. Reid, and Fred P. Rivara, "Changes in Health Care Costs over Time Following the Cessation of Intimate Partner Violence," *Journal of General Internal Medicine* (2010): doi:10.1007/s11606-010-1359-0.

"GeckoSystems' Elder Care Robot Trials' Caregiver Praises New GeckoSchedulerTM," *Green Technology*, http://green.tmcnet.com/news/2010/06/10/4838502.htm.

Susan Griffin, *What Her Body Thought: A Journey Into the Shadows* (San Francisco, CA: HarperOne, 1999).

Robert C. Marshall. "Koreikyo: A Japanese Home Care Co-op Run For and By Seniors," *Grassroots Economic Organizing,* http://www.geonewsletter.org/node/147.

Justin Nobel, "Japan's 'Lonely Deaths': A Business Opportunity" (April 6, 2010), http://www.time.com/time/world/article/0,8599,1976952,00.html

Judith Wallerstein, Julia M. Lewis, and Sandra Blakeslee, *The Unexpected Legacy of Divorce: A 25-year Landmark Study* (New York: Hyperion, 2001).

THERE IS ANOTHER WAY

WAY

Ana-Maurine Lara

part one: survivor's rights & responsibilities

As a survivor of abuse, in any of its forms, I HAVE THE RIGHT TO:

1. NAME RAPE, INCEST, SEXUAL MOLESTATION, ASSAULT, BATTERY, DOMESTIC VIOLENCE, AND ABUSE IN ALL ITS FORMS
2. FEEL ANGRY, HURT, SAD, LOVING, OR FORGIVING OF MY PERPETRATOR(S) AND ANY FRIENDS OR FAMILY WHO HAVE COLLABORATED WITH THE VIOLENCE
3. SPEAK ABOUT MY ABUSE
4. A SPACE TO REFLECT UPON MY PERSONAL HISTORY WITHOUT JUDGMENT
5. THE PHYSICAL AND PSYCHOLOGICAL CARE THAT IS NECESSARY FOR SURVIVING TRAUMA
6. A SAFE AND SECURE HOME
7. SAFE RELATIONSHIPS WITH FAMILY, FRIENDS, PARTNERS, LOVERS, AND SERVICE PROVIDERS

8. CONFRONT PERPETRATORS AND THOSE WHO HAVE PARTICIPATED IN VIO-
LATIONS AND ABUSES

9. LEAVE

10. TAKE ACTION TO STOP THE ABUSE

11. FEEL BEAUTIFUL AND LOVABLE

12. LOVE AND BE LOVED

As a survivor of abuse, in any of its forms, I HAVE THE RESPONSIBILITY TO:

1. TAKE CARE OF MYSELF PHYSICALLY, MENTALLY, EMOTIONALLY, AND SPIRI-
TUALLY—WHATEVER THAT MEANS FOR ME

2. REFLECT ON THE WAYS ABUSE HAS AFFECTED ME AND SEEK APPROPRIATE
FORMS OF SUPPORT

3. UNDERSTAND THE SOURCES OF MY PAIN

4. INTERRUPT PATTERNS OF ABUSE AND SELF-ABUSE IN MY OWN BEHAVIOR
THAT HURT ME AND/OR OTHERS

5. TAKE FULL RESPONSIBILITY FOR MY CHOICES AND BEHAVIORS

6. REACH OUT TO OTHER SURVIVORS AS A SOURCE OF SUPPORT OR TO PROVIDE
SUPPORT

7. LIVE MY LIFE TO THE BEST OF MY ABILITIES AND WITH THE GOAL OF
REACHING MY FULL POTENTIAL

8. STAY PRESENT WITH MYSELF AND ALERT TO MY NEEDS

9. FORM HEALTHY RELATIONSHIPS THAT NOURISH ME

10. CLAIM MY OWN DESIRE

11. ACCEPT MY BEAUTY, POWER, STRENGTHS, WEAKNESSES, AND HUMANITY IN
THE WORLD

12. SURVIVE MY HISTORY, CIRCUMSTANCES, AND VIOLATIONS

part two: what i was thinking

This essay is written for me and other organizers who are survivors of abuse, in any of its forms. I write to make connections between our individual and collective experiences as survivors and our roles as organizers and community leaders.

For many years, with many friends and peers, I have had an ongoing discussion about the effects of abuse on ourselves, our relationships, and our community work. How do we intentionally manage processes of personal healing in relationship to the work of fighting on behalf of our communities? And, how do we name ourselves throughout these processes? Are we victims? Survivors? What are the politics of these identities? What do they indicate about how we feel about ourselves in relationship to our personal histories and the histories of our communities?

Stepping back to consider the larger picture, I want to acknowledge that as people of color, queers, and genderqueers, our histories of resistance are living proof that we do not accept institutionalized forms of violence as inherently true or valid, that we believe in our own worth and right to live life on our own terms. It is important for me to start there because my understanding is that when we extend the definition of oppression to include the exertion of violence in all its forms, we are extending it into an understanding that all forms of abuse are unacceptable, be they institutional racism, compulsive heterosexuality, police violence, date rape, or intimate partner abuse. In other words, if we consider the larger picture of the histories our communities have created through our struggles for survival, we can see that *we already have a basic framework for making the connections between our own individual experiences and those of our communities.*

This is my starting point. Please know that this essay is an attempt to create language for defining my own experiences and my own lessons. Here, I want to share (1) one example of how I survived abuse and the ramifications of my healing process on my community organizing work, and (2) my thoughts on the direct connection between our own resolutions around personal abuse and the ways we affect others as community organizers. Resolving our personal histories of abuse is a life-long process that is more like walking around a well than down a straight road. But when we're aware of our pain, and work to uncover its sources, we become the best allies to our own healing, and can become stronger in our community work.

Without disavowing the incredibly important work of the domestic violence movement, I want to acknowledge that some of the most painful interactions I have experienced occurred in social service or community-based organizations working with survivors and the most disenfranchised members of our society. In the process of reflecting on these experiences (of how community isn't always a safe place), I decided to examine my own history of abuse and survival and the lessons I have learned in the process. I transformed my own lessons learned from surviving abuse into a sort of code for healing behavior in the world beyond myself; one result of that process was the "Survivor's Rights & Responsibilities" statement. For me, these "rights and responsibilities" have served as a guideline for personal and community healing. But I grew frightened that my discussion of the healing process in the language of personal rights and responsibilities could be misinterpreted as some statement about "personal responsibility," rather than what I had intended it to be: a call for considering the ways that violence and oppression work on us and our communities simultaneously, and how sometimes these appear in the actions and decisions of our leaders.

To clarify: healing from our personal experiences is not just a matter of personal health; healing is also a matter of social change. Our communities have suffered lifetimes of abuse: genocide, slavery, colonialism, massive incarceration and deportation, and police violence are only a few of the more obvious examples. The work required to undo the myriad internalized and externalized forms of oppression afflicting our communities is not just about what we do out in the streets, in nonprofits, or in community groups. It's also about how prepared we are to deal with the fallout from our personal experiences with violence. It's about how we treat ourselves and one another in the process. It is hard work to do this. It is really hard. But it is also necessary.

part three: an example from my own life

Many years ago, when I was 23, I dated a woman, "K," who was incredibly abusive—she tried to destroy my friendships, and she demonstrated small but increasing forms of physical violence that culminated in a gun threat. We worked together, and though we were in different buildings, after the destructive break up—which I initiated because I couldn't take her controlling behavior—she followed me around during work hours for about three months. I quit my job as soon as possible and made sure that I changed my social life to avoid the places where she hung out. This sucked for me, but I didn't want to risk seeing her. It didn't matter—"K" always figured out ways to find me.

The moment of personal fury and epiphany came almost two years later when she approached an acquaintance, let's call her "Sarah," and informed her of my so-called betrayal of her love. Sarah, someone with whom I was doing intense community work, was not familiar with the violence I had lived through with this woman. I had never felt the need to talk about "K"—I just wanted to forget about her. Sarah came over to my home one day telling me that they had spoken, and that I had a responsibility to ensure that all of our community was taken care of. I was so upset at the entire scenario: at "K" for trying to reach me through a friend, at Sarah for her one-sided request for my accountability, and at myself for having kept silent for so long. I turned pale. After taking an hour to calm down, to digest what had just happened, I explained to Sarah why I had broken off all communication with "K." Sarah, also a survivor of abuse, indicated that she understood. She started crying, having realized how she had been manipulated by "K."

However, a few months later, Sarah invited both me and "K" to a party, without informing either of us that the other person would be there. When I asked Sarah, whom I considered a close friend, why she had done this, she said it was not her responsibility to value one community member over the other. I left the party. I felt betrayed by Sarah, and I felt that I had been placed in danger. I didn't understand, until much later, how Sarah's own history of abuse manifested itself in the form of manipulating social relationships. I didn't understand how her own blocks against confronting her own abuser meant that she constantly put her friends in situations where they were expected to be able to confront their abusers, even if they weren't ready to do so. From her perspective, she was healing our communities. From mine, she had created a context for potentially perpetuating violence.

If, prior to that moment, I had not done the work of taking care of myself, of ensuring my own safety and mental health, who knows what kinds of violence could have been perpetuated at that party. What if I had tried to confront my abuser and she had turned violent? What if my own anger materialized in the form of violence? The truth is, the community was small—especially that of queer organizers of color. We all knew each other. For me, after my relationship with "K," it had been especially important that I take steps to ensure my personal safety and seek help from friends and counselors. It was especially important because I was working with other survivors, and with people going through abuse in that moment, abuse that is an ongoing reality within my communities. If I had not been working on getting solid on my own stuff, who knows what kind of energy I would have put out at that party, in that moment, with my community. Who knows what kind of energy I would have called forth while being triggered.

That incident became an important catalyst for discussions about partner abuse, as all of my friends who had been at the party realized something was going on. First, because we cared about each other, people noticed I left the party. Second, when folks asked me, days later, I decided to break the silence around what had happened with "K." This in turn encouraged other women in our community to break the silence regarding their own experiences of abuse with "K." When we realized there was a shared experience of violence, we created bridges to hold each other close, to safeguard ourselves and each other. We also created bridges to hold each other accountable, and to generate spaces of healing that were consensual and transparent.

After that night, I never saw "K" again (she recently found me on Facebook—I blocked her). In our community discussions, we asked ourselves to identify the roots of our pain, to define "community" and "community work."

We asked ourselves what it meant to be accountable: how to differentiate loyalty from truth, and how to hold truth gently. We started to analyze the frameworks we were using to define our work. It became clear that a trust had been broken between Sarah and me, and that in order for the work to continue to be effective, we would have to heal and that trust would have to be restored. It became evident that typical movement models of mediation and community work were not what we were using, nor were they appropriate or adequate. What we were attempting required redefining accountability in terms of: practicing total honesty about where we were at emotionally and spiritually; putting the ugliest parts of ourselves out in front of our peers and trusting they would help us grow stronger; taking ownership of our mistakes; and recognizing being nice, loving, and kind as revolutionary values central to our work.

Those discussions at age 23 became super important for my development as a person, artist, and organizer. They were crucial to my understanding of the links between personal experience and community work. Through those shared moments and conversations, I began to understand that our personal experiences of abuse could serve as a road map for continuing or stopping the perpetuation of violent, oppressive behavior. I also understood that it is possible to be, simultaneously, both a survivor and a perpetrator, just as it is possible to be a racist queer, or a homophobic person of color. And that much in the same way we work to not perpetuate racism, we must also work not to perpetuate other forms of violence. There are other ways.

Truth-telling or confronting violence, as in the case of Sarah's party, does not have to be an abusive process, even if it touches deep hurts. The hurt of seeing the truth about ourselves and each other does not have to happen with abusive language or without consciousness around the power we hold in relationship to each other. Truthfulness with each other can lay the foundations for revolutionary consciousness, and for resolving the effects of abuse. Models generated by the most traumatized of our communities—communities of color, genderqueer communities, and genderqueer communities of color—can guide us toward the resolution of multiple forms of violence without reinscribing the trauma that our society inflicts on us every day. We can learn ways to do this work without hurting those closest to us.

part four: what i dream of

Like abuse, resistance takes many forms. Sometimes it drives change, while other times the focus is survival. Sometimes the result is progress, even revolutionary change. Other times resistance is regressive or even colludes with oppression to create more oppression. I know, in my flesh, that my ancestors had no choice about their enslavement. But they did make choices about how to survive that enslavement. They chose profound spiritual power, subtle and direct forms of resistance (including fighting and dying) and, sometimes, participation in the system as overseers or slave owners themselves. Without confusing one context for another, I think history highlights how in our personal and communal lives we can choose to resist through active or passive means, through participation or collusion. We all make choices about how to handle our past and present circumstances, even in the most oppressive conditions. And even when we are powerless over our circumstances, we can still tap into the deepest parts of our own humanity for our own survival.

I want to be clear that I am not talking about having a choice in our circumstances. Rather, I am talking about what we do *with* our circumstances. Our awareness of our circumstances and how to deal with them is what makes us powerful leaders and organizers in contexts that have much wider berth than enslavement. Even with a gun to our head, we have to imagine and act with a desire for the best possible outcome. When we enter into leadership positions (as organizers or otherwise), we must acknowledge what that power means; often, it means that we have choices and responsibilities. That the first choice we made was to put our bodies, minds, hearts, and spirits on the line for a greater good. And that after that first choice, we are accountable for our decisions and our actions. We are choosing to address our own survival, and the survival of our communities, with the tools at our disposal. And as we look out over a field full of greys, we have to first look down to see where we ourselves are standing.

Our ability to make choices is also different from our feelings, our emotions. As human beings, we can't determine how we're going to feel about a given set of circumstances. We are entitled to all of our feelings, but we can determine how we will act once we become aware of them. When someone abuses us, it is usually because that person has made a choice to engage in destructive behavior. We can't account for other peoples' choices, but we also don't have to tolerate their justifications. As organizers, we can stop destructive behavior in all its forms by confronting abuse inflicted by others, and by confronting our own abusive behavior toward others.

As organizers, I know that we don't let racism, transphobia, xenophobia, homophobia, sexism, ableism, or classism stop our work or our collective calls for justice. (In fact, these forms of oppression often form the premise for our work in the first place!) And I know that, as organizers, we actively seek to unearth internalized forms of oppression and the particularly insidious effects of internalizing oppression on our health and movements. From direct observation and from my readings, I know that people who have survived some of the most profound forms of oppression are often the most powerful and necessary leaders of our movements. However, many of us fail to consider how partner abuse—as one of the most intimate forms of oppression—might function within us, become internalized, in the same way that the –isms do. Many of us do not examine the connection between internalized oppression and the violence we inflict and suffer within our own besieged communities. In other words, we often fail to consider the public weight of our personal histories. Many times, we justify our own abusive patterns by using our status within a community, or isolating the truth tellers who reveal our pain. Many times, we allow for the abuses because we are desperate: the work demands that we be alert and ready to respond to crisis at any moment. The work demands that our most brilliant members mentor us, teach us, guide us, and facilitate our own development, even if the way they go about doing it is fucked up.

I can think of many examples of this, but I'll cite one which has stuck with me for a long time. Several years ago, I went to a conference on violence in communities of color. I sat in the audience, excited that one of my sheroes, a veteran queer Chicana leader, was about to speak. I then watched as she yelled, in public and abusively, at a young Native American woman who was simply trying to set up her microphone. We then listened to her justify, to a room of 3,000 women of color, her behavior with the fact of her status in the movement. Needless to say, I was deeply saddened with her choice about how to deal with her frustration. I wanted to remind her that we, all of us in that room, were not the enemy, and that her frustrations about the world would be held in that space. I (and maybe we) was also reminded that the pain of our experiences of violence is always with us, and sometimes, despite our best intentions, we become the vector for perpetuating that violence. I wanted to have compassion for her, but I was mad, and it took me a long time to forgive her transgression. That was okay. I still don't think it's okay that she yelled at a sister like that, but I can only hope she (and everyone who silently witnessed this) learned from that experience, too.

As organizers and leaders, we know we have great responsibilities in assuring constructive social change, and we are aware of the constant pressure of self-development. However, we cannot ignore the impact of our own personal histories on how we approach the work. We cannot forgo our personal health and expect it will not affect our communities. For example, how many times have we seen an organizer who's sick and "toughing it out" instead of going home to rest? For paid organizers, how many times have they been told they won't get paid on sick time, or that they are not doing enough if they don't pull more than their weight? What about this scenario is about control and perpetuating larger forms of violence? What about this scenario is simply survival? We must take care of ourselves as part of ensuring our collective survival. Because we are, all of us together, the community, and this radical mindfulness is the work, the reason we organize in the first place.

It is my hope that as direct or indirect survivors of abuse, we don't also allow our experiences of abuse to become *the* pattern for our interactions with others. It is my hope that we choose to heal and to do things in ways that foment healthier communities, rather than broken ones. It is my hope that as leaders we become models of healing. It is my hope that we, as organizers and leaders, stand on equal footing with one another and others. It is my hope that we, as organizers and leaders, live with enough humility to apologize and approach change within ourselves and our communities as possible. It is my hope that, as organizers and leaders in our movements, we take care of ourselves so that we are available for the long haul.

If we *don't* take care of ourselves as leaders in our movements, or deal with our own histories, how can we be emotionally and mentally prepared to interact with each other in ways that don't replicate the abuse that is familiar and present within our interactions? The personal is deeply political, and not just in terms of identity, but in terms of how we live our lives and do our work as agents of social change.

part five: the imperative tense

In truth, I feel a sense of urgency around all of this. I am now in my thirties, watching yet another generation of young people being abused within our movements. I am seeing that the foundations I helped build in my twenties were not maintained in my communities; those of us who were doing this work ten years ago are watching the wheel get reinvented, without acknowledgment of what has already been done. In other words, the machinations of oppression are alive and well, and, simultaneously, those of us who have stepped up or have been entrusted with doing the work, no matter what our age, must deal with ourselves. We don't have time to watch another generation experience trauma at the hands of movement leaders. We cannot lose the next generation of organizers to the violence of those who are so hurt and tired that they know only to push people to the breaking point. We are living in a state of extreme crisis that is coming at us from all sides. How will we choose to treat and be with each other in ways that will continue to ensure our individual and collective survival?

To lay the groundwork for deeper liberation, we must ensure the perpetuity, health, and safety of our communities. As communities, we must find

the existent models, rediscover old models, and create new models for ensuring our healing. Put another way, we must do much more than survive.
I am asking that those of us who are survivors use our experiences to create
these maps with integrity, love, truthfulness, gentleness, and a vision for assuring the dignity and safety of our collective humanity. I am asking that we
do the hard work needed to leave the destructive patterns behind and trade
them in for new ones, that we survive our histories and circumstances, and
allow ourselves to feel beautiful and be loved so that we can create beauty
and love for each other.

part three

(re)claiming body, (re)claiming space

MANIFESTO

Vanessa Huang

We believe in home   all home all beautiful   home enough bellies breathe & sigh
enough skin rest dance free   enough courage carry all life   this a home no landlord
tenant bank imagine   no passport jail shelter claim   no developer gift no reparation
furnish   this home free a bodycrossing & shame   free a memorybreak   no shame
all beautiful   this home pray for lost & stolen   home now free a traveling fence
finger & sky breaking open   free enough many home many body home & whole
together   home safe & full spirit prayer   bodyprayer full desire   home wider song
& cookin   wider shape a wood brick & stone   home wider shapes weave together
full & wide enough spirit return to body   enough whole body each body heartbody
holy beautiful   holy so holy body homeless turn home again

We want home   all home all beautiful   home alive so alive heartbrave thunder shake
out a hiding   so holy beautiful & so holy brave every body home & every body free

WITHOUT MY CONSENT

Bran Fenner

My first adult experience with intimate partner abuse started right before college. While having sex, I suffered a flashback to a sexual assault from my childhood. I had to stop, and started to cry. My partner at the time held me for about 20 minutes, and I started to feel better—but then they asked me to continue with the sexual act I had stopped doing. I felt sick to my stomach and confused, so I just said I wasn't in the mood. Rather than respect my decision, my partner whined, begged, and pleaded until I cooperated. Until I gave in.

I didn't want to go through a long process of saying NO. From prior experience, I knew the other person wouldn't listen, and eventually I would have to give in or find a substitute; cooperate. In this moment, I experienced major feelings of guilt: guilt that I had a history of sexual abuse and, later on, depression that would sometimes hinder my sexual desire, especially around specific acts my partner desired. This was a running theme throughout the relationship: I was made to feel bad and mean for not wanting to have sex. Though this behavior was less aggressive than the time this person held me down while I tried to get free and pleaded NO repeatedly, it was still violent and scarring.

"I just wanted to make you feel good." This was the excuse my former partner provided for physically restraining me, for showing up unannounced at my mother's house in the middle of the night, for each time they coerced me into sex. Later I realized that it was never about me—it was always about their satisfaction. I just got good at faking it so it would be over as soon as possible.

Fortunately, this relationship ended, and as traumatized as I still am from some of its different aspects, I've learned a lot from it. The most important thing I learned is that cooperation is *not* consent, and my first NO should be the final NO. The excuse "But I want to make you feel good" is not an excuse, it's a self-serving rationalization for abusive behavior. NO is often easier for me to say to strangers. Since then, almost all of my partners have been sexually responsible. Learning how to say NO and being okay with other people's hurt feelings increased my sense of self-worth, allowing me to reclaim my desires. This experience also helped me relate more respectfully to other people. I'm more aware of respectful touching and not assuming what's comfortable for people, as well as understanding that many people in my community have been sexually assaulted. I want to do everything in my power not to replicate those patterns. We are, however, only human and sometimes fuck up. The point is not to go to a place where you focus only on how what you did was harmful, but instead to figure out how to grow and change and have your actions show that.

My ex may never know why I refused to be in the same spaces as them or how many female-bodied people have felt sexually disrespected by them. They did not listen throughout the relationship, and there seemed to be a point when they stopped engaging with anyone who would challenge their behavior. That point seemed to come after they were isolated and talked about in the community. Although this person might still blame me for their "ex-communication," most of the stories that were circulating in the community came from other people's direct experiences, many of which were similar to mine.

Since this person was surrounded by enablers, it is easy to imagine how they would not move to a place of truly looking within and understanding male-bodied privilege, consent, and healthy relationships. Worse, this person's abusive behavior, pushing women and trans men into unwanted sex or sexual acts, seemed to be ongoing; and some of these people, I knew. Admittedly, I see the appeal of shaming and community call-outs. But ultimately, I think this helps stunt the perpetrator's growth process, creating a false sense of relief for the person (and community) wronged. Accountability could mean so many different things. It could mean one person is asked to stay out of certain social events and seek counseling. The other person may require support as well to begin to let go of the damage suffered. As in organizing, I believe in the escalation model as part of an accountability process. Using the escalation model involves finding people who can commit to working with both parties to heal while creating and maintaining realistic boundaries. Escalation becomes necessary when perpetrators refuse to engage in the process, maintain agreements or change their behavior.

There are a lot of things we are not in control of, particularly if we are poor, brown, female-bodied, queer-bodied, and/or disabled. Our ability to decide what happens to our bodies can be compromised not only in our interpersonal relationships, but also within the larger systems that shape our thinking and behavior. So many of our communities are under constant attack by pervasive police surveillance, harassment, and brutality, as well as other forms of state violence framed as "protection." Yet, in some ways, I am even more dismayed that some social justice activists are also perpetrators of sexual harassment, assault, sexual manipulation, and rape. Too often we remain silent as a community when confronted by cycles of abuse, allowing violence to fester like a wound on someone's forehead. We all see it but try not to look. Why?! What are we afraid of? Is it the significant amount of work it takes to create a long term vision for alternatives to policing, the complications of organizational impacts? I am tired of our seeing a community member abuse their partner without response—or with an inadequate one, where we have one meeting, take great notes, and subsequently drop the ball. I'm sick to my stomach when I remember that the person who violated my body and boundaries was constantly surrounded by community people who never held this person accountable. Meanwhile, several female-bodied folks (most being young folks I worked with) confided in me about unwanted advances from the same person. We were all silent, but I was blamed for this person's isolation by their friends. This was beyond invalidating; it was humiliating and contributed to a severe depression that lasted years.

Though neither of us was willing to engage in conversation, at the same time, isolation was not the answer. To ensure that the process of accountability for the person who "fucked up" continues, the community needs to support all parties involved. For example, we need clear boundaries for all parties and community events. Both people may get triggered when they see each other; reactions can be damaging and lower community morale. And what about people who are less willing to be held accountable for sexually inappropriate behavior? How do responsible community members at least watch out for the people who may be at risk for their abusive behavior? Do we post guidelines for fund-raisers and house parties around consensual behavior, notifying all attendees that those who do not adhere to them will be asked to leave? Why not? I personally believe that many of the rules clearly posted at the door of many sex clubs or play parties should be universal. Why not expect people to ask if they can touch you; why not suggest code words to use if you need someone nearby to intervene? We have to be dedicated not only to institutional change, but also to transforming our interpersonal dynamics. We cannot allow the fear of not being liked to prevent us from setting boundaries as a community. To me, there is a big difference between kindness and niceness. More often than not, "being nice" (which is not necessarily about being genuine) tends to lead to passive-aggressive behavior and unhealthy repression, and ultimately can undermine what is required to build a community that loves and protects all of its members. If we are serious about ending violence within activist communities, it is crucial that we set community standards for acceptable behavior and that we are committed to fiercely maintaining them.

With all of the lessons I have learned, I now feel a sense of empowerment each time I let someone know they're dancing too close, or that I want them to dance closer. I know that I have the ability to forgive someone who has fucked up and is actively working to change. That said, the biggest task I have ahead of me (and before the recommended forgiveness of the community member who repeatedly violated my body and tried to take away so much of me) is to forgive myself and heal the other part of my past—the child who was repeatedly violated and unprotected, the child whose early wounds were left uncared for. For a long time I held on to the fact that I chose to stay in a sexual relationship with this person. The fact that I chose to stay was a primary reason I felt unjustified in walking away earlier, why I let guilt run things. For some time, I started to believe this person's words when they berated me for saying NO. Now if someone begs and pleads that I do something sexual for them, I know I can walk away. It is always okay to say NO and that can give you a new and beautiful understanding of what YES really and truly means for you. My prior relationship was not always clearly abusive to me until after the fact. There were ways in which the abuse was more obvious but I felt a need to focus on the coercion and manipulation that ran the majority of the relationship. I appreciate my story being shared; reading this all those years ago might have validated my feelings enough to have helped me end the cycle earlier.

BELOW ARE TIPS GATHERED FROM MAINLY PERSONAL EXPERIENCES, COMMUNITY DISCUSSIONS, AND PAMPHLETS ON PARTNER ABUSE:

Are you listening? "I don't know" and "maybe" do not mean YES. YES does. Everything else means NO! If someone says NO, stop pushing. It's not cute, it's not smooth—it's sexual harassment.

Are you being responsible? If your date is drunk or passed out, that is not an invitation for sex. You are responsible for everything you do; these are choices you make. Sometimes what was a yes may become a NO when someone sobers up and that needs to be respected too.

Are you respecting someone's decision? Don't make people feel bad for saying NO to one, a few, or all sexual acts. Being in a relationship or on a date does not mean you have any rights to someone's body. You are not entitled to anything except mutual respect.

What is consent? Consent is freely and voluntarily agreeing to do something. Consent is not giving in to someone who is harassing you to do anything. Consent is not when you or the other person are heavily intoxicated, not when someone is sleeping, not when someone has said NO. (And remember: only YES means YES!)

Remember: Touching someone while they are sleeping or falling asleep because you find yourself turned on is selfish. How many important decisions are you asked to make after being woken up in the middle of the night? If you think there is a possibility you might want to have sex with your partner in the middle of the night, talk to them beforehand and make agreements. For some people, it could be hot to be woken up in that way, but unless your partner has given you permission that is fully consensual, you are raping them.

No one is obligated to get you off sexually. If you are horny and the other person is not, you do not need to show your disappointment. Remember, you can always jerk off. If it becomes a consistent problem, you may need to adjust your relationship; if you're monogamous, it could mean figuring out how to open up your relationship for a bit so your sexual needs are met. If it continues for a long time, it could be a sign of a bigger problem or dynamic you can evaluate together. Sex involves reading body language and listening to the desires of all people involved; how responsible or considerate are you being if you succeed in wearing someone down to the point where they give in to your needs rather than respecting their own wants and boundaries?

If the other person says no to a sexual request, that should be taken seriously. Someone saying NO is not an invitation to beg, plead, or cry for sex.

Sometimes you can't help but cry. This may mean after being told NO you might need to take some time to yourself to calm down. Being sexually rejected by a partner, date, or friend can trigger many difficult emotions, such as lowered self-esteem, anger, and sadness, as well as a lack of confidence, and body issues. These are all very real feelings that you will have to figure out how to deal with. Making the other person feel guilty or bad for setting a sexual boundary is neither okay nor helpful. Try listening first, then maybe talking to a friend whom you trust, especially a friend who is a good communicator and is good at seeing issues from multiple sides. Some friends may automatically side with you, especially if they don't like your partner. Try getting support from someone who can better separate the people from the actions.

Many aspects of my life have been affected by this experience—negatively, positively, and everything in-between. I continue to struggle with maintaining my boundaries and staying present in my body, though it has gotten easier. Disassociating was a skill I developed to protect myself many years ago and it served me well. Now I work hard to develop new skills but my process is long from over.

Good luck in every part of your journey.

A SLIDING STANCE

N.

I **stand** in the stone corridor, looking at the uniformed court officer with wide eyes. I am here checking out the space before my court date to get a peace bond against my lover.

"What do you mean we all wait in the same space?" I ask.

"Don't worry—just ignore him, dear."

"Ignore him...right."

Later, the judge will call my lover "mister," give her masculine pronouns despite her obviously female name.

I will learn a lot through this process about the gendered assumptions surrounding relationship violence.

We didn't fit their framework of understanding.

The truth was, though, in their own way, my queer feminist activist communities didn't know any more what to do with me or us than the courts did.

I sometimes felt profoundly alone, like I was drowning in the collective silence and judgments built around me. And in very different ways, I wouldn't doubt this also to be my lover's experience. In either case, nothing on offer seemed very helpful.

I didn't love the option of engaging the court system, it being an institution embedded in racism, classism, patriarchy. At demos, cops were always on the other side, a force we were generally fighting against. It wasn't a decision I made easily or lightly.

Unfortunately there didn't appear to be a lot of other options available. I didn't trust my lover to hold herself accountable, and who else would be there to deal with whatever came next? However conflicted my decision, in the absence of community alternatives it offered me some promise of response, some authority where I felt like I had none. My refusal to see her didn't stop her from showing up at my house. My shouts didn't stop her fist.

It is the morning of filing my statement with the police, who would now hand deliver the court summons to my ex-partner.

My new lover thinks this is an occasion to celebrate: "You must be relieved."

No, my choice paradoxically involves giving over control, an uneasy space I occupy after a relationship where I felt so little of it.

I feel an overwhelming grief I have been staving off by procrastinating until the deadline. That our relationship is over is undeniably real to me in this moment.

How could I say that even after everything, part of me still longed for her? It is a difficult thing to explain to anyone who hasn't been there. From the outside, this possibility seems unimaginable. From the outside, things seem clear and straightforward.

From the inside, life is held in powerful contradictions. I lived our profound intimacy that, when good, was quite magical. The person with whom at times I felt the most safe, the most alive, was the same person at times I both dreaded and feared. The person who could be big and angry could just as easily be intensely vulnerable and incredibly loving. For all her suffering, I thought I could love her pain away—that I just had to love her bigger, better.

Once out of the relationship, I worked hard to see the hooks. How deep our socialization runs—part Catholic upbringing to honor commitment no matter what, part fairy-tale belief that true love only comes once—that somewhere inside of me I clung to my values, and my fear clung to me. To my homophobic family, how much I wanted to show you that queer relationships could be healthy and long-lasting—that I could have what you have, that I could be just like you. And how, because of this, I have kept my silence, and you don't know me as well as you might.

It would be easier to tell you that the story ends there, that I picked up the pieces and moved on, but it doesn't. After I got a peace bond against her, I violated the bond myself, some time later, by seeing her and getting back together with her. Some were brave enough to say I was betting on the wrong horse, but I wasn't ready to hear that.

My house held a meeting with us during which my partner listened to and addressed their concerns about how her behavior had eroded their sense of safety too. She would have to earn back their trust. And I believed she would, because things were different...for a while. But this new narrative, though useful, left no room inside the relationship to name old behaviors, old ways, if they didn't exist anymore.

Soon enough the narrative began unraveling, but in the face of people's judgment and my own hope for change, how could I admit this to anyone, even myself?

Rarely did I get time alone to even think such thoughts. She accused me of using my femme and "passing" privileges against her through the court process; using my class privilege when I didn't pay for this or that; of not knowing what it was to be a "real" survivor. When she disclosed affairs, my hurt and anger was evidence of my lack of internal security and radical politics.

Everyone has a bottom line. Sometimes you just don't know what it is until you hit it. Mine came in a moment that, in the bigger picture, was a more ordinary betrayal. Another "poly" agreement broken, knowingly, and right in front of me. Humiliation aside, I experienced a moment of pure clarity when I realized this will not stop. This will not stop, no matter what I do or how much I love her. I decided I was finally done.

WHEN YOUR
PARENTS MADE
YOU

Leah Lakshmi Piepzna-Samarasinha

When your parents make you, it is Chile, 1974
They think they will raise you in a revolutionary sunlight
but you are born in a refugee camp to a mother alone
as your father sits in Pinochet's prison

When you show me the one photograph of your childhood
you are four. Your delicate fro spreads like sunrise
as your wide open eyes stare away, fully disassociated
At the refugee kitchen table
your mother rocks thick black eyeliner and wings of hair
holding a cigarette over a smile insisting

She looks like her hummingbird heart is about to explode
Your father grips her heart
like a cigarette between his fingers
He is the one about to explode
Your heart flies off someplace else

At fourteen you run away from them
sleep on couches and stairways
spray TORONTO IS HUNGRY everywhere
When the L.A. rebellion explodes for your birthday
you smash all the windows of the McDonald's
and make the front page of the newspaper
You cross the border in the trunk of a car

You hitch to L.A.
where the national guard is still on the sidewalk
Your eyes are still somewhere else
as you beat up skinheads,
throw some off a roof
get trailed for years by that one cop
You soak stamps in rubbing alcohol delicate
write letters longhand to prisoners
walk across the city on one falafel

We have sex the first night
after watching *Brother from Another Planet* on video
I am trying to look like a South Asian Kathleen Cleaver
You have two pairs of baggy pants and one twin futon mattress
You have *The Angry Brigade* and *Wretched of the Earth* in your bookcase
We tag Pepita and Chanchito '97 on the walls of the underpass
The security guards tell us to stop kissing in the lobby

You pull out your knife as we try to have sex in the playground
when a man jumps out with his dick in hand
You tell me you've always wanted to die
but feed me, give me books
I've never been this happy

I pull you back from the window,
jam my shoulder in the door
to the room where you're trying to cut
your wrists with a pink daisy razor

Everyone has thought you were crazy for so long
you're bi, talk about abuse, being crazy
Being lightskinned tortures you
like an itch that never once stops
You try to rip your eyeballs out their sockets
because you think they're blue
You sneer, at least when they think you're white
they think you're Italian.

I meet your mother and she and your dad take us out
before the food comes you and your dad are circling each other
in the street. go on, hit your old man
this is why you left
but almost 10 years later you want your parents
You start to say that, after all
your father was driving a cab all night
working another job during the day, going back to school
to learn what he already knew
on papers the government declares useless
You start to treat me like he treated you

Eyes disassociated but fixed on something else
Years pass, I leave
I can't make your eyes focus
I can't stop the relentless step
of the skinheads and fathers and fists
in your head

You always said you would go crazy if I told these stories
that you'd go to the cop shop and kill as many as you could
but this is my story I'm telling, not yours
my story of where violence comes from
where it goes
You tell your own story
I hear second hand
where you say you just slapped me once
Me sweetheart,
I tell a different story

FREEDOM & STRATEGY / TRAUMA & RESISTANCE

Timothy Colm

In 2007, I attended a workshop at the Trans Health Conference where the facilitator told a story about a guy who, after having top surgery, threw a party at which he burned all the pictures that existed of him before he physically transitioned. People have all kinds of ways of relating to their past selves. Like the boy in the story, I'm a trans guy. But this story unsettled me for other reasons.

When I was fourteen and fifteen years old, I was in an abusive relationship with my best friend. Eventually, after my other attempts to end the abuse had failed, I decided to stop talking to him and going to his house. For a few months I managed to avoid him, until mutual friends of ours visiting from Georgia came to town and stayed at his house. On their last night in town, he convinced me to stay over too. The next morning, after they left, we were folding up sleeping bags and he started touching me. I managed to stop him, and left his house. This was the last time he tried to mess with me. But for the next three years we still attended the same high school. Our classes overlapped. We still had all the same friends.

The story of the photograph-burning party stayed with me because it reminded me of when I wanted to destroy the person I used to be, to burn up the remnants of my past and start fresh. I wanted to become a healthy, whole person, the person I pretended I was most of the time. For a long time, I hated and feared the girl I had been at fourteen. I was afraid she would show up someday and ruin everything that was important to me. For so many years, I never talked about what had happened when I was fourteen. I was afraid if I told the people I loved, the people who loved me, what had happened, they would see me as the person I had been then. I believed this would drive them away from me.

here is a photograph of me at fourteen: I'm laughing at the camera, standing outside in the grass. It's early autumn. I have a brand-new buzz cut. I'm wearing a bright green sweatshirt, his sweatshirt. He took the picture. I never had a copy of it, so I can't show it to you now. The image comes back to me as a surprise, a marker of a moment I'd forgotten: before the abuse started, back when he was still my best friend.

When I think of myself at that age, I feel fiercely protective. I remember this loudmouth shy-eyed kid, kind of a dyke but still figuring it out. I had just cut off all my hair; I was trying out being at home in myself.

When I was nineteen, the boy who abused me wrote me a letter explaining that all the awful things he did to me were part of his desperate attempt to be a "successful heterosexual man." (He identifies as queer now.) I'm not sure if he was asking me to absolve him for what he did. Part of me wants to cite examples here, give you a list to prove how awful it was. But I don't remember it as a list. I don't remember it as a narrative. It's a flash of many moments, layered on top of one another, without much order or sense. What he did to me, during the abuse and for years afterward, caused me pain and disgust and a deep sense of shame. It was all senseless, out of context, and it got all over me; I couldn't disentangle myself from the awfulness. I didn't understand it as, "what he did was terribly wrong, and it hurt me." There was no clear logic to how it lived in me: the terribly wrong and the hurt and me and him were all jumbled up together.

I didn't respond to his letter. But years later, I would write him a letter of my own: *I believe it's possible for people to change, and that you've changed in some ways. I hope you have people in your life who will support you but also be critical of you, who will hold you to standards of accountability. The best way you can show me that you've really changed is by respecting the following: (1) I don't want to see you. What this means: If you know I'm going to be somewhere, don't come. If we're in the same social situation—a party, a bar, whatever—it's your responsibility to leave. (2) I don't want to talk to you. Don't talk to me, or look at me like you expect me to talk to you. (3) I don't want you to ask people we both know, or friends of yours with whom I've interacted, for information about me.*

My letter would come later. When I received his, I was nineteen, mired in college activist work with another boy who'd assaulted me. He lent me Borges's *Labyrinths,* burned me a free-jazz Coltrane album. Then he persuaded me to sleep in his bed when I didn't have a place to stay. I woke up to his hand down my pants. I avoided his gaze for many years, through meetings of the white anti-racist group where we'd talk about building trust with each other, reaching out to other white students, accountability to people of color. Afterwards, I'd go home with the sweet girl I was dating and freeze up and shake while talking in her bed.

I joined a campus support group for survivors of sexual assault and abuse. There I started to realize that the considerable difficulty I had owning my experiences and integrating them into my sense of myself was not due to some special personality defect, but was in fact a typical repercussion of trauma. I found that other survivors faced similar difficulties processing the abuse they had experienced. This was when I first began to use the term "survivor" to talk about myself. In the support group, I found comfort and solidarity, but I also had to sacrifice pieces of who I was to access the space. Statements were regularly exchanged about how we were all women and that made the space so safe, while I bit my lip and stared at my hands. It took me a full year after coming out as trans to tell the group. I didn't think I could be there anymore if they knew I was a guy.

During college I was also a counselor on the sexual assault response team. I led workshops on consent and assault for new students. At any given moment in the cafeteria or at a party, I could typically point out at least four known perpetrators of sexual assault. But, all that time, it never felt possible to stand up to the people who had assaulted me. I never knew I could write a letter that said, *Stay the fuck away from me, stop smiling at me, and stop talking shit about me to my friends.* I never knew I could tell the boy who assaulted me in college that I couldn't do organizing with him, that he needed to leave the white anti-racist group and stop coming to my friends' parties. What I found in the survivors' support group helped me feel less lonely and unstable, but it didn't include a vision for transformation. None of the work I was doing at the time gave me the courage and momentum to challenge the world around me to become a place where survivors of abuse could live fully and wholly, and be believed and respected.

Just before I turned twenty, I lost my dad to cancer. I needed all the love and support I could get. For a while, I tried to just get over my abuse history and move on with my life. I had already lost so much community and connection solely because I was trying to avoid the boy who abused me in high school. I was sick of having to choose between protecting myself and seeing people I loved. I was sick of distancing myself from old friends because they were still friends with him. Some of them tried to talk to me about him, even arguing with me from his perspective, or at least as he told it: "He said he thinks you two were in love back then. You know, it's hard for him to see you, too, especially when you ignore him."

fast forward a year and a half. It was summer. I was at a picnic—a top surgery fundraiser in Prospect Park for a guy I barely knew. I'd come with a new, wonderful friend. I knew she went to college with the high school abuser but we never really talked about it. I just told her we had fucked up history and that I didn't talk to him. I was having a good time. After the picnic, she and I were headed to a music festival at Coney Island. But then he showed up, the high school abuser, with other friends from high school, the ones I'd been keeping my distance from but really loved and missed and fuck it, I just wanted to be normal and so off we went on the subway to Coney Island, the whole group of us together. I was fine. I was fine. Except when we got there and started drinking, I freaked out and ran into a dirty sweetheart art punk that none of them knew and wandered off with him and we got Coronas in brown bags and drank them on the beach and I just kept saying, "I'm so glad I ran into you. I hate that boy I'm with." He nodded with soft eyes. I never explained and he never asked. Then I met back up with the others, and we took the subway to a tiny, boring party and then left quickly again, because someone was driving—driving!—back out of the city and they could give us a ride home on the way. Except I was stuck in the backseat of the car, four across in a space made for three, and pushed up next to me was the high school abuser. His body against mine, I was suddenly flooded with memories of the abuse, how he used to force me to do things while his hands were all over the back of my neck. So that years later, it still makes my skin crawl sometimes when people touch me there.

A few years later, I moved to Philadelphia and started meeting people doing radical organizing around sexual assault, people whose visions of possibility were informed by this work. I joined a group called Philly's Pissed, whose mission is to work against sexual assault in our communities by supporting survivors. There I found myself, every week, in meetings with people who had baseline politics and beliefs that lined up with my own: Part of healing is taking back power that's been taken from you. The criminal justice system will not protect us or end the violence in our lives. People of all genders experience partner violence and sexual assault. Maybe most important of all, there were other trans people in the group. During this time, I experienced many things that might seem small but were actually hugely important. For example, I had friends and lovers who validated my sense of betrayal after the weekend home when a friend invited me to a bar without telling me the high school abuser would be there: "Wow, that's not okay. You don't have to see him. It doesn't have to be a secret. You might want to just tell a bunch of people at once. And you can ask them not to invite him to their parties."

When I'd done survivor support work and sexual assault education in the past, it had been with people with wildly variant political outlooks and personal investments. So it felt different to be doing this work with Philly's Pissed. I felt safe, alive, energized. These people really for real had my back, and not only because they loved me and saw how my past was destroying me, but also because they knew survivors of abuse and sexual assault need to be able to speak about their experiences and articulate what they need, with the knowledge that they will be believed and supported.

After years of keeping quiet, holding so many awful secrets, and being challenged by people I considered my friends when I did talk about the abuse, I had found a space where I could speak from my experiences of trauma and begin to extract wisdom from them. I have so much love for the few dear friends who held me and listened while I whispered memories during the worst years. But hours spent in their beds couldn't undo the rest of the world. In Philly's Pissed, we were doing the work of supporting survivors together, out of a collective vision of transforming our communities and ending sexual assault. For the first time, identifying as a survivor felt like a source of power, rather than a site of trauma.

This process of coming into collective power was how I came to finally write my own letter to the boy who abused me in high school. It took him three months to write back. In the interim I figured that was that; he was going to continue showing up in my life, over and over, sitting across the table from me at some hipster bar, staring at me while I tried to talk to my friends, trying to talk to me, shifting around awkwardly when I didn't respond. All the while, my body shivered with so many flight-desires, so many fucked-up memories.

But even if he refused to change, I knew that in writing him I had shifted something forever. Now it was on the table. I had called him a perpetrator of rape and sexual assault; I had called him on his manipulative and abusive behavior. I didn't phrase it as an accusation, a confrontation; I just said it casually, a matter-of-fact accounting of our history and dynamic. Now I had some steady ground to speak from, if he showed up at a bar, at a party, in my friend's living room. Now I could say, "I asked you not to be here, I asked you to leave if you saw me." That kind of confrontation still terrified me, but I'd laid some groundwork to help myself no longer stay silent.

What's more, I knew if he didn't do what I asked, there were steps I could take. Working with Philly's Pissed to support other survivors had expanded my sense of the choices available to me. I took the process we used, which was to help survivors identify, step by step, what would increase their sense of safety and healing, and I began to apply it to myself. I could tell more of our mutual friends about his abusive behavior, and ask them to back me up in my desire not to share space with him. There was no guarantee they'd agree, but in asking I'd be honoring this belief I hold, somewhere deep in my heart, that I deserve to have a buffer from him, to never have to see him again, to feel safe, to be safe, to have control over my life. I was willing to tell people if I had to (deep breath), and to stand firm in my belief that we all deserve to fully inhabit our bodies and lives.

I knew he talked a lot of feminist and gender theory, and thought of himself as someone who would Never Do That Again (as he said in the first letter he wrote me). He knew what he'd done was deeply, deeply fucked, and he believed that he was different now, that he had changed. He seemed to want me to witness and confirm this change, and I wasn't going to do that. What I was willing to do was tell him the simple, small things he could do to stop hurting me. So I did. And after three months, he wrote back and said he would do the things I asked of him.

To build radical communities which really, truly support survivors of rape, abuse and sexual assault, it's necessary to describe the fear, shame and terror some of us go through, to make clear why it's so important to support, hear and believe survivors. To that end, I will tell you that the month I was writing the letter, I felt pretty crazy and scared much of the time. When I decided to write it, I thought, *Oh I've worked through that stuff, I'm solid now, I'm tough and I don't dream about it anymore and I don't choke every time someone says the word "blow job" and I can have fun, casual sex without being triggered and I can refer to being assaulted without instantly floating a million miles away and/or feeling insanely vulnerable.* Writing a letter to the boy who abused me in high school that told him to step out of my life was something I was certain I wanted to do, as soon as I realized it was something I *could* do. But the process of writing the letter brought me right back to being the scared vulnerable kid I thought I'd left behind years ago. I hurt myself for the first time in years, I got deep into panic and fear, I struggled a whole lot. What was it? It wasn't so much digging up memories, though there was a little of that. It was more that writing the letter made me confront every one of my fears about the high school abuser and the world as it related to my abuse history. I was afraid he would tell all our mutual friends and acquaintances I was a jerk; afraid they would think I was unreasonable, that I lacked compassion. I was afraid they wouldn't believe me about the abuse and rape (even though somewhere I had a letter from him where he admitted to it). I was also afraid that they *would* believe me—or rather, that if they did believe me, they'd forever see me as weak, vulnerable, damaged because of it. As a trans guy, I felt especially vulnerable about people learning that I'd been assaulted when I was a girl. Maybe it would confirm their fucked-up perception of transsexuals as damaged people who hate their bodies, or their theories that sexual abuse has made us trans.

Mostly, the fear boiled down to this: he was someone who had hurt me so deeply and messed with me so profoundly, who had coerced and manipulated me into staying quiet about the things he was doing, who cleverly and persistently took away so much of my power, my voice, my ability to negotiate circumstances for myself. Although it was seven years since he'd laid hands on me, I still couldn't rid myself of the sense that he had an enormous amount of power in my life. I was afraid to challenge him and was deeply, irrationally terrified that he could somehow destroy me, destroy the beautiful and good life I had made for myself. In some ways, he did have a lot of power: a rich, white, non-trans boy in a world that, by and large, doesn't believe survivors, dehumanizes trans people, and ignores the existence of survivors who are boys. So in some ways, my fear was not at all irrational. But I had brilliant, visionary people on my side, people who loved me and people who had my back because they believed in self-determination for survivors and everyone else. What's more, I knew writing to him was a small but necessary part of creating a world that believes and supports survivors and trans people, and, moreover, a world that also believes and supports survivors who are trans and/or gender nonconforming.

Working with Philly's Pissed to support survivors, and seizing back power from the boy who abused me in high school both opened up new space in my life and new possibilities for how I could relate to my past. I feel lucky I was able to get him to step out of my life a little—lucky, only because I know so many survivors don't ever get that space, not because it's such a huge thing to ask. In the end, he didn't stick to his promise. Just over a year later, he showed up in my life and space again and broke other parts of our agreement, too. But as difficult as it was to deal with his reappearance, drawing lines and making demands had irrevocably changed my power in the situation. I'm no longer afraid of what he'll do to me if I tell people how he abused me ten years ago. For years, I had to choose whether to stay numb, hovering above my body, in order to keep old friends, or to fully remember and honor my past and create a new, unrelated life. I went back and forth between these two options, the either/or, but part of writing him that letter was refusing to be the one who was pushed out. I want to be part of the transformation of our communities into places that support survivors in speaking the truth and taking up space, because we shouldn't be the ones who always have to leave. I'm working to remember and reintegrate parts of myself I sequestered away for so long. These pieces of my personal history are no longer just sites of pain and vulnerability, but together form a foundation for a powerful wisdom that I've built with other people working to end sexual assault. I want to keep building this wisdom together, transforming the trauma that keeps us isolated into collective resistance.

part four

WE ARE READY NOW

BEAUTIFUL, DIFFICULT, POWERFUL

Ending Sexual Assault Through Transformative Justice

The Chrysalis Collective

The Chrysalis Collective formed when a friend and member of our community experienced acquaintance rape by another local activist. "Diane" was a woman of color involved in several local organizing projects. Through her activism, she befriended "Tom," a white male grassroots organizer working full time in primarily poor, people of color communities. As their friendship grew, Tom expressed his romantic interest. Diane made it clear to Tom that she was both unavailable and uninterested. A few months later, Diane felt that Tom betrayed their close friendship by manipulating her into sexual situations that she did not want. Their friendship abruptly ended. After several months of confusion and anxiety, Diane painfully realized that she had experienced acquaintance rape.

Aware that the state and its prisons are the biggest perpetrators of violence against our communities, Diane looked elsewhere for solutions. As infuriated and upset as she was with Tom, Diane knew that putting him in jail would not bring about the healing, justice, and peace that she wanted for herself, Tom, and the community. She gathered her close friends and formed the Chrysalis Collective. We were a group of womyn and trans folk of color with experience organizing around reproductive justice, queer health, racial justice, gender justice, youth issues, immigration rights, and food justice. At that time, we didn't know how to build a Transformative Justice (TJ) collective, how to make Tom accountable, what TJ models already existed, or what our next steps might be.[1] But we did believe in TJ as a path of individual and collective healing through community accountability, compassion, and commitment. It was a way of creating a system of community-based justice grounded in the humanity—not the brokenness—of its members and in our creative capacity to transform and heal from living in a violent and imbalanced society. Instead of turning to the state, we drew on the strength and resources already in our community to end sexual assault and build safer, healthier relations among and between activists.

This is the story of our process, what we did, how and why we did it, what worked, and what didn't. Our story won't apply to everyone, or perhaps even to anyone, but we hope our offering to this beautiful, difficult, and powerful movement for TJ will inspire the work folks do in their own communities.

step 1. gathering: form a survivor support team (SST)

Our first step was to form a Survivor Support Team of folks who wanted to turn this community accountability idea into a reality. Diane called together a team of trusted friends and organizers. Some questions we considered were:

— Whom does the survivor and her allies want in the SST?
— What are the goals of the SST?
— What are the expectations, skills, commitment levels, and availability of the SST? What resources does the SST need to prepare and gain confidence for the work ahead?

The first SST meeting was a two-day gathering that included a lot of tears and tissues, visiting the ocean, and expressing a commitment to support Diane and see this nascent TJ process through to the end. During this initial meeting we also developed our initial goals for the TJ process. We created separate goals for Diane, the SST, Tom, and our communities, including:

— Help Diane seek a healthy, healing path, join a survivors' group, not blame herself for what happened, and keep a journal.
— Have Tom agree to work with the accountability team (AT) we planned to organize, seek counseling, share with friends that he is in a TJ process, and admit to the assault.
— Ensure that the SST and AT commit to a survivor-centered TJ process, recognize Tom's humanity, create a community-based alternative to the state, and eventually share their experience with community organizers and groups.

At the time, we had no idea how we were going to meet these goals or whether it was even possible. Yet the aspirations we named when things were new, raw, and unmapped have remained our guiding force throughout the entire TJ process.

Since neither Diane nor our Support Team had much experience in TJ or accountability work, our next step was to read everything we could find on the subject. Our team spent several months learning, brainstorming, and talking about how to approach Tom. We needed this time to be intentional about our work, build our trust as a group, learn enough to move forward, and give Diane the space and support she needed to heal. There were times when we felt overwhelmed by what we were reading, when we were uncertain about what we could do, and when Diane had some rough nights. We built our trust by continuing to show up for Diane, for each other, and for ourselves.

step 2. expanding: form an accountability team (AT)
Next we began the process of forming the team that would be responsible for working with Tom to hold him accountable. Early on, the SST had concluded

that we did not want to take part in working with Tom. We wanted to be able to focus on Diane's healing and also felt that we would not be able to distance ourselves enough from our anger at Tom to work compassionately with him. So we formed the AT as a separate team of people whose task was to hold Tom accountable. First, we made a list of community allies who could be potential AT members. Since the AT would be in closest contact with Tom, it was vital to choose folks who not only believed in our definition of TJ but could also commit the time and energy, and be willing to develop the skills needed, to engage with an aggressor.[2] We asked ourselves the following questions:

— What experiences did they have with sexual assault, transformative justice, or community work?
— What other skills could they offer the TJ process (e.g., patience, clarity, compassion, political vision, commitment)?
— What leverage did they have in the community (e.g., positive reputation, community elder, financial resources, connections)?
— Would it be helpful if the AT was drawn from diverse communities across lines of race, gender, sexual orientation, class, organizational affiliation, and age? In our case, the aggressor was a middle-class, straight, white male with a pattern of not listening. We felt that an AT led by working-class womyn of color would be less effective than a predominantly white and/or male AT.
— And, finally: Did they know Diane and/or Tom?

Forming an intentional community of people as the AT was key to the process of creating safe spaces for Diane and Tom, and crucial to our TJ work. For us, the TJ process was not about shaming or threatening the aggressor; it was about a deep transformation based on radical reflection, community accountability, and love.

Next, SST members contacted the folks individually on the list. Since their vocational circles overlapped so much, Diane chose to keep her and Tom's identities confidential. Without divulging identities, the SST informed the potential ally that a sexual assault had occurred in the community and that the survivor was starting a TJ process. We shared the SST's framework for rape, sexual assault, and TJ, and made sure that folks shared a similar analysis. Although most folks did not have much training or experience with a TJ process, we emphasized to them that they could still join the AT, pool their skills, and learn together.

At the end of our vetting process, our AT included four incredible activists who shared a radical political vision and a strong gender justice framework. Three of the members were well-respected activists in the social justice community with decades of community work and organizing experience, a few had previous experience confronting perpetrators of sexual assault, and one was involved in ongoing prison-abolition work. The majority of the AT team was white, male, and straight, reflecting our intentional strategy, and one of the veteran movement activists was a person of color. All of them knew Tom and/or Diane, and several had close working relationships with one or both of them. The AT's deep compassion and commitment guided them through the early months of negotiating their working and personal relationships with Diane and Tom. As with the SST, the AT members would progressively build on each other's strengths to create a trusting, powerful group.

After introducing the AT members to each other, the SST gently revealed the identities of Diane and Tom. As some AT members knew Diane and/or Tom, this required some time to process, especially since there was an awkward period of time when the AT knew about Tom's identity before being ready or prepared to confront him.

Around this time, the SST and Diane compiled a list of "talking points." These talking points included information that the AT could (and could not) share with Tom, i.e., a very brief summary of the assault from Diane's perspective: that the assault occurred by manipulation, not physical force, and other details. Crucially, Diane reported that this phase was extremely stressful. Sharing her story with the AT was a huge, public, and sometimes terrifying step. She felt a lot of fear, self-doubt, and anger, so the SST took extra care in supporting her process. They sat with her, listened to her worries, affirmed her commitment to healing, and reminded her that she was not alone in this difficult, but good and important, journey.

step 3. communicating: defining the relationship between teams

For each group, we outlined clear expectations and roles. However, we kept open the possibility of shifting them as needed.

THE SURVIVOR SUPPORT TEAM:
— Focused on Diane's needs and desires throughout the TJ process.
— Educated themselves about TJ by checking out resources in books/zines, on the web, and in our communities.
— Supported Diane's healing process as an individual and within the TJ process.
— Initiated, monitored, and evaluated Tom's accountability process through the AT.
— Communicated between the AT and survivor, making sure the AT knew Diane's needs and gave Diane updates of the AT's process while respecting how much/little she should know with respect to her healing process.

THE ACCOUNTABILITY TEAM:
— Committed to a survivor-centered praxis at all times in their work with Tom.
— Educated themselves about TJ with an eye toward supporting Tom's transformation with compassion. (Our AT also had to balance taking the time to be fully prepared with the urgency of transforming Tom's behavior.)
— Worked directly with Tom to achieve accountability and transformation. (As a group, they had to gain Tom's trust and commit to honoring his humanity. For example, they consistently reiterated their commitment to TJ, rather than to legal or retaliatory justice.)
— Conveyed *and* translated ideas and suggestions from the SST to Tom. For example, the AT developed specific exercises and discussion tactics to convey the concerns of Diane and the SST to Tom.

The SST and AT had two fundamentally different roles, lenses, and responsibilities; yet they were connected by their shared commitment to TJ principles and by a similar analysis of the various forms of sexual violence and oppression. Building a solid foundation between the AT and SST laid the groundwork for what was to come. Regularly scheduled communication between the teams addressed Diane's process, Tom's transformation, logistics, coordination, questions, and any other issues. Our understanding of TJ required that each perspective be balanced: the AT needed to hear from the SST to continually see their work with the aggressor from the survivor's perspective, and the SST needed to hear from the AT to monitor Tom's progress and be reminded of Tom's humanity despite the harm he committed. When the groups were working and communicating well, they formed a continuum from Diane to the SST to the AT to Tom, allowing for direct lines of communication as well as the distance necessary for Diane's healing, safety, and confidentiality.

step 4. storming & developing: create a transformative justice (TJ) plan

We found that it was crucial that the SST and AT develop a TJ plan before they approach Tom. The purpose of the plan was to outline our steps toward TJ if and when Tom agreed to work with the AT. We created a document where we outlined potential "steps" and then brainstormed ways of pushing Tom to accomplish the best-case outcome, ways of protecting ourselves from the worst-case scenario, and some of the possibilities in between. Our TJ plan included:

— Our goals.
— Ideas for how to first approach Tom.
— Warning signs of covert aggression from Tom.
— Backlash precautions (i.e., maintaining Diane's safety and using our leverage were Tom to respond by counter-organizing or trying to contact Diane).
— Establishing guidelines for meetings with Tom (e.g., building trust between Tom and the AT, and offering resources, "homework," and goals for each meeting).

— Working with Tom's accountability process, which involved overcoming denial and minimization, improving survivor empathy, changing distorted attitudes about power/privilege/gender, learning good consent and intimacy practices, and cocreating a relapse prevention plan.

The actual TJ process proceeded differently than what we had imagined in our brainstorm. Some ideas were never used, and others had to be developed along the way. Even though not everything was used, it was really helpful for the SST and AT to have thought through these issues together and anticipated possible reactions and outcomes. Our plan was imperfect, incomplete, and did change, but it was much better than having no plan at all. We drew on the good resources we already had—and embodied—to make the plan as strong as possible.

step 5. summoning: prepare for the first approach

Our AT and SST spent several months mentally and emotionally preparing for the initial approach and first meeting with Tom. The SST and AT lined up, vetted, and interviewed local resources, such as therapists, men's groups, and other TJ resources. We found that local community resources for aggressors in relation to sexual assault and TJ were weak, so we explored regional and national support networks as well. We also asked:

— Where and when would the first approach occur?
— Which members of the AT would approach Tom? How would they invite Tom to the first meeting? Where, when, and how would they tell Tom that a survivor was seeking his accountability for rape?
— How would the AT communicate with the SST about the first approach?

We wanted an approach that would model concern (rather than punishment), confidentiality, and community safety while still giving us enough leverage to compel Tom to participate in the TJ process. In our discussions, it was helpful for us to distinguish our tactics for the "initial approach" when we would ask him to come to a meeting about a community concern, and the "first meeting" where we would tell him that the community concern was his behavior and Diane's experience of rape. It was agreed that two folks whom Tom respects would do the initial approach and keep the exchange brief and general to avoid tipping him off as to what the meeting would be about.

We felt that this plan would maximize our chances of getting him to the table to listen to our concerns, be willing to participate in the TJ process, and minimize any reaction that could endanger Diane. The success of the "initial approach" would rely on the fact that Tom cared about the community and would want to be part of the solution to a community problem; the success of the "initial meeting" would rely on the fact that these concerns would be brought to him by people he trusted and respected, and that it would be done in a way that was not about shaming or punishing him.

Preparing for this step was important because Tom's reaction could not be predicted, and how the AT responded could influence Tom's participation in the TJ process. What if Tom refused to engage with the AT, leaving everyone unhealed and the community endangered? What if Tom freaked out when his behavior was named as rape? What if everything went as planned? We simplified our preparation for the first approach by assuming a best-case scenario, but we also developed a list of tactics to influence and raise the stakes for Tom in case he resisted (e.g., going to his friends and colleagues).

The AT chose two members whom Tom respects and who have worked directly with him. After a community event they all attended, the two members casually approached him and said, "Hello, we would like you to join us for a meeting about an important matter concerning a member of our community." They diverted Tom's questions about the community member's identity by saying, "There are issues of confidentiality. We'll talk about that at the meeting." Neither the assault nor the TJ process were mentioned. For the first approach, we felt the less said, the more likely Tom would participate in the first meeting (where the details would come out and the real work would begin). We were wary of sharing any more information about the assault or TJ process with Tom for fear it would scare him away, trigger aggressive reactions, or turn him off. Our primary goal was to invite Tom to a first meeting, and fortunately he agreed to attend.

Immediately after the initial approach, the two members processed the experience with the rest of the AT and the SST, as everyone was anxious to know how it went.

In hindsight, we've realized that this approach had the extra benefit of activating within Tom the mental frames he and we needed for this process: responsibility, caring, trust (we were going to trust him with a community concern), at the possible cost of him feeling betrayed by our half-truth. In contrast, an "authoritative" approach would likely activate an offense/defense response in Tom so he could regain "his way"—the opposite of what was needed in the process. (And truthfully, we just felt uncomfortable with acting in an "authoritative," top-down manner, rather than modeling horizontal cooperation.)

Although this first invitation to the process seemed simple enough, it was an extremely stressful time for Diane, the SST, and the AT. We supported Diane and each other through our feelings of doubt and anxiety about whether the first approach and meetings would be effective. Unfortunately, we were not prepared for the growing internal stress in the groups. Our SST and AT lost some folks due to the increased intensity of the process and the time commitment. This was a time when folks really saw and felt how the TJ process would roll out.

step 6. building: the first meeting

The AT planned the first meeting with an eye toward Tom's potential responses. This would be the first time Tom would hear that Diane had experienced rape, that she had been deeply harmed by his behaviors, and that we would be asking him to engage in a long, complex process of TJ. We considered the following range of feelings that Tom might experience and/or express:

— *Ganged up on.* To minimize the chances of this happening, we limited the first meeting to the two AT members we had selected—community leaders and elders who modeled cooperation, not domination—to make the initial approach because among us they were the most trusted and respected by Tom.

— *Denial, outrage, remorse, shame, guilt, fear, and defensiveness.* With these feelings in mind, we didn't expect much at first. We set and kept good boundaries, and used active listening.

— *Betrayal by the survivor and AT.* We tried to build trust and safety right away by compassionately (but critically) listening to his experience, giving him space to feel betrayal and denial, and allowing him to offer some input on his TJ process.

— *Overwhelmed by too much information.* To avoid this we kept things simple at first.

At the first meeting, the two AT members gently told Tom that a community member experienced his behavior as rape. They revealed Diane's identity and shared a few of the SST's talking points. The AT folks explained that Diane and the community had experienced a harm which must be healed in a responsible way. These points were communicated both verbally and in a written document for Tom to reread and process later. Some of those points were:

— The AT was there to serve the needs of Diane and the community.

— The AT would support Tom in his accountability and transformation process.

— The AT would provide Tom with a simplified statement or version of Diane's experience, rather than a detailed account that could lead to a debate over what happened.

— The AT acknowledged that Tom's intention and experience might be different than Diane's.

— The AT set clear boundaries around the survivor (i.e., do not contact Diane).

— The AT valued Tom's contributions to the community.

— The AT and Tom had a mutual interest in stopping sexual assault in the activist community.

— The AT invited Tom to bring his needs and goals to the next meeting.

The AT members were also prepared to:

— Validate Tom's story, feelings, and experience, if offered; repeat our support of the survivor's experience if Tom tried to blame Diane for what happened.
— Deflect questions or challenges about the incident, violation, process, or Diane until the next meeting.
— Avoid volunteering any additional information "to be helpful."
— Ask if Tom had friends to process with afterwards.
— Establish that Tom should communicate with the AT through a predesignated point person.

After this meeting, the AT members debriefed, updated the SST, supported each other, and relaxed as best as they could. Their work had just begun.

step 7. transforming: meetings with the accountability team

Fortunately, the initial approach and first meeting led to regular meetings between Tom and the entire AT. During each meeting, the AT allowed generous time for check-ins and emotional processing. As expected, our personal feelings, such as anger and judgment, arose, so we consistently reemphasized the entire team's commitment to TJ—not to punishment—and to building a climate of trust and respect.

In the initial meetings, the AT gave an overview of the process that we expected going forward. We solicited boundaries from everyone and developed shared goals, ensuring a place for Tom's voice in the process. We also learned not to expect much from him during the initial meetings. The work ahead was likely to be long, and we figured it was most important that each meeting lead to the next one.

As we've continued, the AT has played many expected and unexpected roles, such as supporter, friend, challenger, therapist, investigator, contract negotiator, and judge. Always, the AT and SST have worked together to make sure that the survivor-centered TJ process be guided by the goals of the TJ plan. The AT also focused on the shared goals produced with Tom. They respected Tom's needs while prioritizing the safety of Diane and of the community.

MEETINGS WITH TOM HAVE FOCUSED ON THE FOLLOWING:

— *Challenging rape culture:* Pacing the information slowly, starting with sexual-assault definitions and statistics; studying and discussing relevant zines and resources; repeating our understanding of rape and how it differs from the criminal definition and mainstream myths; exploring the difference between intent and impact; and challenging the primacy that rape culture gives to an aggressor's intent over the consequences of the aggressor's behavior for the survivor and the community.

— *Exploring unrelated scenarios:* Describing situations involving culpability, intent, and manipulation, and then connecting them to the incident; asking what taking responsibility would look like even if Tom were blameless.

— *Focusing on the survivor's experience:* Asking Tom how something looks and feels from Diane's perspective; asking "What did you take from that statement?"; asking who got what they wanted; restating the survivor's experience; pressing for feelings and empathy; understanding the meaning and practice of good consent.

— *Connecting with Tom:* Connecting to his activism and using various anti-oppression frameworks that would be familiar to him; involving Tom in problem solving; pushing Tom to places of discomfort; asking Tom to imagine he is on an AT for someone else; assigning and discussing homework; practicing active listening and mirroring.

We also expected Tom to manipulate conversations to avoid accepting the painful reality that he deeply harmed Diane and, by extension, the community.

AT members attempted to avoid this by:

— Practicing role-plays about defensive behaviors.

— Developing mantras for tough situations (i.e., "Diane experienced that as harm").

— Debriefing together after every meeting with Tom, with a particular focus on detecting manipulation.

— Debriefing with the SST after every meeting or two to check in with the TJ process.
— Trusting the experiences and wisdom of the group members.

Throughout this process, one difficult and recurring question was whether the AT and Tom had met their goals. The AT had clear goals for Tom, i.e., that he admit to rape and seek professional counseling. At the same time, we have been frustrated by how to measure or evaluate these goals. The AT not only wanted Tom to change his language and behavior; they also wanted him to internalize what he was learning and emotionally "get it." Observing behaviors and statements were one way to measure change, but we realized that there was no guarantee that he was really "getting" it. Given the difficulty in measuring our success, it has been crucial to set clear goals for Tom from the beginning of this long process of transformation.

GOALS FOR TOM:
— LEARN about sexual assault, consent, privilege, patriarchy, gender socialization, and rape culture.
— RESPECT physical and communication boundaries for Diane's safety.
— EXAMINE his past behavior for other experiences of manipulation and assault; acknowledge and be accountable to that history; and keep the community safe in the present and future if this is repeat behavior.
— SEEK professional counseling for aggressors or join an aggressor recovery group.
— SELF-EDUCATE to deeply understand the incident, his intent, and behavior, and the subsequent harm to Diane and the community.
— DISCUSS & MODEL consent behavior for future relationships.
— COMMIT to acts of restitution to Diane and the community.

step 8. evaluating: lessons learned
As much as we prepared, there have been important lessons that we did not anticipate in our TJ work:

— The situation—and many rapes in activist communities—involved coercion, manipulation, and/or entitlement, not sheer physical force, and reflected how deeply rape myths and culture are embedded within our own activist circles. Male entitlement, racism, and an ignorance of rape culture made it that much harder for Tom to recognize his behavior as rape.

— It was hard to balance Diane's need for confidentiality with the need to warn the community about Tom, and this remained an unresolved tension in our TJ process.

— Diane's and Tom's transformations needed to follow their own paths, which might mean that Tom might be ready to offer restitution before or after Diane is ready to receive it.

— We should have been more serious about communication between the AT and the SST. It sounded easy enough, but it sometimes felt overwhelming to schedule another meeting or call. No matter what the excuse, we have learned to make time to check in. It is worth much more than we first realized.

— The aggressor accountability process got so involved that the SST started to lose track of Diane's healing process. At one point, our meetings were all about Tom's progress, and we would run out of time before addressing what Diane needed. We are learning to put Diane's well-being back at the center of our process through things like expanding our support circle, reading zines together, and making a trigger plan. (A trigger plan is a way for Diane to identify and overcome her triggers. When she experiences a traumatic memory or reaction, the trigger plan that we developed together helps her identify what is happening and the steps she needs to take to feel safe.)

The Chrysalis Collective is still actively engaged in our survivor-centered TJ process. The more we learn about TJ, the more we realize that it is a deep commitment requiring a lot of energy and patience. Our unfinished process has lasted almost two years so far and we have gone through stressful times.

Yet healing and transformation is clearly, slowly, steadily happening for everyone involved. This experience has connected each of us in unexpected and powerful ways that reaffirm our collective commitment to transforming ourselves and our communities.

working definitions

— **RAPE.** Nonconsensual sex through physical force, manipulation, stress, or fear; the experience of sex as the unwanted physical, emotional, mental, or spiritual violation of sexual boundaries; not an act of caring, love, or pleasure; sexual violation of trust.

— **SEXUAL ASSAULT.** Any unwanted physical, emotional, mental, or spiritual violation of sexual boundaries.

— **CONSENT.** An understandable exchange of affirmative words and actions regarding sexual activity; agreement, approval, or permission that is informed and freely and actively given without physical force, manipulation, stress, or fear.

suggested resources

generationFIVE: Ending Child Sexual Abuse in Five Generations

http://www.generationfive.org

Hollow Water: Community Holistic Circle Healing

http://www.iirp.org/library/vt/vt_bushie.html

Indigenous Issues Forums

http://www.indigenousissuesforums.org

INCITE! Women of Color Against Violence

http://www.incite-national.org

Communities Against Rape and Abuse (CARA)

http://www.cara-seattle.org

Center for Transformative Change

http://transformativechange.org

Angel Kyodo Williams, "Doing Darkness: Change Vs. Transformation," *Transformation: Vision and Practice of Transformative Social Change* (October 2009). http://transformativechange.org/docs/nl/transform-200910.html

notes

1 After a lot of phone calls, web searches, conversations, and networking with amazing activists around the country, we found incredible resources. We are grateful for the wisdom and work shared by the TJ activists who came before us, especially the folks from generationFIVE, Hollow Water, Indigenous Issues Forum, INCITE! Women of Color Against Violence, Communities Against Rape and Abuse (CARA), and the zine "The Revolution Starts at Home: Confronting Partner Abuse in Activist Communities," eds. Ching-In Chen, Jai Dulani, and Leah Lakshmi Piepzna-Samarasinha (2008).

2 The Chrysalis Collective deliberately uses the term "aggressor" throughout the chapter for reasons similar to those offered by a collective of women of color from CARA: "[W]e use the word 'aggressor' to refer to a person who has committed an act of sexual violence (rape, sexual harassment, coercion, etc.) against another person. Our use of the word 'aggressor' is not an attempt to weaken the severity of rape. In our work of defining accountability outside of the criminal system, we try not to use criminal-based vocabulary such as 'perpetrator,' 'rapist,' or 'sex predator.'" See CARA, "Taking Risks: Implementing Grassroots Accountability Strategies," in *Color of Violence: The INCITE! Anthology,* ed. INCITE! Women of Color Against Violence (Cambridge, MA: South End Press, 2006), 302n1.

MAKING OUR STORIES MATTER

The StoryTelling & Organizing Project (STOP)

Rachel Herzing & Isaac Ontiveros

Today, more and more people in anti-violence and broader social justice movements are calling for alternatives to imprisonment and policing in response to intimate and interpersonal forms of violence. But many are frustrated and discouraged in their efforts by a lack of concrete examples of existing alternatives, which in turn reinforces a continued reliance on criminalization as the only effective response to intimate violence. Additionally, among many activists there exist old and emerging critiques of the social-services approach. Despite the availability of an array of domestic violence services specifically targeting communities who have historically been denied access to resources, including shelter, advocacy, and legal services, the scope and impact of these services remain limited. The typical interventions might be appropriate for those people leaving violent relationships but do not address the needs of people unwilling or unable to choose this option. Similarly, many people will not use conventional domestic violence resources due to language and cultural barriers and fears of contact with criminal legal and immigration systems. Finally, current options tend toward interventions at advanced stages of violence, after long-term physical and mental health impacts have already occurred.

Creative Interventions is an organization that developed in response to the environment described above. Rather than assume that the relationships, families, and communities in which violence occur are sites of irreparable, unchangeable harm, Creative Interventions imagines those relationships, families, and communities as locations of potential change and transformation. We view learning about violence intervention as an important and necessary aspect of community health and organizing. By sharing stories in which everyday people have intervened in situations of violence without relying on the state or social services, we begin to add to a toolbox of shared resources that enable us to respond to violence as community organizers with a focus on long-term change and shorter-term intermediate steps, collective rather than individual action, self-evaluation and assessment with the goals of improving strategy and tactics, and shifting power away from the state and toward our own self-determination.

Creative Interventions' StoryTelling & Organizing Project (STOP) developed as one of the primary means through which the organization responds to the gaps in current responses to interpersonal violence. STOP seeks out, documents, and analyzes stories from people who have used community-based interventions to violence within their own families, among their friends, and/or within other social networks without relying on the criminal legal system or social service agencies. Whether it's Korean and Latina mothers protecting their children from physical and sexual harm, youth standing up for a friend who had been sexually abused by someone in their neighborhood, a mother who taught her son to stop rape, or a Maori family coming together to stop a father from beating his son, hearing the stories of concrete actions people like us have taken to stop continued violence might help prevent violence from happening in the future.

As new stories are shared through the project, we turn the audio and textual documentation of the storytelling into products that can be shared with others interested in intervening in situations of interpersonal violence. Short audio pieces are available on our website, as are excerpts from the story transcripts. We are also working with our organizational partners to develop a range of additional STOP-related tools and materials that will support their ongoing organizing and advocacy efforts, including video pieces, poster projects, and study guides documenting the ways different organizations and communities have drawn and applied lessons from the stories.

STOP's vitality and strength comes through collecting stories from everyday people who have successfully ended violence in their lives and the lives of their loved ones, showing us that ending violence actually is possible. These audio-recorded and written stories offer lessons on how we can help ourselves and others organize to share tested strategies and build capacity to stop violence right where it happens: in our homes, on our streets, and in our communities. Through the partnerships we have developed through the project, STOP has been able to build a network of individuals and organizations from different parts of the world that have worked collaboratively to strengthen community-based approaches.

At Creative Interventions, we have seen how storytelling brings knowledge, resources, and power back to our communities—especially to those closest to and most impacted by violence—to support survivors, and to confront and demand accountability from people when they are abusive. Storytelling offers information, tools, and an orientation toward collective organizing that can equip a community to make interventions effective. Storytelling, as an organizing strategy, shifts the dynamics of power that allow violence in the first place. The stories collected through STOP remind us that alternative strategies for dealing with violence have a long history in our communities and are still being tried all the time. They emerge from our collective experiences, practices, and values, and provide lessons of continued value for future generations. They highlight how change is incremental, while helping us take the necessary steps toward more fundamental shifts.

A community that is able to support safety and self-determination for all of its members is a community with the power to challenge the other injustices it faces. We do not need to rely on state violence to end violence—we have the needed resources and wisdom right where we live.

If we understand community organizing to focus on long-term change, prize collective action over individual action, engage in evaluation and assessment of our approaches, and strive to shift power to marginalized communities, then STOP's storytelling and story collecting can most certainly be seen as community organizing practices.

One of the basic premises of the stories we gather through STOP is collective action. The intervention experiences described in the narratives could not have happened through individual action alone. Each instance required some level of collective responsibility and accountability. They also proceed from the foundational assumption that the collective (the family, an organization, a neighborhood) impacts and is impacted by both the harm done and the responses to that harm.

The telling and retelling of the stories of our interventions in situations of violence establishes, in our collective memory, the idea that these kinds of actions are possible and happen regularly. Importantly, this process also encourages us to view the stories as documentation of our movement. Individually, each story has the power to instruct, inspire, and suggest new paths toward liberation. Taken collectively, the stories also help us to evaluate the contexts in which we encounter violence and assess which tools and tactics have had the greatest impact in a given situation. By assessing different situations of violence and different intervention strategies, we can imagine ways of uniting elements from a variety of interventions into new approaches.

The acts of telling and listening to people's stories, and of translating those stories into organizing tools, help create meaning, pass on traditions, and explain how common practices come to be. In the tradition of raising up people's histories, organizing projects like STOP build community resources and help create environments in which people feel confident and competent to test new intervention strategies (or intervene at all) for interrupting and ending violence. Sharing experiences by way of telling stories helps communities acknowledge the tools and expertise they already have and encourage them to build their capacity even further.

The challenge for STOP is for the stories collected through it to be more than just a catalog of oppressive situations. While naming and opposing violence serves to break the silence surrounding it, STOP challenges us to go even further, incorporating the stories into our organizing. This work raises a number of questions: How do we use these stories in the work we do? How can they inform the way we do our work? How do we translate whatever learning happens around these stories into a methodology that moves our work forward; that moves us even a few steps toward shifting the balances of power and strengthening communities' agency and practice of self-determination?

When a story is told or collected, silence is broken. This is no small thing. Isolation is a key factor and tool in perpetuating violence. Survivors of violence often find themselves silenced and stripped of power by their abusers, by the criminal legal system, or by the shame and fear that often accompany survival. Sharing stories allows the telling and retelling of what survivors—people who so often have been told that their voices are not worth hearing—have weathered and withstood. At its strongest, the act of naming the violence breaks an essential circuit in the cycle of violence. When a story is told and collected, it acts as a direct challenge to the survivor's isolation. And the bond created between the storyteller and the story collector has the possibility to reverberate and grow. The act of storytelling, the act of story collecting, and the relationship created between the two processes can translate into increased senses and practices of agency.

If the story is told and collected within a collective environment, the potential for people to exercise their own power may grow even stronger. Once the story collector is not simply an individual collecting a story, but a member of a family unit, an organization, a coalition of organizations, a community whose work has brought them together, our organizing work has already begun. When our communities unite to organize collectively, we maximize our ability to address, confront, and struggle against the systemic and intimate forms of violence so many of us face.

What follows is an excerpt from a transcript of a story offered to the StoryTelling & Organizing Project. It has been lightly edited for clarity. This story is just one example of the ways that community members, acting collectively, have taken steps to intervene in violence without engaging the criminal legal system.

RADHIKA'S STORY

About three years ago, I was part of an Asian Pacific Islander (API) women's group and also a young writers' group. The API women's group provided mentorship and taught some of the classes with the young writers' group. One of the young women who was in the young writers' group approached those of us who were in the women's group and said that a youth artistic director of an API theater group had had a sexual relationship with her when she was a minor. He was in a position of power, being the youth director, and she was part of that theater group, so there were a variety of ways in which this was completely inappropriate.

She had come to us looking for guidance. She didn't want to have to deal with him anymore. She didn't necessarily want to seek any kind of criminal justice route, but what she said again and again was that her ideal would be [to] never have to see him again, never have to deal with him again. And given that we were this API women's artist group and that this was an Asian theater group, there were relationships between the two. And we believed the young woman. I don't think that was actually ever a question. We knew that she wanted something to happen. We knew she didn't want it to be criminal justice-related. We were in a somewhat awkward position that way because she didn't want to be identified.

[We] brought it to the attention of the theater group, and said, "Look, this has happened and we heard about it from this young woman." And so it was also somewhat awkward for them because they're a nonprofit and had employment

policies and all kinds of things. So [that approach] got brought from their board. I guess they did whatever was an equivalent to their internal investigation....

He ended up saying yes, that they had had a sexual relationship but that it was consensual and not an issue. And of course we had a couple of problems with this. [His position alone] made it impossible for her to have been in a consensual sexuaol relationship with him. We also had a problem with it because what we started hearing was that he had made sexual advances to other young women who were in the 16-18 range as well.

He was very well-liked in the community. He was able to resign and to give family reasons for his resigning. And so he resigned and it looked like, "Oh, he's being the good son and taking care of his family and that's why he's leaving the theater company," when it was actually because of this young woman's complaint.

It was difficult for our women's group because there was at least one person in our group who was very good friends with him, and had known him for years. She was put in a particularly difficult position, because she also had the strongest relationship with the theater group. So they were looking to her to provide some information [and] guidance, and I think it may have felt for her that she was [asked to kind of choose with whom] her loyalties lay. It was also somewhat stressful for the women's group because some people were all ready to take street action and name him publicly and make it a very visible accountability, and other people wanted to talk to the organization, let [the theater group] handle it. So, there was some tension about that as well.

There was a convening of town hall meetings to discuss the older Asian American men within the Asian American community, particularly in the artist and activist community, taking advantage of, preying on, young API folks. Clearly this incident was what sparked it, and there were people who had varying degrees of familiarity with exactly what had happened or what was involved, who was involved, all that kind of thing. For some people, they wanted the town hall to have nothing to do with what happened. Other people wanted the town hall to be [only] about what happened.

[The town halls] became mostly educational [discussions] about the issue of sexual violence and how it plays out in the community, so there was a lot of addressing myths and facts—almost like a Sexual Assault 101, and helping to explain and understand that boundary.

There were people from the theater group who were involved in planning the town halls, who were very protective of the man in question, and said, "Well, there's no way that we can know what exactly happened, and, how do we know that she's telling the truth? And, even if she was telling the truth, he's no longer part of the organization, so we're fine," as though that were all that it took. We started talking about it being a larger issue, because as this started getting addressed, we started hearing more about something happening here, and something happening there, within circles that really were meant to be safe and progressive and all of those kinds of things.

Overall, I think the young woman in question did, to a large degree, get what she was looking for. We clearly rallied behind her, took her seriously, took her story seriously, understood it as a harm. We felt very protective of her. But I think the other thing was that the more complicated the relationships are between people, the harder it is to see a clear path as to what it is that people are looking for.

I think this intervention was successful because the man in question no longer had his job in the theater group working with youth and because the young woman in question felt supported by the people that she went to [for support. However,] as far as I know he's still working with young people, just in a different place.

I think that the other limitations were that we were dealing with an organization that had its personnel policies, etc., so there was a way in which we could kind of bring it to the attention of the organization, but felt like we weren't really a part of the process after that. How the organization is going to deal with it is very dependent on their understanding of the issue, and kind of [on] what facts they have. Like I said, the young woman didn't necessarily want to identify herself, so they have a representative from the women's group who is speaking on behalf of this young woman, but they [don't] have the young woman [there to speak for herself.] And we have this guy that they all know and love and respect, and he is telling his side of the story. So I think that was probably one of the challenges. The women's group, we came up with a public statement around the issue more broadly that we disseminated [at the town halls]. How much people were able to take in the issue of sexual violence, the issues of power and boundaries; I don't know how much that sank in.

We wanted the same thing in terms of this young woman feeling safe and [that we were] taking her seriously and doing something about it. But after that, what do we all want? And it was just very different. And, you know, we all kind of ended up in this particular case just having different opinions about all of that. This wasn't something that broke our group or something that destroyed us, but it was a very difficult process that took a lot out of people.

WHAT DOES IT FEEL LIKE WHEN CHANGE FINALLY COMES?

*Male Supremacy, Accountability &
Transformative Justice*

Gaurav Jashnani, RJ Maccani & Alan Greig
THE CHALLENGING MALE SUPREMACY PROJECT (CMS)

Since 2008, the three coauthors of this essay have been working together as the Challenging Male Supremacy Project (CMS). Thus far CMS has aimed to be an intervention into the organizing and activist communities of New York City, an effort to concretely shift the personal and political practices of cisgender (i.e., non-trans) men as well as form better allies to feminist, queer, and trans justice struggles and movements. Each of us has previously participated in organizing to end child sexual abuse, either with generationFIVE or other organizations that believe (1) there are systems of oppression that must be thoroughly transformed as part of this work, and (2) state systems are themselves purveyors of harm and will not provide useful long-term solutions to the violence within our communities.

In the following account, we share our collective experience of forming CMS, organizing and facilitating a nine-month "Study-into-Action" group, and holding a public event (as well as some of the political analysis that brought us to this project). We bookend the essay with a detailed, first-person account of one of our experiences supporting an accountability process—in this case, RJ's experience co-facilitating an accountability circle around a situation of abuse and doing follow-up work for the two years since. Because one of our explicit goals is to have more cisgender men doing the work of holding other men accountable, we spend some time exploring RJ's involvement in this accountability process, including some of the fears and uncertainties raised for him. Our intention is to explore some of the complexities of cisgender men trying to actively and explicitly challenge male privilege while at the same time systemically benefiting from it.

Through formal collaborations and individual relationships, we support the work done primarily by cisgender women, transgender, and gender nonconforming organizers to challenge male supremacist violence in transformative ways. At the same time, we believe that cisgender men must take on more of this work, rather than continuing to let it fall disproportionately upon the very people who bear the brunt of this violence. Further, we also believe that more cisgender men in activist communities need to do advanced work specifically around male privilege and violence in order to enter future organizing efforts with more shared analysis, capacity, and commitment. (We made a conscious decision to use the still somewhat unfamiliar term "cisgender" in doing this work, a term coined by transgender activists used to describe those of us who identify with the sex and gender identity we were assigned at birth and are therefore accorded certain privileges by society.[1]) We hope this piece illuminates some of the ways we can make our communities healthier and safer by creating liberatory responses to violence, as well as the ways that these responses can push the cisgender men involved to more deeply challenge their relationship to male privilege; we offer it as part of a broader effort to find responsible and useful roles for cis men as allies in this work.

a (not so) typical story

In 2006, two young women came together who had been lied to, and one of them sexually assaulted, while involved with the same young man. All three of them worked together as student organizers. The two young women decided to break their silence and do something about it together. Dissatisfied with the "typical" options (e.g., shaming, retaliation, calling the police) available for addressing sexual violence and male supremacy within activist scenes, they contacted Danielle, a member of the Rock Dove Collective, a radical community health exchange in New York City, with experience setting up "accountability circle" processes.

To build an effective accountability process, Danielle believed it was essential to involve people whom the person who caused harm cared for and respected. For this reason, one of the young women contacted me (RJ), as someone who this young man (we'll call him "Mr. X") respected, in the spring of 2007. Although I had some years of experience working with organizations building community-based responses to harm, first in Critical Resistance NYC and later with generationFIVE, I had never before facilitated anything like an accountability circle. This would also be the first time Danielle facilitated an accountability circle for sexual assault, a task she viewed as uniquely challenging.

Needless to say, it was disappointing and infuriating to learn from this young woman that Mr. X, who I knew as a friendly acquaintance in activist circles, had been abusive toward multiple women. He was a very visible and vocal leader within a citywide network of student activists, and held a great deal of social capital (e.g., likeability, influence, credibility) and power among his peers. He was also irresponsibly engaging many women within this network and, in several cases, sexually assaulting them; for some of the women, this harm was compounded by the fact that he was someone they—and many people they knew—had been inspired by and respected a great deal. He was even a part of the accountability council within their student network for addressing just such behavior, and had participated in confronting other men.

Listening to this young woman describe the harm caused by Mr. X brought up a mix of feelings in me, including sadness and shame as I thought of my own sometimes reckless sexual behavior, spanning from my late teens through my mid-twenties. I mourned friendships I had damaged or lost and opportunities for organizing I had ruined.

Unfortunately, this story is not exceptional in left and radical communities; situations involving a charismatic male figure in the movement behaving in sexually irresponsible or other harmful ways are quite common, just as they are in many communities. Throughout the process, the women he had abused made it clear that what they wanted was to feel safe and to see Mr. X change, so that he wouldn't cause them or anyone else in their communities more harm. This was about intervening in "business-as-usual"—taking action not only to address this specific person and the harm he was causing, but also to challenge male supremacy within the communities tolerating and even colluding (through silence, excuses, and so on) with his inappropriate, misogynist, and violent behavior.

As I began to prepare for the process, I experienced a number of emotions: I felt very committed to supporting the women who were harmed and to building an accountability circle around Mr. X; I also felt some apprehension knowing that since I was stepping up around challenging his behavior specifically and male supremacy more broadly, I was going to have to hold myself to a higher standard and that it would bring up ways I wished I had behaved differently in the past. As common and structural as the behaviors that Mr. X was exhibiting were, I also believed that he could really transform them if he committed to it. After all, the past few years of facing my own experiences of being sexually abused as a child and teenager had seemed to provide me with a key to moving forward in bridging the gap between my own sexual politics and my practice. Why couldn't that shift in practice also be the case for him?

After some preparation, Danielle and I approached Mr. X to inform him that we knew about his abusive behavior toward the two young women, and to see if he would be willing to participate in an accountability circle to address the harm he'd caused. We proposed that he work with us to compile a list of people close to him (other activists, friends, family) to invite into the accountability process. The circle itself would be a facilitated gathering, where we moved through a series of questions as a group; Mr. X would make specific commitments to address the harm he had caused and the factors that contributed to it; and some of the other participants would commit to supporting Mr. X in taking his next steps.

Danielle provided a list of what these circles are, and what they are not:

ACCOUNTABILITY CIRCLES...

— ARE opportunities to air emotions, issues, tensions, fears, ideas, facts, stories and ARE NOT places to attack, degrade, punish, harm, or demean
— ARE collaborative and ARE NOT led by the facilitator
— ARE NOT a way to determine guilt/innocence (not a trial) and ARE a way to determine a response to a harm
— ARE focused on an incident or set of incidents and the best response to them and ARE NOT limited only to that incident
— ARE a way to hold people accountable in a compassionate way and ARE NOT a way to isolate or alienate someone
— ARE NOT only about the "perpetrator" and ARE an opportunity for a community to take a role in a person's healing process
— ARE (probably) uncomfortable and ARE NOT perfect or easy
— CAN BE transformative, powerful, beautiful tools and ARE NOT ends in themselves

Mr. X acknowledged that he had caused the harm we were seeking to address, and agreed to work with us in organizing the circle. Although it was a very slow process at first, we felt like we were making progress by compiling a list of people to invite to the circle. Something that became clear, however, was that Mr. X had few truly deep friendships and that approaching family was not going to be an option. This was a challenge that Danielle and I partially expected, not just from what we knew of him but also from the lack of community we saw among many people around us. We recognized that organizing this circle was also about supporting him in building some of the community he would need, both to be held accountable for the harm he caused and to grow and change in the future.

It would take over a year before the circle itself came to fruition: Mr. X dragged his feet in many ways, and the rest of us were juggling multiple commitments while trying to push this process forward. Over a year to pull Danielle and me, one of the two women who had initially come forward, Mr. X, and five other people who had some relationship to Mr. X (either current or former friends, or concerned community members) into the same room at the same time. As facilitators, Danielle and I also brought to the circle the expectations of the second woman who had stood up to address the harm but did not want to attend the circle meeting.

With everyone seated in a circle, Danielle and I went over again what a circle is and is not, and described the basic mechanics of the process. We would work through a sequence of questions, moving clockwise around the room, giving each person a chance to respond to the question. The person whose turn it was to speak would hold a talking stick in their hand and pass it when they were finished. Before posing the opening question, we facilitated a discussion to establish some ground rules, which we made sure would include some form of confidentiality, respecting time-outs and showing respect in general, listening to each other, honoring the silence or speaking of the person holding the talking stick, and a commitment to not making threats. Then we set out working through the questions:

— How are you feeling now?
— What are you hoping to get out of today/why are you here?
— What is your relationship to what happened? What happened? What did you do/have you done?
— How did you feel about it at the time? When it happened/When you found out?
— How do you feel about it now?
— What concerns you most going forward?

— What are some things that could address those concerns? (Brainstorm concrete ideas and go multiple rounds if necessary.)
— Which of those things are feasible (e.g., willingness, time, resources, appropriateness, value, consensus)?
— Who should be responsible for what?
— Are they willing to do those things?
— What specific agreements do we want to leave with today?
    * Are those attainable?
    * If so, who is responsible for each aspect of the agreements (including primary responsibility, support roles, and follow up/check in)?
— How are you feeling now/closing comments?

After six arduous hours, Danielle and I thanked everyone for their commitment to the process and we closed. Mr. X had verbally committed to honoring requests concerning his presence and behavior around the specific women he'd harmed, as well as broader requests addressing issues (mental health, substance abuse, and misogyny) that had contributed to his actions. Others within the circle committed to providing support for the different pieces of work that lay ahead of him.

working together to challenge the culture of male supremacy

Together with many others, we (Alan, Gaurav, and RJ) recognize male supremacy as a system causing a great deal of violence and harm not only in the world at large, but also within our own radical and Left movements. Whether physical or sexual abuse, talking over others, being needy without asking first or reciprocating later, or shrugging off emotional and logistical work, practices of male supremacy often work to undermine solidarity and community. Male supremacy harms, traumatizes, and pushes people away, placing even more obstacles in our collective path to social transformation.

Male supremacist behavior within our organizing spaces often goes unchecked because many of us have internalized the male supremacist notion that the "real struggle" is elsewhere, whether in the streets or the halls of government. In addition, some of the most obvious forms of this behavior, such as male sexual violence, can feel especially difficult to address for those of us who recognize that the police and prisons not only fail to prevent this violence but actually produce and reproduce systems of heteropatriarchy, white supremacy, and capitalism. Left unaddressed, however, male violence within our communities reinforces the status quo and undermines the belief that a better world is within our collective capacity to create. The joint statement "Gender Violence and the Prison Industrial Complex" issued in 2001 by INCITE! Women of Color Against Violence and Critical Resistance is particularly instructive on this point, urging "all men in social justice movements to take particular responsibility to address and organize around gender violence in their communities as a primary strategy for addressing violence and colonialism. We challenge men to address how their own histories of victimization have hindered their ability to establish gender justice in their communities."[2]

Through co-facilitating or supporting various accountability processes, we've also learned that men who have caused harm are often easier to reach if they are engaged by people they already trust, and are frequently more likely to be accountable if they can maintain preexisting relationships or even build new ones. When we address the problem through this lens, it becomes clear that the responses often employed to address male violence—public shaming, physical punishment, exile from spaces or a community, calling the police, or just doing nothing—are insufficient for transforming either the specific harmful behavior or the surrounding conditions. Demonization, isolation, retaliatory violence or state intervention offer, at best, only partial solutions, and can be especially destructive for communities that are already scapegoated and targeted by the prison industrial complex (PIC).

The question, then, is how do we respond to these widespread harms in ways that build solidarity, create community, and support the healing of those who have been harmed, while also challenging the male supremacist context within which the harm occurred? How do we do this without relying on unnecessary violence, exclusion, or state systems? We might call responses that meet these criteria "transformative justice" (TJ), to the degree that they seek both to address the specific instance(s) of harm and transform the convictions and structural conditions that facilitated the harm happening in the first place.[3]

Helping to bring together the accountability circle strengthened RJ's commitment to actively challenge male supremacist violence around him, and led to the three of us sitting down to explore how we could do this work together and, eventually, founding the CMS Project. Over several months we spoke regularly about what we wanted to see and help to create in terms of community responses to violence. (One framework we found particularly inspiring was the "Transformative Justice Collaborative" model initiated by generation-FIVE, a Bay Area–based organization focused on ending child sexual abuse by organizing "toward equity and liberation rather than maintaining the inequality that the current State and systems maintain.") In an attempt to bring more cis men into this work, as well as to meet an expressed need to challenge male supremacy within various New York City social justice organizing communities, we facilitated our first "Study-into-Action" group process from May 2009 to January 2010. For nine months, this group discussed, read, and reflected on male supremacy in our personal and political lives.

Facilitating this process for a diverse group of cis men from all over the city, we tried to construct spaces and practices for confronting male supremacy in its concrete manifestations, as it intersects with other systems of oppression. For example, in one session we broke into groups to analyze how different racialized masculinities are represented in mainstream media. This was instructive for exploring both how we had related to our own particularly racialized masculinities growing up and how we have been targeted, privileged, or otherwise stereotyped in the popular imagination. One of the questions that remained at the end of this session was whether we were seeking to construct new and better masculinities or move beyond masculinity altogether.

Foundational to our monthly Study-into-Action sessions was our practice of Somatics, an integrative approach to healing and transformation that understands and treats human beings as a complex of mind, body, and spirit. With support from generationFIVE cofounder and longtime Somatics instructor Staci Haines, who co-facilitated our first session, we tried to employ Somatics as a tool to address shared privilege and power. We communicated to the group that we incorporated Somatics not simply as a practice of self-help or self-improvement—which is often socially decontextualized and strongly individualistic—but because we believe that we cannot just think and talk our way out of male privilege and male violence. This felt particularly important to us as so much of this violence manifests in relationship to bodies and what we do with and to them. As we shared in the group, we need to work with our whole organisms and transform ourselves at the level of everyday behaviors in order to shift our practices of male privilege.

Over this first cycle of work it became clear that there were recurring dynamics we needed to address and particular skill sets we needed to build. One key area is the development and valuing of emotional intelligence and the capacity to provide and seek appropriate support. Here we aim to root out specific tired and destructive behavioral norms—cis men who act needy and/or emotionless, cannot or do not notice their own or others' emotions and emotional triggers, and so on—and encourage men instead to reciprocate the support they receive and provide care for others (including other cis men) in a way that challenges patriarchal social relations. A second area of focus is on developing a profound grasp and consistent practice of consent, moving from a legalistic framework of soliciting permission to a deeper and more nuanced understanding of power. In our work, we try to reframe consent—and particularly the word No—as something that can make healthier relations possible for all parties, and allow us to maintain connection in the future. At the same time, we've strived to question our basic assumptions about sexuality and desire, denaturalizing our sexual desires and examining how historical and cultural forces help to shape and produce them. The third area of development involves learning to identify and share work that has historically been—and continues to be—relegated mainly to women, especially in the home or in formal political settings. This area builds on the work of feminist writers such as Silvia Federici and Selma James; in the Study-into-Action, we used an excerpt of Federici's book *Caliban and the Witch* (New York: Autonomedia, 2004) to frame the ways in which the work of social reproduction is devalued and overwhelmingly forced upon women as part of a system of capitalist exploitation. So far, we've worked in these areas through education, skills-building, and mobilization with other cis men, and also in collaboration with feminist, queer, and trans organizers to build radical analysis and practice together.[4]

Before beginning our Study-into-Action, we decided to approach some of the groups in New York City that do related work and formally partner with them in planning this project. In the role of Accountability and Support Partners, these organizations gave us feedback on a curriculum outline several months before our first session, helped to shape its structure and content, and met with us halfway through the nine-month program to again provide insightful feedback. The groups included the Safe OUTside the System (SOS) Collective of the Audre Lorde Project, Sisterfire NYC (a collective affiliated with INCITE! Women of Color Against Violence), Third Root Community Health Center, the Welfare Warriors Project of Queers for Economic Justice, and individual members of the Rock Dove Collective and an emerging queer people of color anti-violence group. Incorporating our partners' suggestions, we fashioned each Study-into-Action session to open with group-building activities and an introduction to Somatics, followed by activities mapping the history of our understandings of masculinity—how different forces of privilege and oppression have shaped us as cis men. From there, we centered the sessions on political education, historicizing male violence, and forming a shared, intersectional analysis of male supremacy and male representations in media. The second half of the curriculum moved toward a more experiential focus, honing in on what male supremacy, violence, accountability, desire, and transformation (could) look like in our personal and political relationships, and what commitments we can make to challenging male dominance. Over sessions six through eight, we explored how male violence manifests in our communities; how, when we observe male privilege and/or violence, to intervene as bystanders without reproducing male supremacist dynamics; what accountability for male violence looks like in a TJ framework; and how to relate differently as cis men to desire, connection, and intimacy. In our final session, we evaluated our process together and discussed our concrete commitments to challenging male supremacy in our personal lives and political work.[5]

As the name suggests, we were hoping to culminate the Study-into-Action with some sort of collective action in support of and useful to one or more of our partners. Lacking a clear opportunity to do so, we instead organized a reportback event in March 2010 (two months after the end of the 9-month program), to which we each invited friends, family, and members of our communities. The goals of the event were to organize something collectively among the three of us who facilitated the Study-into-Action and the nine participants who completed it, to broaden the dialogue and share our commitments with a larger group of people to whom we are accountable in different ways, and to create a platform for this dialogue within the context of our accountability and support partner organizations—who also participated in the event—as a way to continue building connection and collaboration. The need for this kind of work was reflected in the packed room of over 100 people who showed up for the reportback, representing a rich cross-section of the city.

We find ourselves at present in a moment of reflection, where we are attempting to synthesize all the learning and feedback gained from our experiences with accountability processes, the Study-into-Action, and the collective event we hosted. Our relationship with generationFIVE, with whom we are deepening our understanding of TJ and training in Somatics, will continue to be crucial in our next steps following this assessment process. We recently completed production with generationFIVE on a DVD of "men's digital stories to end child sexual abuse." The digital stories and accompanying discussion guide are a teaching tool to explore the relationship between child sexual abuse and male supremacy, as well as the multiple positions that young men often hold in relation to violence.

Based on all of the learning and feedback we've gained from both partner organizations and participants, we are currently revising the curriculum developed for the Study-into-Action in order to share it with people who are interested in building similar projects and to improve the next round of the Study-into-Action. We are also continuing our participation in the StoryTelling and Organizing Project, a website and international network of organizations that provide a forum and a model for "collecting and sharing stories about everyday people taking action to end interpersonal violence," and whose audio stories we have used in some of our work. Perhaps most importantly, we are looking for ways to deepen collaboration with our Accountability and Support Partners locally while continuing to engage and support the Study-into-Action participants and their communities. Whether we remain in our current formation or shift toward something else will depend greatly on these two groups' needs and desires.

As allies to feminist, queer, and trans struggles against interlocking forms of oppression, we must acknowledge that we cisgender men cannot simply will our privilege away or make a quick and painless transition to different ways of being in the world. This work cannot happen unless we learn to acknowledge that there are all sorts of privileges and benefits we stand to lose by challenging male supremacy—but also, that we have honest emotions, healthier relationships, greater dignity, and a fuller humanity to gain.

and the story continues...

And Mr. X? We had decided not to include him in the Study-into-Action process, as it did not seem clear that he was authentically committed to transformation. It had been a difficult year. He'd left the city and country several times and didn't put much effort into working with me (RJ), despite the fact that I was the person responsible for checking in on how he was keeping his commitments overall. When I surprised him by showing up at one of his parties, he commented—perhaps half-joking—that I was not "his parole officer." What?! I'd just gotten off of a 9-hour shift taking care of restless children, and I was stopping by because he wasn't getting back to me by phone or e-mail. It wasn't my ideal way to start a Friday evening. Especially in times like this, the friendship, solidarity, and commitment of Danielle, Gaurav, and Alan, with whom I could vent and debrief on how to honor the commitments laid out in the accountability circle, have been crucial.

The fact is that it's been difficult to figure out how to orient myself to the responsibilities I had agreed during the circle to take on: I'm tracking his behavior through checking in on him and with people around him, though I'm not a social worker (much less a parole officer). On the other hand, although I care about him, I'm not a simple "friend." And he may confide in me, but I'm not a counselor or therapist. I'm something else. I worry about how much to empathize or connect. Will I be enabling in some way, or will I come down too hard on where he's at right now? (One thing that we've learned through the multiple accountability efforts we've been a part of, and from talking with more experienced folks like Support New York, is that this question—When do I express care and support, and when do I push for more?—is one of the hardest parts of engaging with someone who has caused harm.)

In June of 2009, a month after kicking off the Study-into-Action group and a year into the accountability process, Danielle and I checked in with each of the participants in Mr. X's accountability circle. Speaking with them, and considering the reports from others who had been around him and our own infrequent communication with him, it became clear that Mr. X wasn't living up to the commitments he'd made in the circle. It was also clear that we had not established sufficient means for checking in around his various commitments, nor had we articulated a clear outcome were he to fail to keep those commitments or remain in contact. We checked back in with Mr. X, sharing this feedback and what we thought it might mean. Although a bit snide and defensive at first, he seemed to come around and engage in a way that he hadn't previously. With support from Danielle, he found a therapist and various groups to address his alcoholism while building a group that he's comfortable with, and committed to starting sessions with me around misogyny and male supremacy.[6]

It's been over two-and-a-half years since two young women stepped forward and initiated this accountability process. It is very heartening to see them continue to be engaged and making important contributions in their radical political work, and to hear from them that they feel very supported and affirmed by our efforts. Their courageous actions were a major inspiration for CMS, and our broader, everyday efforts to take on the work of challenging male supremacy in more active, thoughtful, and radical ways. There is much work ahead, and some of the outcomes can be difficult to measure. Through building processes like the Study-into-Action and the accountability circle, it is our hope that we are creating responses to harm that make our vision for a better world—one that offers safety without depending on prisons—not only more likely, but also more credible.

notes

1   For a more thorough explanation of "cisgender" and related terms, see http://juliaserano.livejournal.com/14700.html

2   See *Color of Violence: The INCITE! Anthology,* ed. INCITE! Women of Color Against Violence (Cambridge, MA: South End Press), 2006.

3   For more information on transformative justice, you can check out a short essay or the longer online resource "Toward Transformative Justice: A Liberatory Approach to Childhood Sexual Abuse and Other Forms of Intimate and Community Violence (A Call to Action for the Left and the Sexual and Domestic Violence Sectors)," both from generationFIVE: http://resistinc.org/newsletters/issues/articles/towards-transformative-justice and http://www.generationfive.org/downloads/G5_Toward_Transformative_Justice.pdf.

4   In founding the CMS Project, we've joined a patchwork landscape of organizations and collectives in New York City working to eliminate violence against female/queer/trans individuals and communities and/or build alternative forms of safety and accountability beyond the PIC. We've learned from and collaborated with Support New York, a collective which has been doing work around survivor support and community accountability for several years; we've also been in touch with members of Reflect, Connect, Move around our shared work on gender violence,

while CONNECT—an organization focused on family and gender violence—has shared space and resources with us. We continue to be inspired by Critical Resistance NYC and the People's Justice Coalition, who are building community-based responses to state violence: the former (as part of a coalition) recently won a campaign to stop construction of a new jail in the Bronx, while the latter is working to foster and support a citywide culture of observing the police as a tactic for deterring abuse and brutality on their part.

5   As facilitators, we consistently tried to cocreate a space in which all of us acknowledged how much we each have to teach each other, balanced against the fact that three of us had written a curriculum with set topics informed by external input from allied organizations. Similarly, as facilitators, we took on a number of roles within the group, and walked a difficult line at times between leading and participating.

6   A feminist therapist who lives in my neighborhood has worked with one of CMS's partners (Queers for Economic Justice's Welfare Warriors) and has experience in harm reduction. She provided support for me in preparing this one-on-one work. One of her first pieces of advice was that Mr. X and I negotiate and establish clarity around our respective roles before beginning this work together.

resources

Audre Lorde Project: http://www.alp.org

Critical Resistance: http://www.criticalresistance.org

generationFIVE: http://www.generationfive.org

Generative Somatics: http://www.somaticsandtrauma.org

INCITE! Women of Color Against Violence: http://www.incite-national.org

Queers for Economic Justice (QEJ): http://www.q4ej.org

Rock Dove Collective: http://www.rockdovecollective.org

StoryTelling and Organizing Project (STOP): http://www.stopviolenceeveryday.org

Support New York: http://www.supportny.org

Third Root Community Health Center: http://www.thirdroot.org

GOALS FOR THE CHALLENGING MALE SUPREMACY STUDY-INTO-ACTION:

1. Build an understanding of the workings of male supremacy in relation to other systems of oppression, in our own lives and histories, and those of our communities.

2. Build a practice of confronting male supremacy as it intersects with other systems of oppression toward eliminating intimate and interpersonal violence in our personal and political relationships and institutional violence in our communities.

3. Create a space of and practices for accountability and support for cisgender men so that we can further the work of owning and changing our own oppressive behavior, while challenging gender binaries and heteronormativity.

4. Recognize the ways in which masculinities are racialized within our society and hold ourselves to a complex understanding of how this impacts our experiences of male supremacy.

   * Make room for the histories of trauma and violence that people bring into the room, and connect people with resources that can support them in engaging with these histories transformatively.

   * Strengthen the relationships between us, in order to help us hold the work we will do together.

   * Build a practice of solidarity with feminist, queer, and trans struggles and movements.

   * Work with and toward a vision of dignity and self-determination for all people.

May: FORM. Lay foundation of CMS group, including expectations and support mechanisms; introduction to Somatics; begin exploration of male privilege.

June: SHAPE. Explore the forces of privilege and oppression that have shaped us, and the changes that will move us toward our commitments.

July: FRAME. Deepen our understandings of male supremacy as one component of interconnected systems of oppression; locate sites in which to resist male supremacy in our lives.

August: REPRESENTATION. Identify (and question) distinctly marked masculinities—as they differ along lines of race, class and sexuality—and how they support the most privileged men.

September: RELATIONSHIPS. Examine the ways in which we reproduce systems of oppression/privilege in our personal and political relationships; explore how to hold space with others in a way that honors the full humanity of everyone.

October: VIOLENCE. Reflect on (our) experiences of violence, from the perspectives of survivors, bystanders, and those who have caused harm.

November: ACCOUNTABILITY. Discuss TJ and what it would look like to be genuinely accountable for male privilege in our lives/relationships.

December: DESIRE AND CONNECTION. Explore intimacy, isolation, consent, abuse, and histories of violence, as they apply to us and our (potential) partners.

January: MOVING FORWARD. Discuss action component; consider paths for bringing our work to other circles, as well as for future TJ work; honor and appreciate one another.

MOVEMENT BUILDING STARTS WITH HEALTHY RELATIONSHIPS

Transforming Silence Into Action (TSIA) in Asian Pacific Islander LBQT Communities

Orchid Pusey & gita mehrotra

Transforming Silence Into Action (TSIA) was a series of national gatherings between 2003 and 2008 that brought together a national network of advocates and activists addressing intimate partner violence in Asian and Pacific Islander (API) lesbian, bisexual, queer women, and transgender communities. The conversations and analyses development generated during TSIA gatherings were unique in centering the experiences of queer API people who are part of the movement to end domestic violence. These gatherings gave queer API women and transgender people the opportunity to build capacity and leadership through dialogue that (1) recognizes the complexity of these issues across our diverse communities and experiences, and (2) understands that movement building starts with healthy relationships. TSIA participants met to collectively create new ways of understanding and addressing violence in our relationships, and contribute new and important ways of thinking to queer movements, the broader anti-violence movement, and other movements for social change.

The following pages document some of TSIA's history, values, and core analyses, all aligned with the goal of building the strength, visibility, institutional memory, and sustainability of this work. What follows reflects one moment in the evolution of our analyses; we hope that it can spark and support further discussion and action around abuse in queer API relationships and communities, and contribute new perspectives to anti-domestic violence efforts in all communities.

history

The TSIA initiative grew out of an early network of queer API women addressing domestic violence in their communities that gathered three times between 1998 and 2001. During that time, the Asian Women's Shelter (AWS) also organized a series of focus groups with queer API women in the San Francisco Bay Area on their understanding and experience of relationship violence.[1]

From 2001 to 2003, the AWS launched the TSIA initiative with partners who had been doing similar work in Seattle and Hawai'i, and selected Hawai'i as the site for the first national gathering to directly address the marginalization of Hawai'i and the Pacific US territories in most national efforts, and the under-representation of Pacific Islanders in the early network itself. The gathering aimed to bring together advocates and activists to share information, resources, and strategies to address relationship violence in API queer communities. From 2004 to 2008, AWS coordinated three more TSIA national gatherings, each expanding the network, its analyses, and its capacity to more effectively address issues of gender justice and the exclusion of transgender communities and other marginalized API queer communities from analyses and spaces devoted to gender-based violence. The dialogue and information shared at the gatherings evolved significantly over time, reflecting a deepening analysis within the network, the growth of queer anti-violence efforts in local communities, meaningful community-building within the network, and a self-reflective organizing process that refined the national gatherings over time.

Each gathering comprised small- and large-group discussion and strategizing sessions, as well as peer presentations about work in local communities and resource-sharing. Participants shared training curricula (for use in API communities) on LGBQT issues, homophobia, queer domestic violence, and other relevant topics. Across gatherings there was also a desire to discuss community accountability models and concrete community-based interventions, to solicit feedback on local strategies and challenges, to build healthy relationship skills training curricula, and to explore other creative ways of doing anti-violence work within queer API communities. The meetings were largely informed by participants' own activist, advocacy, and personal experiences, and structured to encourage a meaningful exchange between the resources, skills, analyses, and alliances developed during TSIA gatherings and participants' local community work.

Approximately forty participants from across the US attended each gathering as a result of an invitation process that prioritized former participants and people from un- and under-represented API groups. Attendees were a mix of concerned community members, organizational representatives, progressive activists, and domestic violence advocates. Together they represented Pacific Islander, West Asian, South Asian, Southeast Asian, East Asian, and mixed Asian communities living in the US. In an effort to build coalitions and dialogue with those doing related work, TSIA organizing committees decided to invite participation in each gathering from five allies who were queer women and transgender people from other communities of color, including African American, Alaska Native, and Latin@ communities.

core themes and key ideas[2]

TSIA's work exists within the context of the broader domestic violence movement and the wider movement to end violence against women. We believe gender-based analyses of domestic violence are critically important, given the pervasiveness of male violence against women and girls, heavy currents of sexism and straight male privilege in our communities and society, and misogynistic backlash against the domestic violence movement. Gender-based analyses of domestic violence reflect the nature and pattern of direct patriarchal violence against women and girls, and help us address misogynistic community- and systems-based responses to it. But existing gender-based analyses are not an easy fit for queer relationships and communities. As part of the queer domestic violence movement, we must strengthen our assessments of violence and power within relationships in ways that take into account complex gender dynamics in our communities and do not rely on gender-based violence assessment shortcuts (e.g., the primary perpetrator is the more masculine person, the bigger person, etc). The TSIA network is committed to doing the following:

1. Support work that challenges sexism and the oppression of women and girls;
2. Simultaneously advance understandings of intimate partner violence in ways that (a) reflect experiences in queer relationships and, in particular, address API women and trans people's uses of violence to exert patterns of power and control over their partners; and (b) deconstruct gender binaries[3] to reflect gender complexity and diversity, and expand safety from all forms of gender-based violence; BUT
3. Do so in a way that strengthens (rather than dismantles) our feminist, anti-oppression, and community-based analyses of violence against women; AND
4. Strategically and proactively address how certain groups and individuals (e.g., fathers' rights movement) use queer analyses to support claims of "gender symmetry" or the idea that violence is committed with equal frequency and intensity by women and men.

The analyses and questions presented here are primarily developed out of and informed by on-the-ground experience. They emerge out of years of peer-to-peer conversations and storytelling, and are an attempt to synthesize a wide range of ideas from participants' personal and community experiences. They also bring together examples of community responses to violence shared by TSIA participants whether or not they viewed them as successful.

We are developing models for understanding domestic violence in queer API relationships and communities.

What does violence and abuse in queer API relationships look like?

TSIA participants generally agree that:

1. Most people have learned and survived violence and have the capacity to use it in some form.
2. Violence does not have a singular definition, and tactics of abuse exist along a broad spectrum of behaviors.
3. Just as with violence in all other relationships, abuse in queer API relationships can cover the entire spectrum (e.g., name calling, financial control, sexual abuse, attempted homicide, murder).
4. Patterns of behavior and uses of violence must be assessed and understood within their relationship contexts rather than in isolation.
5. Shared understanding and analysis about the spectrum of abusive behavior should inform our development of corresponding prevention and intervention strategies.

How do we assess and understand queer API relationship violence amid the challenges presented by the traditional "survivor/perpetrator" framework?

TSIA participants have long struggled with what we call here "the survivor/perpetrator dilemma." Over time, we have acknowledged myriad complex dynamics that show up in different relationships, and that do not easily fit into dominant analyses in the broader domestic violence movement, such as:

1. Some people in relationships get stuck in an unhealthy pattern in which two people use forms of violence in response to conflict, but the uses of violence are not patterned attempts to exert power and control over the other person.

2. Some people continually survive violence in a relationship and develop defensive or retaliatory responses to it that are also not patterned attempts to establish their power and control over the other person.

3. Some people use violence as a means of asserting power and control over their partners across multiple relationships.

4. Other people survive patterns of violence in one intimate relationship and then perpetrate them in another. Or, they survive violence during one period of a relationship and perpetrate it during another period (in the same relationship). Participants knew that these, like the preceding three situations, were not true of all manifestations of domestic violence, and recognized their potential to be wrongly wielded by individuals, communities, or systems trying to deny the existence of a pattern of violence for which one person actually is accountable.

For more than thirty years, a broad domestic violence movement has worked tirelessly to increase societal acknowledgment of domestic violence as a significant community issue, and specifically to expand public awareness of survivor/perpetrator power and control dynamics. Raising that awareness continues to be critical in straight and queer communities. And, in TSIA discussions, participants have grappled with the "survivor or perpetrator?" binary. Does it *always* apply in queer API relationships in which there is violence? Conflicting perspectives arise repeatedly.

Some participants reject the survivor/perpetrator dichotomy, asserting any of the following:

1. Everyone is capable of violence in some circumstances.

2. Anyone of us might use various forms of violence at some point in our relationships.

3. People's lives hold complex relationships to violence that cannot be summed up by the terms "survivor" or "perpetrator."
4. Labeling people as survivors or perpetrators is dehumanizing and does not contribute to healing and reintegration into the community, and ultimately diminishes our efforts toward community transformation.

Others believe that the survivor/perpetrator framework remains useful, asserting any of the following:

1. Understanding domestic violence requires the placing of violent incidents within the context of power and control.
2. The survivor/perpetrator dichotomy helps us differentiate between unhealthy behaviors or moments, and patterns of imbalanced power and control.
3. Drawing this distinction between isolated incidents of unhealthy behavior and patterns of violence used to establish power and control helps TSIA participants name some patterns of emotional and physical violence which they have identified as belonging to the latter category— relationship violence of a type and severity that they think is appropriately named within a very clear survivor/perpetrator paradigm.
4. This distinction can become crucial if partners must, or choose to, engage certain systems such as social services, shelters, family court, or the criminal legal system.

The TSIA network's challenge is to shift this internal debate by reframing the question: When and how are aspects of the survivor/perpetrator dichotomy (and power/control analysis) useful and appropriate in understanding domestic violence in queer API communities, and when and how can aspects of these frameworks be harmful or limiting?

Violent, manipulative, controlling, and otherwise harmful behaviors in relationships must be meaningfully assessed. And those doing that assessment must be deeply aware of their own assumptions and biases. When someone who has used violence against their partner, but whom we see and identify more readily as a survivor (e.g., a queer woman, a trans person of color, an immigrant from our home country, a friend) asserts that they are "the survivor" or that their partner uses the same amount of violence that they use, what do we do? What effect does, for instance, their gender identity and expression—and that of their partner—have on our interpretation of the situation? Do we ask questions to learn more? What questions? Do we take their word at face value and conclude that the survivor/perpetrator analysis doesn't apply to queer relationships? Or do we recall that though men in heterosexual relationships can be survivors of violence perpetrated by their female partners, there is some statistically justified skepticism of straight men who berate their partner's behavior and unequivocally claim their own status as abused and controlled? There is no statistically justified skepticism in the realm of queer domestic violence, but we have seen some tendencies in communities to skip an assessment of power and control upon hearing one person's assertion that they are (or were also) "the survivor." To fully explore this complex set of questions while expanding our practical assessment skills, the TSIA network strives to ensure that:

1. If there is an abusive dynamic in a relationship and more than one person is using or has at some point used violence, we acknowledge and assess all of the violence; discern and recognize the patterns and context that make the situation one of domestic violence; accurately assess who in the relationship is perpetrating a pattern of power and control; and take steps toward safety, accountability, and change.

2. If there is a situation in which two people have an unhealthy dynamic and are both using violence as a response to conflict in their relationship, we do not force our understanding of the situation into the binary of survivor/perpetrator simply because we have no other ways of assessing violence in relationships.

As we build tools and skills to support queer API communities responding to domestic violence, other questions emerge: What types of behavior and contexts of violence lead us to define a relationship dynamic as "unhealthy?" As "abusive?" As immediately dangerous or lethal? How much violence can a person perpetrate within a given relationship context and still be considered the survivor? How can we better identify dynamics of power and control when relationship violence surfaces in our communities?

As we expand our analyses of relationship violence within queer API communities in the context of anti-domestic violence organizing, we also face important assessment considerations. We want to support everyone in our communities in moving toward healthier relationships. We know this will create stronger and healthier queer API people and communities. But supporting a community in moving toward healthier relationships involves encouraging everyone to identify and unlearn their uses of violence and other unhealthy patterns, whether or not they are currently involved in an abusive relationship. And if we create community norms that encourage everyone to identify and unlearn their uses of violence, we will likely prop open the door for some in our communities to misuse those norms to "blame the victim" or deny wholesale the existence of survivor/perpetrator dynamics in abusive situations. In our ongoing attempts to expand upon existing assessment tools, we currently arrive at the following:

1. We can understand a complex relationship situation when we vigilantly recognize when reliance on the survivor/perpetrator binary impairs our responsiveness to violence and blocks creativity in developing interventions, and when it enhances responsiveness and promotes access to safety and accountability.

2. We help end violence when we encourage everyone to unlearn harmful patterns and educate ourselves and our communities on how to identify power and control patterns, assess for risk and safety, and call out (rather than collude with) victim-blaming and survivor self-blame.

3. We effectively expand analyses of gender-based intimate partner violence when we mold them to reflect the realities of queer relationships, including their unique patterns of power and control, and dynamics that impact

how the abuse is viewed (e.g., by queer communities, straight API communities, social service providers, the court system), in collaboration with other anti-violence movements.

The complexities of queer API identities and experiences complicates the development and implementation of effective domestic violence interventions.

As part of the movement to end domestic violence, TSIA recognizes that successful interventions must take into account the social contexts of people's lives and relationships. Queer Asian and Pacific Islander identities vary enormously across age, English language proficiency, ethnicity, immigration history and status, gender identity, gender normativity, ability, geography, class, body size, and other factors. (One key factor of difference—the degree of recognition and support one receives from family, ethnic and faith community, work environment, and local community—is deeply significant to one's life and cannot be easily summarized.) Through the course of the TSIA national gatherings, we have heard numerous perspectives from participants about the impact of these factors on their lives and relationships. Participants have voiced realities that include but are not limited to:

— I am depending on the acceptance and support of my ethnic community.
— I am either invisible in or ostracized from my ethnic community. I am considered either part of that community, or queer. No one accepts and sees me as both.
— My ethnic community faces overlapping issues of oppression, violence, and survival. There are "bigger" issues there than queer relationships or domestic violence.
— I have never been part of any single ethnic community. I have no place there.
— I am depending on the acceptance and support of my queer community.

— As a queer Asian person, I am either invisible or exoticized in the white queer community and/or by other queer people of color.
— There is no queer community where I live. I am isolated and closeted.
— I am depending on the acceptance and support of my community.
— My progressive community faces "bigger" issues than queer relationships or domestic violence.
— I am depending on the acceptance and support of my family. I cannot tell them about my relationship.
— My family rejects me. I am depending on the acceptance and support of my friends and/or relationship.
— I am alone. There are individuals who matter to me, but there is no whole community whose opinion matters to me.
— Homo/bi/transphobia is deep and widespread. It impacts everything.

These statements reflect some of challenges facing API queer women and transgender people trying to understand and respond to relationship violence in a larger social context shaped by homo/bi/trans/phobia, racism, xenophobia, and other forms of oppression. Such challenges reveal that, oftentimes, community members' experiences of identity, social context, and oppression amplify their reliance on the very things that interventions to violence ask them to risk: the security of their relationships with their partner, close friends, and/or queer, progressive, or ethnic communities.

TSIA gives us an unprecedented opportunity to discern what kinds of interventions may work in these varied contexts. While we acknowledge that interventions will often be as diverse as individual situations of violence, we also strive to analyze which aspects of interventions are useful in what types of circumstances, and to locate and map important patterns and trends (e.g., of explicit and implicit conditions that create opportunities or "success" in varying community contexts).

We are exploring concepts and practices of community accountability as potential models for responding to domestic violence.

Participants in the TSIA network know that queer API community members face multiple barriers when attempting to access existing domestic violence and sexual assault services and systems. TSIA participants also generally agree that, like violent and abusive behaviors, appropriate interventions to relationship violence exist on a spectrum and might range from community education to calling 911. An intervention could look like "calling someone out" or supporting someone to change their behavior over a long period of time. No single type of intervention is "right" for addressing violence in API lesbian, bisexual, queer women's, and/or transgender relationships and communities. Some API queer community members experiencing relationship violence have chosen or needed to call the police, go to the hospital, get restraining orders, fight custody battles in court, and seek safe, confidential housing in domestic violence shelters. Many TSIA participants had experience expanding accessibility and reforming systems to increase safety and support for queer people in those and other systems. Participants also readily acknowledged that many would risk entry into those systems only as a last resort, and rely heavily on the support of their peer networks and communities. Also, they acknowledged that there are very few spaces in which to focus on efforts that are separate from systems reform or accessibility development in existing services. Therefore, community-based education, prevention, and community accountability intervention models, as well as the importance of peer networks, have been a central theme and discussion thread of the TSIA network gatherings.

Community accountability—as it has been discussed and framed during TSIA gatherings—is perhaps described most succinctly by the Oakland-based organization Creative Interventions[4] as "an umbrella term for many models and processes for community responsibility for, and control over, ending violence."[5] Throughout TSIA national gatherings, participants have, for the most part, assumed (1) the necessity of developing community accountability models, and (2) that there are ways in which the often marginalized, small, and close-knit nature of our communities can increase our reliance on them, and thereby make community accountability both more possible and more difficult. Over the years spanned by four TSIA gatherings, more and more participants tried new community-based strategies to address intimate partner violence in their relationships and communities. But most approaches focused on early stages of community engagement, such as creative outreach and education in queer API community spaces. We had fewer examples demonstrating how to practically implement community mobilizing and/or accountability as violence intervention.

While the "why community accountability?" discussion has thrived at TSIA gatherings, and in other progressive communities, the "how" of actually doing community accountability work has proven much harder to identify, implement, and replicate. What follows are common challenges and lessons learned from TSIA conversations about the nuts and bolts of community accountability. They are not meant to make community accountability seem impossible. Instead, they are an honest accounting of what we have faced and know we will face again; laying them out in the open reduces confusion and frustration, and helps us prepare for the future.

i. we're dealing with extra dirty laundry

Many individuals and communities (particularly within marginalized social groups) facing domestic violence will deny, suppress, collude, and/or victim-blame—indeed, try nearly anything to avoid airing their "dirty laundry" in public. TSIA participants generally agree that many factors make domestic violence in queer API relationships and communities feel like "extra dirty laundry." First, experiences of domestic violence are difficult for any survivor to disclose and challenging for any community to face. Second, racism, anti-immigrant sentiment and attack, and other social realities isolate participants' ethnic communities and further encourage community members to handle their "dirty laundry" privately. And finally, homo/bi/transphobia attacks the basic essence and existence of queer people's lives and relationships. This compounds people's defensiveness and protectiveness of their relationships. It heightens their resistance to say or do anything that could be used to bolster existing hatred of queer people, API people, and queer API people. In combination, these factors can make it incredibly difficult for an API LBQT survivor to come out about their experience of relationship violence.

ii. denial, denial, denial
Communities often want conflict to just go away or resolve itself, and will deny its existence in myriad ways including wholesale denial, minimizing its impact, or ignoring its escalation. Most of us have been raised to deal indirectly with conflict, and have limited comfort with, and skill in, conflict resolution. This often leads to community responses that involve denying, avoiding, or ignoring abuse. Those responses show up in different ways. Community members may feel that they don't know the people involved in an abusive situation "well enough" to get involved. Or they may be hesitant to "choose sides" by supporting the survivor or "calling out" the abusive partner's behavior. Or they may simply refuse to believe that someone who is "fine" to them could be abusive to someone else.

iii. identifying unhelpful and harmful uses of community power
Community tendencies to minimize or deny violence can cause: (1) community members not to intervene; (2) survivors to remain silent about abuse; and (3) perpetrators to continue violent patterns.

Ironically, the same community-based power that makes community accountability possible can also silence potential interveners and create a culture of collusion and silence. Those bystanders or friends who could put community accountability into action can be silenced by fear of the same risk (loss of acceptance or approval within the community) that we hope to harness to engage perpetrators and build safety within the community.

iv. looking out for "s/he said–s/he said"

Oftentimes people who are perpetrating abuse are the first to spread word throughout the community that they are being victimized by their partner. When friends and community members have limited ability to assess what is happening or make assumptions based on gender shortcuts—or even simply believe whoever claims to be the survivor first—they can act in ways that are harmful to the situation, and/or do nothing at all. Community responses can become entrenched in "s/he said–s/he said" camp-building. In these situations, it is important for key people involved in the intervention to open communication channels, reduce gossip, and take leadership to assess power, violence, and safety needs in the situation while working with others to address them.

v. "we have to look out for our own"

In their desire to spare an abuser from being ostracized from their already marginalized group, communities can and often do deprioritize a survivor's need for community and safety. Many often find it easier to silence the survivor, victim blame, or wrongly deny any evidence of a survivor/batterer dynamic, than to intervene and engage a person to stop and unlearn their unhealthy or abusive behavior.

vi. it takes more than "community"

It can take time to build common core values and a shared understanding of what constitutes intimate partner violence, what a successful accountability process might look like, and what role, if any, community members should take in it. Community accountability requires coordinated time, effort, and a level of emotional commitment that is difficult to sustain. Already juggling multiple demands on their time and other (often limited) resources, people typically have inadequate support or structure in their community accountability efforts and so want to "just move on" as quickly as possible. Given how hard confrontation and conflict are for many or most people, those involved in community accountability processes (from any perspective) need support, respite, and understanding.

*vi. strong friendships and effective direct communication contribute to lasting
efforts*

When based on support, trust, constructive direct communication, and a willingness to challenge each other to grow, friendships and other personal relationships are a crucial element in the community accountability process. Friends and support people can and are drawn into violence interventions from all sides, including: friends of the person taking accountability, friends of the survivor, friends who are trusted facilitators, and other community members who want to contribute resources but don't want to be fully involved. These relationships need to make it through what is likely a complicated process of negotiations and teamwork. And, unfortunately, many factors impact what kinds of peer networks people may have, the degree of established trust in friendships, and the extent to which those friendships can endure a process as potentially challenging as community accountability. Care, patience, and practice with communication and conflict resolution have the potential to help these relationships emerge renewed and strengthened.

vii. survivors and community members can disagree

Serious conflict can arise between what survivors want/need and what community members think is an appropriate way to "call out" abuse or intervene in a violent situation. Understandably, survivors often fear retaliatory violence from the abuser, the abuser's community, or from the community at large if others speak up on their behalf. And community interveners often start out with strong feelings and differing levels of consciousness around domestic violence, and sometimes rally behind interventions that could put survivors and key interveners at heightened risk of harm. A survivor may want personal support but wish to keep the violence a secret, insisting it's not a community issue while their supporters feel that relationship violence is an issue that affects the community and that community members should come together around it. During TSIA gatherings, participants shared and troubleshot situations in which it had been challenging to determine what to do because the survivor did not want any form of intervention. On the flip side, disagreements can arise when (1) community members do not want to or do not have the capacity to intervene with the perpetrator in the way that the survivor wants, and (2) when interveners or the survivor change their minds along the process in ways that others don't understand or uphold. Solid and consistent communication and safety planning between survivors and community interveners ensures that risks taken in any community-based intervention are calculated and negotiated from multiple perspectives.

viii. figuring out what counts as "accountability" and when the process is "done"
Situations of relationship violence emerge in communities and can generate crises and high intensity engagement by those most affected by them. Friends and supporters can engage perpetrators and survivors of violence in different ways to try to stop the immediate violence, but rarely is the situation a single, isolated incident that can be quickly and wholly resolved. Lasting, positive behavioral change requires a slow, supported process during which progress can be frustratingly unclear, unknown, or even backwards. That said, an accountability process can't remain at the same level of intensity forever. There must be markers of observable or measurable accountability. Community teams need to talk together about what will signal that the team's process is "over" (for whatever amount of time).

ix. homophobia can isolate relationships from community
Community accountability implies the influence and presence of a community, even if that community is made up of just two or three people. But homo/bi/transphobia forces many queer relationships into a state of isolation in which they have limited, if any, community support. The increased vulnerability of the relationship itself, of both people in the relationship, and the survivor in particular can have devastating effects. This increased pressure and isolation impacts every aspect of the situation—it's harder to get support, to increase safety, to leave the relationship, to risk homophobia

(against both people) from systems and services, to rebuild a sense of self-worth and self-confidence, and to have hope for a healthy and happy queer relationship in the future.

x. challenges to accountability in activist communities
Neither taking accountability for our actions nor changing our behavior is easy, and we all know how common it is for folks to resist and avoid being accountable. In progressive and activist communities, this resistance can take many forms: over-intellectualizing the accountability process, challenging the analysis or language of those asking for accountability, using experiences of oppression (or another's experiences of privilege) as an excuse for using violence, framing any questioning or challenge of our behavior as abusive and disempowering (or as white, bourgeois, academic, classist, sexist, homo/bi/transphobic, racist, ableist, etc.), and directing all of our anger, shame, and trauma on the interveners.

Such tactics are quite effective because they emerge from the cultural norms of so many progressive and activist communities. Because we always want to take issues such as process, language, oppression, and privilege, and the context of someone's experience and use of violence seriously, we often back off from calling them out even when we suspect there are smokescreens or aggressive tactics being deployed by someone trying to avoid taking responsibility for violence. Calling these tactics into question takes both individual and collective courage, challenging a progressive community to expand beyond its own dominant norms and support a process that makes real accountability and change possible.

That said, no two communities or situations of violence are exactly the same. Sometimes, community members (including survivors in a situation) holding someone accountable will blame the full history of their anger and trauma on the person whom they want to hold accountable. They can generate or demand accountability goals that are impossible for anyone to meet.

In these situations, it is important for community members to remember that the pain and harm caused by situations of relationship violence cannot be undone or erased by a single community-based accountability effort. Community-based interventions are just one element of many in the process of individual and community healing.

It is impossible to fully control how, when, or whether intervention efforts lead a person to change their behavior in a lasting or meaningful way. And community accountability efforts cannot be expected to work at all stages of intervention in all situations of domestic violence.

But despite challenges to creating safety, change, and/or transformation through community accountability efforts, there is a broad range of possible positive impacts that includes and expands beyond that which a team initially names as goals for accountability. Even if community accountability actions do not achieve the originally intended result(s), they can contribute to building values-based community and even accomplish unintended positive results that can be documented, evaluated, and shared. Community accountability work can also serve as an example to others about the community's values and "bottom lines," and impact the future such that:

1. Domestic violence is addressed not as "dirty laundry" but as an issue of community health, safety, and wellness.
2. Shared values and behavior around nonviolence are developed alongside shared identity and shared politics.
3. Communities hold abusers accountable for their violence and support their transformation.
4. Peer groups resist conflict-adverse tendencies toward denial and minimization, and instead face and intervene in domestic violence as it emerges in their social networks.
5. Communities nurture cultures of healthy relationships and build shared values around relationship violence and the implementation of a range of community interventions.

In the meantime, to build more collective understanding of when and how to use community-based interventions, TSIA participants continue to discuss these questions together:

1. What behaviors or relationship dynamics compel community members to intervene?
2. Are there abusive behaviors or situations that cannot be effectively addressed from within the privacy of a particular relationship, and/or through community engagement and accountability?
3. When and how might individuals or communities integrate state systems (e.g., law enforcement, social services) of intervention and accountability?
4. What are communities' "bottom lines?" Are there actions or behaviors that must always be addressed?

THEME 4:

We need more practical tools and models for identifying and unlearning uses of violence by others and ourselves.

The TSIA network recognized that there are few tools or models for doing this kind of work within grassroots communities or within the broader anti-violence movement. We understood that people have complex relationships to violence (e.g., having perpetrated it, survived it, witnessed it, colluded with it). And carefully examining our histories and uses of violence can help us in our own lives as well as better equip us to support others who are committed to unlearning and being accountable for their violence. For the third and fourth TSIA gatherings, we designed the "Identifying and Unlearning Our Own Violence" workshop to break the silence typically surrounding the issue of our own violence (and other harmful behavior) within progressive communities. Workshop exercises and discussions focused on the following goals:

1. Respond to the strong interest in this topic within the TSIA network.
2. Build the value of critical self-reflection, accountability, and change within the network, within activist and anti-violence spaces, and within our communities.
3. Provide tools for identifying and unlearning potentially unhealthy behavior(s) and/or abusive behavior within ourselves.
4. Build capacity and resources for doing this work within queer API communities.
5. Begin to lift the shame and silence around these behaviors in a constructive, direct way.
6. Generate new norms for healthy relationships and self-motivated change in our relationships and communities.

Workshop participants used individual journaling prompts, sharing in pairs and small action groups to reveal and work on—rather than hide and deny—their own problematic behaviors; they also shared some of their friends' experiences. Workshop participants found the process powerful and useful for thinking about their relationships and anti-violence work. We hope that participants will build on the work started here to further develop effective and practical tools that support healthy relationships and communities.

moving forward

How do we maintain the viability of this work in queer API activist communities? Most work on domestic violence in our communities has been initiated by progressive queer API anti-domestic violence advocates and activists. However, many activist communities have not historically taken on intimate partner violence as a community issue. To help maintain the viability and sustainability of anti-violence work within progressive/activist communities, the TSIA network is committed to the following:

— *Linking macro- and micro-level analyses and action.* We often see progressive groups articulate macro-level analyses of issues (such as white supremacy, imperialism, and/or globalization) without prioritizing skills and capacity building to address interpersonal violence. When interpersonal violence occurs in those same groups, they often deny or minimize the violence (at least at first) and eventually become mired in stress and dysfunction because (1) they disconnect interpersonal violence from the "real work" of social justice movements (e.g., "it's just about social services, it threatens our solidarity, it's personal and not systemic"), and (2) they lack skills and practice in articulating and enacting values that support healthy communication and relationships. The ensuing drama and hardship harms individuals, organizations, communities, and movements. We are committed to upholding macro-level analyses and to connecting them with investment in healthy relationships and experiences in facing the complex realities of interpersonal violence in our communities.

— *Bridging the divide and strengthening the relationship between direct service and community engagement.* In our view the enormous division between direct service and community organizing work has limited the vision, scope, quality, and effectiveness of both, and subsequently weakened the overall viability of efforts to end domestic violence in queer API communities. We seek to broaden perspectives within certain progressive communities that otherwise elevate the importance and value of community organizing work over direct services, which they see as "band-aid" social service models that do not take into account long-range analyses and visions for social change. Conversely, we also seek to broaden the viewpoints of those anti-violence advocates who might otherwise overlook or minimize the potentially transformative power of community-based initiatives not housed in traditional social service models.

— *Simultaneously building analysis, practical skills, and concrete action.* Analyses of intimate partner violence that stray too far from the on-the-ground emotional dynamics of real situations of violence in our communities also hamper the viability of our work. For example, in TSIA discussions participants often voice a desire to engage batterers and hold them accountable for their behavior while ensuring their support and integration in the community. But when sharing real experiences and recalling the emotional realities of people who are hurt, crushed, broken, defensive, aggressive, dismissive, irrational, or manipulative, participants reveal different personal responses. Somewhere between an idealized, abstract analysis and the complex and intense impacts of violence on a community is where we want to be. We seek to bridge the gaps between analysis, skills building, and action so that they increasingly inform each other.

— *Creating a cultural shift toward movement-building that encourages healthy relationships and meaningful self-reflection and change.* Within TSIA, we believe that how we do our work is as important as the work itself, and we know that healthy relationships free of violence and oppression are, in a very real way, the foundation of strong communities and movements. Health and sustainability—for ourselves, our communities, and our movement building efforts—is strengthened when progressive activist groups take on issues of internal power dynamics and healthy interpersonal relationships as expressly linked to the "real work." The hard part is this: meaningful self-reflection and change is critical to healthy relationships; yet self-reflection and change (especially in regards to identifying and unlearning violence we use) can be deeply challenging and uncomfortable, and counter to many activist cultures.

We strive to equip our communities with tools with which to identify and respond to domestic violence when it is happening, and to support those needing safety. And we support all those who have learned to use violence as a maladaptive response to conflict or grasp at power in their lives, to grow and change.

This is hard work. But we know we are on our way. We are responding to intimate partner violence in API LBQT communities, and building healthy relationships. We are infusing the network with the value and practice of self-reflection, and participants are literally transforming silence into action. And as we model and share these values and approaches in our local communities, we know that in this case, bringing the work home is a healthy thing to do.

notes

The Transforming Silence Into Action (TSIA) project has been built upon the energy and insights of those who carried this work years before TSIA began, all TSIA participants, and those who served on local organizing and national advisory committees, and who hosted gatherings in their hometowns and cities. TSIA thrived due to the visionary fundraising of the Asian Women's Shelter's (AWS) founding Executive Director, Beckie Masaki, who created a partnership with the Office on Violence Against Women (OVW) to fund TSIA as a demonstration site for community-driven initiatives led by underserved/underrepresented communities. OVW also supported AWS in subcontracting with the API Women and Family Safety Center in Seattle, WA; PACT Family Peace Center in Honolulu, HI; and with Kalei Kanuha at the University of Hawai'i to share funding and support other local initiatives and community research projects addressing violence in API queer communities. The authors wish to thank all of the above and more, especially Kata Issari and the staff of PACT Family Peace Center, AWS staff, and those National Advisory Committee members who were able to consistently give their time and talents across all four TSIA gatherings.

1   A report titled "Raising Our Voices" documents the results of those initial focus groups. Available online at http://endabuse.org/userfiles/file/ImmigrantWomen/ Raising%20our%20Voices.pdf.

2   *Terminology:* The terms people use to identify themselves and their experiences are layered with private and public political and social meaning, and vary depending on context. These differences and the concepts behind them are too complex to analyze here. It is our intention to use terminology in a flexible way to promote and open up dialogue. The language we use here is not meant to suggest a "right" way of discussing and defining these topics. We have included a few comments below on several terms that we use repeatedly in this writing.

- *"Domestic Violence," "Relationship Violence," "Intimate Partner Violence."* We are aware that these terms can connote different contexts and meanings to different people. Participants at TSIA used all three. Thus we use them here interchangeably.

- *Asian & Pacific Islander (API).* We use API to refer to people of East Asian, South Asian, West Asian, Southeast Asian, Pacific Islander, and/or Central

Asian descent. For more on how we use "API," please visit http://www.apiahf. org/apidvinstitute/definition/htm.

- *Queer, Lesbian, Bisexual, Transgender.* We value inclusive language and recognize that people's identities and experiences are complex to a degree that we cannot accurately or consistently reflect throughout this document. We use the terms queer, lesbian, bisexual, and transgender broadly while also recognizing that these are certainly not the only four terms used to connote gender and sexuality. The term "queer" has been reclaimed and used as a more inclusive term by some, while others dislike it due to its historical use (and use in some current contexts) as an oppressive term. We recognize that we simultaneously engage and risk alienating different people by using the term "queer." We also recognize that there are people in nonheterosexual relationships who do not identify with any of these terms.

- *Community/Communities.* In our view, "communities" based on race, gender, sexuality, geographic region, political beliefs, and so on are rarely intact or homogenous. Often, references to "the _____ community" really refer to the most dominant and visible members of that group. For example, references to "the Korean community" often overlook or deny the experiences of people marginalized within the Korean community (e.g., because of being poor, being fat, being divorced, being gender nonconforming). References to "the queer community" are also rarely inclusive of those who are marginalized within that already marginalized group, such as queer API people or queer people with disabilities. Based on these and other realities, we recognize that the concept and experience of community is often complicated. For the purposes of TSIA (and especially in our discussions about community accountability), we use "community" to refer to any group of people who are aligned with each other in some way through shared experience, identity, location, and/or friendship. We do not make any assumptions about group size or composition, and believe that there is value in differentiating between larger communities (e.g., the Afghani community), and smaller, more intimate communities (e.g., a survivor's community of three close friends).

- *"Relationships" and "Communities."* When discussing locations of domestic violence, we use "queer API relationships and communities" while acknowledging that: (1) Generally speaking, domestic violence is not enclosed within individual relationships but plays out in and affects communities; (2) However, there are queer relationships that are deeply isolated, either because they are largely (or entirely) closeted or because they exist in local contexts in which there is no queer/queer API community; and (3) When discussing "queer API relationships" we refer to a relationship in which at least one member identifies as API.

3   A "Gender Binary System" is a social system that defines, acknowledges, and allows for exactly two "natural" and "opposite" sexes/genders that are assigned at birth, and aligned with corresponding behaviors and roles (i.e., male = man = masculine, which is the opposite of female = woman = feminine). In this system, there is no recognition of, or room for, diversity, ambiguity, change, or mixing of biological sex and gender traits.

4   "As of January 2010, Creative Interventions [CI] has transitioned from a nonprofit organization to an ongoing web-based resource to support people, groups, and organizations developing community-based responses to violence" (http://www.creative-interventions.org).

5   Mimi Kim, founder of Creative Interventions, shared this definition as part of her presentation at the third TSIA national gathering in June 2006.

additional resources

The Asian Women's Shelter and TSIA value anti-oppression–based structures and practices as much as justice-oriented goals and outcomes. We were not able to expand upon these aspects of TSIA in this essay (e.g., organizing and advisory committee structure, guiding values and process behind invitee selection and agenda development). If you are interested in learning more about these aspects of TSIA or would like to read reports or materials about TSIA organizing efforts, please contact AWS directly. Examples of materials include:

- "Creating Community, Hope, and Change" (documents the background and proceedings of Transforming Silence Into Action I)
- "Relationships So Loving and So Hurtful: A Study of Intimate Violence in Asian and Pacific Islander Queer and Lesbian Relationships" (an exploratory research

project by Valli Kalei Kanuha, detailing interview respondents' understandings of their experiences of intimate partner violence in API women's relationships)

- Identifying and Unlearning Our Own Violence (training curriculum)
- Statement on Diversity in API Communities
- Gender Justice Statement
- Invitee Agenda Survey

contact us

Asian Women's Shelter

Queer Asian Women & Transgender Support Program (QAWTS)

3543 18th Street, #19

San Francisco, CA 94110

phone: 415.751.7110

http://www.sfaws.org

THINK. RE-THINK.

Accountable Communities

Connie Burk

For nearly a quarter century, The Northwest Network of Bisexual, Trans, Lesbian, and Gay Survivors of Abuse (NW Network) has worked to end domestic violence and create the conditions needed to support loving and equitable relationships. For much of that time, NW Network advocates have endeavored to develop a tenable practice of "Community Accountability" in activist communities.

We knew the need was urgent from our own experiences and from people who sought our services. We watched, over and over again, as the community mobilized unwittingly to defend abusive people. We sat in poetry slams while people who battered publicly degraded their partners in politically charged rants, the activist community swooning at their feet. We endured the petty power plays of batterers rallying activist groups to retaliate against networks of friends, other organizations, or our organization for helping their partner. We saw popularity and coolness dictate who would be salvaged and who would be savaged. We hoped that by building strong, transparent Community Accountability processes, we could confront some of these pernicious problems of harm and collusion as part of our long-term work toward transforming our communities into spaces that could foster loving and equitable relationships.

As we worked and struggled through the Community Accountability process, we noticed recurring limitations in the application of many of its central principles. Some of these limitations are discussed below.

THE IDEA OF "HOLDING SOMEONE ACCOUNTABLE."

Community Accountability processes often center on a group holding an individual accountable for their actions. This has contributed to a distorted understanding of "accountability," i.e., the mistaken idea that accountability is at its most fundamental level an external process rather than an internal skill.

The NW Network is a very survivor-centered place. We understand people who are surviving abuse to be agents—people who are the subjects of their own lives, not simply objects of abusers' control and exploitation. As survivors, we recognize that being able to think critically about our own choices, knowing that what we do matters, and being able to be accountable to ourselves for our actions (even while locating those choices within the context of abuse and exploitation) are hallmarks of "being in charge of one's own life." For survivors, being accountable to the people who are battering them is not a real option. Folks who batter use their partners' mistakes to further their own control: *Who are you to talk? If they knew what you've done, they'd never help you! You can't leave me, you owe me.* But, like all people, survivors need the products of accountability: release from guilt and shame, reconciliation with oneself and one's community, being out from under the obligation that comes from harming another. Even when actions are wholly justifiable in their context, folks who have remorse or grief about their actions can benefit from accountability.

Accountability is not something that happens to bad people. Accountability is a human skill. It is a skill that each of us must commit to developing as an internal resource for recognizing and redressing the harms we have caused to ourselves and others. Cultivating deep skills (and community investment) in personal accountability also better equips us to respectfully request accountability from others and to be aware when someone is highly resistant to taking responsibility for their actions. As more people develop these skills, the community becomes better able to expect and support ethical, organic accountability processes.

As long as most people in our community have rotten accountability skills, people who abuse will be able to get away with their abuse. Their lack of accountability will not be particularly noticeable or interesting until it is too late. Folks who abuse will manipulate others with their compelling sense of victimization and entitlement forever—or until the harms of their actions are absurdly blatant, or the community falls apart under the weight of defending or managing them.

WHO IS THE ABUSER?

In heterosexual relationships, sexism privileges men's power over women and so it is likely in an abusive relationship between a person raised as a girl who is a woman and a person raised as a boy who is a man that the man is the abuser. (This is not true 100% of the time and everyone should have more refined ways of identifying abusers.) But, if you had available only one predicting factor, the gender of the people in a heterosexual relationship would be the most predictive. This is not the case for queer relationships. Gender, on its own, is useless for predicting who is likely to be the survivor, or who is likely to have abused.

In activist communities, who is believed? And beyond that, what is the harm being addressed? Is it abusive power, control, and exploitation? Is it certain violent acts? Is it the exercise (or simple presence) of privilege? A survivor of domestic violence is likely to use violent behaviors to resist the objectification of being abused. A person who is battering can report actions taken by their partners that are mean, cruel, scary, or confusing. Out of context, they could be seen as abusive. In context, they can be understood as resisting power and control. People have the mistaken idea that batterers are "bad" and survivors are "good." Battering is bad. Surviving battering is good. But, batterers and survivors are people. Understanding a given survivor's actions when they confound our notions of the "good victim"—or interpreting a given batterer's charming manipulations—is not simple. In our experience, folks in activist communities too often end up confused and mobilize against the survivor.

People who batter can use their own vulnerabilities (such as their own experience surviving racism or homophobia, dealing with a mental illness or a previous assault, or facing exploitation in their family of origin or in the workplace) to control and manipulate friends, lovers, family, colleagues, and comrades. They set up loyalty tests. They believe that they are the victims. Often their vulnerabilities are real—and everyone's vulnerabilities matter and merit reasonable attention—but their sense of persecution and entitlement is devastating to their loved ones and the community. Activist communities may believe that we are immune to such manipulations, but that's simply arrogant and wrong of us. We are the least immune because we are the most compelled by the interplay of the individual condition with the systems of oppression operating in our world. Activist communities are particularly susceptible to manipulation by abusers because we are most likely to have compassion for how abusers experience institutional oppression and to understand how they are victims of unjust systems. Our empathy confounds our ability to see people who face oppression as people who could also be capable of, and should be accountable for, abuse.

On the ground, when choosing whom to support in a conflict, people tend to believe that their friend is in the right and that the person they are less connected to is in the wrong. For example, if my friend is screaming at their partner, I may reflexively identify with the anger that they are expressing and assign responsibility for it to frustrating behaviors from their partner, behaviors I may be more willing to consider as manipulative, exploitative, or hurtful.

On the other hand, I am more likely to see someone screaming at my friend as abusive, and may be less open to the possibility that the yelling could be a strategy of resisting abusive power and control. Choosing sides based on "natural alliances" is not sufficient.

The ability to get clear about who has abused is additionally complicated by the fact that survivors often blame themselves for the abuse. Many batterers blame their partners for everything that goes wrong. Over time, survivors may internalize that blame and begin to hold themselves responsible for every problem, concern, or mistake that comes along. When a survivor is willing to "take responsibility" while a batterer is happy to blame their partner, an abusive situation can be even more confusing for the community to sort out and understand. That self-blame can feed into the batterer's attempts to mobilize the community to their defense.

Still, we know that even an accurate assessment of which person's behavior is abusive does not guarantee a positive outcome or an ethical process.

FRAMING COMMUNITY ACCOUNTABILITY PRIMARILY AS AN "ALTERNATIVE TO THE CRIMINAL LEGAL SYSTEM" IS A PROBLEM.

Community Accountability has been presented in activist communities as an alternative to accessing law enforcement or prosecution in response to harms within the community. Some activists are interested in Community Accountability processes primarily as a rejection of the criminal legal system. "Not calling the cops" becomes a litmus test for radical realness. Community Accountability processes are rarely convened to address late rent payments, someone driving drunk, stealing or other such harms. Instead, these processes have been applied almost exclusively to "gendered" violence: sexual assault, sexual harassment, stalking, domestic violence. The mix of Community Accountability as a rejection of the criminal legal system and as a test of realness has at least two significant consequences: it creates the false idea that we can eliminate the harms of the criminal legal system through Community Accountability, and it requires women to bear the brunt of the Community Accountability learning curve.

While the mainstream anti-violence movement has participated in the massive criminalization of intimate partner violence and developed an absurd over-reliance on the criminal legal system, most folks in every community avoid law enforcement and prosecution. For most people, whatever their circumstances, the criminal legal system will suck and be consistent only in its stunning failure to meet survivors' needs or expectations. From our experience, most queer folk—activists or not—just don't expect the legal system to be safe, relevant, or useful. And, across the board, folks are more likely to tell a friend or family member that they have experienced an assault than to seek police or prosecution, or even civil court remedies.

It's just that most of our friends and family fail at helping survivors, too.

Community Accountability tries to replicate the helpful functions of law enforcement (interrupting harmful acts) and prosecution (determining responsibility for and redressing harm), but outside the framework of the State. The thing is, good intentions are not enough to avoid replicating the harmful consequences of the criminal legal system—for victims or for those accused of doing harm. The criminal legal system is desperately flawed. But Community Accountability processes are humbling, for while in our experience it's proven nearly impossible to achieve the idealized outcomes of the legal system (justice, restitution, rehabilitation), it is fairly easy to replicate its "revictimization" of survivors. We have seen this happen again and again with Community Accountability processes: survivors are exhausted, the community divided and angry, and the folks who caused the harm suck up the attention, community resources, and all the air in the room.

Meanwhile, without the important protections of due process that exist in the criminal legal system—the right to face your accuser, the burden of evidence, the right to a timely trial, and other basic protections for defendants—it's easy to cause harm to the accused as well. Despite the limits they impose, no justice system process can function absent protections for the accused. In turn, though, those same protections make it difficult to substantiate charges of domestic violence, sexual assault, rape, harassment, and stalking. The prosecution has the burden of proof, even if it is very difficult to prove that an assault happened when there are no eyewitnesses beyond the accused and the victim. The accused has the right to cross-examine evidence brought against them, even if that means a victim is re-traumatized by the public discussion of the violence committed against them.

Whether in our family room or in a court room, these harms are hard to prove and hard to prosecute. Another framework is needed. Instead of being used as a way to reject the criminal legal system, Community Accountability could be used to transform our friends', our families' and our own frail and sometimes harm-compounding responses to violence into something useful.

COMMUNITY ACCOUNTABILITY PROCESSES CAN FEEL CONTRIVED & IMPOSED.
People may experience the language, frameworks, and priorities of these processes as drawing more from therapy or professional nonprofits (i.e., "middle-class ideas") than from diverse sources of knowledge. If we experience something as contrived and imposed, it's easy to attack or dismiss it, even if it has a lot of merit. But, when we attempt to salvage something more "authentic" from our various cultures of origin, we face challenges as well. For one, the various cultural practices for Community Accountability created by our diverse communities have been largely lost to the vagaries of assimilation. Perhaps trickier still, many of the cultural models we have for accountability were never fully realized in their original contexts. Many of the methods that communities have devised over time to curtail the harm caused by its members have been largely theoretical, and have had less success in practice than in establishing broad cultural perspectives on how accountability should be done. They may have been as flawed or aspirational or simply as mythical as the myth of the US justice system, or the myth of activist "community accountability." Our hope is to find something usable, but we can be fairly certain that there is not much to simply revive and replicate.

A little over a thousand years ago these observations were codified in the Jewish canon; Rabbi Elazar said: "I would be surprised if there is anyone in this generation who is able to accept reproach." And Rabbi Akiva answered: "I would be surprised if there is anyone in this generation who knows how to give reproach." It's both chilling and oddly comforting that these words still resonate so powerfully today: chilling, because so many smart and committed people have failed at this task for so long; comforting, because we can be assured that we are asking a meaningful and enduring question. All this to say: at least we join most groups of people throughout time in being frankly mystified at how to get folks to do right, and in being equally confused about how to do right while trying to get folks to do right.

LIMITATIONS IN ACTIVIST COMMUNITIES' ANTI-OPPRESSION ANALYSIS.
While "reverse isms" are not possible because of the lack of institutional power to subjugate folks in privileged groups, oppression (and the intersections of its various manifestations) does not operate in the linear or binary manner frequently represented in "power and privilege charts." This can present challenges to activist groups attempting to apply ideological frameworks when evaluating and responding to abuse in intimate relationships. The personal is political, but the personal is frankly a lot messier than our dogmas can articulate.

As our praxis learning around Community Accountability grew, we realized that we rarely designed, implemented, or participated in processes that worked in the ways they were intended to or with outcomes on par with the huge input of time and energy and human endurance that they seemed to require. A satisfying, useful resolution was much rarer than generating a new hot mess that needed its own accountability process! Even with our best work, most critical thinking and deepest commitment to sound practices and fierce compassion, our attempts felt more like hauling millstones than creating liberation. We know that there have been some incredible triumphs through Community Accountability processes, but we found those successes very difficult to achieve reliably.

With a lot of love and humility, it became clear that our activist communities do not presently have the skills, shared values, and cultural touchstones in place to sustain Community Accountability efforts. Instead of continuing to struggle with (and frankly, suffer through) Community Accountability within these limitations, we have been experimenting with an alternative framework. This framework, which we call "Accountable Communities," may be a precursor to Community Accountability models, or perhaps it will grow in a new direction that will result in different goals. We certainly hope that, as an idea or practice, it can also be helpful to current and future Community Accountability projects undertaken by our allies.

accountable communities: a different approach

Accountable Communities shifts the emphasis from a collective process for holding individuals accountable for their behavior to individual and collective responsibility for building a community where robust accountability is possible, expected, and likely.

An Accountable Communities approach promotes the individual and collective ability to assert choices (self-determination) and take responsibility for one's actions within their full context. To understand one's actions in their full context, a person must understand that systems of institutional oppression and privilege, personal challenges and aptitudes, and situational conditions profoundly impact the options s/he has to choose among.

The limitations themselves do not exempt one from taking responsibility. However, the context matters. The context shapes what it looks like to "take responsibility" for the choice.

A survivor of battering, for example, might evaluate her decisions to pressure her abusive partner to have sex. The tactic of pressuring her partner for sex may have prevented a violent attack by her partner, earned her money that she needed to pay for childcare, helped her demonstrate her attraction to her partner and allayed accusations of infidelity, or stopped her partner from targeting someone else for sex. The community and the survivor should understand that choice in its context of surviving abuse. But, there is no reason to minimize or deny it as a choice, or to minimize the possible cost to the survivor for having acted outside of her values, in this case by not respecting others' boundaries. Being "accountable to" the batterer is not a useful solution here. But, support for affirming her own values of respecting sexual boundaries and taking steps to create the conditions in her life that would allow her to act consistently within her values while staying safe might be. Some hallmarks of an Accountable Communities approach might include:

— The shared expectation that people develop their individual accountability skills as a precondition of collective accountability processes.
— Skill building for individuals and groups to better understand the complex dynamics of abuse beyond a list of concerning "behaviors." By increasing a community's ability to consider the context, intent, and effect of observed or reported behaviors, people may be less vulnerable to misidentifying resistance as abuse.
— Raise the expectation of loving-kindness in our communities. Do not collude with trash talking, gossip, and the false sense of being an "insider" that comes from participating in isolating someone else. This will help reduce incidents of unwitting mobilization against survivors.
— Promote "engagement before opposition." That is to say, when confronted with negative information about people in our communities, we should commit to reaching out to them instead of acting reflexively based on reports about them. For both individuals and organizations, the impulse to react with opposition (whether a passive cold shoulder or an active boycott) is strong. We want to show our loyalty to the harmed party, we want to demonstrate that we are aware of the issues, that we don't tolerate harmful actions, or we just want to show that we "get it." But we could try a different approach and resist fracturing relationships by taking an engaged stance toward people or projects with whom we take issue. In other words, we can start from a place of curiosity: What do you mean? What happened? How are you being responsible for this choice? Can I explain our position on this issue? By placing direct engagement like this ahead of automatic opposition, we may learn new information that will change our assessment of the situation AND be more effective in moving the community toward a positive solution.

— We can understand Accountable Communities to include the work of engaging friends and family to strengthen their response to abuse and violence and to create the conditions that would promote loving and equitable relationships. Beyond potential abusers changing their own behavior at the source, survivors, along with their friends and family, are best positioned to recognize signs of emerging abuse. Friends Are Reaching Out (F.A.R. OUT), a NW Network project discussed later, activated support networks as both assistance for survivors during an abusive relationship and as a way to create shared values and agreements that would promote self-determination and caring relationships among friends and family groups. Our best use of these resources then is to begin intervention as early as possible to interrupt isolation at the first opportunity and build new models for relationships that reduce the likelihood of future harm.

— We can invest in recovering and advancing culturally relevant practices for fostering Accountable Communities. I offer this knowing full well that folks have already worked on this for a long time, from many traditions, but we continue to need to lift up and share these perspectives. For example, when I think about the essential tasks involved in creating Accountable Communities/Community Accountability, I am reminded of the Jewish principles of *Tshuvah* and *Tochecha*. The first is difficult to translate: connoting repentance, accountability, and redemption, Tshuvah literally means "to return." It is a set of progressive steps required for a person to be fully reconciled with her/his community. Only after all these steps have been successfully completed has a person "returned." And only after all the steps of Tshuvah have been completed can one ask for forgiveness. In a very illuminating cultural twist, it is only permissible to forgive someone after they've made Tshuvah, not before. Tshuvah is considered a vital human experience that is necessary for the person who has done the harm to heal and become restored. If we go around forgiving people (which includes holding them blameless and removing the obligation of restitution), we are de-mechanizing the process that is necessary for someone to internalize positive change.

One can complete Tshuvah out of fear—fear of a beat down, or fear of incarceration. (If one desists from the wrongdoing, even motivated by fear instead of true remorse, Tshuvah can be achieved.) And, one can complete Tshuvah out of love—love of community, of the harmed other, of the self—or out of a desire to return. Tshuvah out of love is better than Tshuvah out of fear, but either is better than continuing the harm. However, if one does not desist from the wrongdoing, no matter how aware, sorry, up to date on restitution payments, or any thing else that they are—they have not made Tshuvah. *Not doing the harm is the most critical expectation of the return.* Tochecha, on the other hand, means "to rebuke"—to correct or to call for accountability in another. While we are obligated to rebuke others who are missing the mark, we are commanded in no uncertain terms to carry out the task of rebuke with humility, love, and careful attention to the experience of the rebuked person. If we rebuke someone and embarrass them, we have harmed them. But if we do not rebuke someone and they continue to cause harm, we become implicated in that harm. If we had rebuked them, perhaps they would have stopped; we are then responsible for the transgressions that our rebuke could have prevented.

At the NW Network, our work with the Accountable Communities framework is evident in various organizational "artifacts" such as our Values Statement. But our efforts in this area are perhaps most widely known through two specific Accountable Communities projects: our Relationship Skills Class (RSC) series and our F.A.R. OUT framework.

RSC is a six-week skill building class that explores all forms of relationships—including but not limited to intimate partnerships—using the lens of "personal agency" (making choices and being responsible for our choices) from a number of perspectives. The RSC series originated in a support group for queer domestic abuse survivors held at our organization. After spending a long time working together on issues of power and control, signs of abuse, ways to safety plan, and so on, group members asked for more information on building the skills they needed to create the relationships that they wanted to have. They had learned a lot about relationships that involved abusive patterns of power and control, and now they wanted to shift their focus to what kind, loving, sustainable, relationships would look and feel like, and in particular, how to envision such relationships relevant to their diverse cultural backgrounds and personal identities. For instance, when sorting through information in a new relationship, how do we decide when it's right to compromise, and when we should stand our ground? The support group provided the initial content for the RSC series, which has been offered regularly since 2002.[1] Designed and implemented by and for queer women of color, F.A.R. OUT organized friends and family to support domestic violence survivors in their social networks and to build a shared critical analysis of violence. Close friends and social networks discussed relationship values and goals, how to get (and give) support without putting one's business in the street, what being responsible for one's own choices in context might look like, what agreements they wanted to make about open communication and resisting isolation, and how to respond when abuse occurs. Some people hosted large dinner parties, others met for coffee one on one.

As the project developed, the organizers realized that F.A.R. OUT's approach would require continuous tweaking and adaptation to fit specific friends' needs; their methods of implementation would work best when "made to order." Across the board, participants felt they had developed more awareness about relationships in their communities generally and the risks for abusive relationships specifically. Through the F.A.R. OUT framework, they also reported gaining new tools for reaching out to loved ones who might be in difficult relationships and for supporting themselves and others in their efforts to live in congruence with their values. Whether in a "Relationship Skills" class, a domestic violence support group, or around a friend's kitchen table, cultivating an awareness of how we show up for friends and family—and ask others to show up for us—has become a basic building block of our work.[2]

Our work in conceptualizing an "accountable community" is still new and continues to evolve and challenge us. We have been joined in this work by many individuals in our community who have attended RSC, participated in F.A.R. OUT, or otherwise contributed to the realization of these ideas. We have been so grateful to be supported in this work by colleagues and comrades from many activist communities. We hope that by implementing the same thoughtful approach that so many have used in examining Community Accountability, we can continue to develop practical tools and skills that will be of benefit to both projects.

Our work toward liberation challenges us to think and rethink our approaches to change. Revolution requires that we continuously ask ourselves what it would take to stay here, to work toward the liberation of the person across the room, across town, across the globe. Such revolution does start at home, where our beliefs are formed by the daily practices of our lives. At times, this work feels overwhelming: how can we transform a violent world, call mighty governments to account, and repair generations of injustice when we are still unable to stop activists committed to liberation movements from abusing their partners, sexually harassing their comrades, or otherwise harming people in our communities? Accountability, understood as a human skill, offers each of us a path forward when we miss the mark.

notes

1   Over the years, many people have worked on the various classes by adding content, refining ideas, expanding the perspectives, and so on. From the beginning, class instructors drew from their own experiences, from their families and diverse cultures of origin, from the unique culture of queer people, and from the wisdom shared among abuse survivors. *What have we always known? What have we learned? What did we wish we knew then? What do we still need to know?* RSC's consistent theme is one of becoming aware of our own values, goals and dreams, and of deciding how to live in alignment with this self-awareness, which is the basis of solid relationships. In the end, being "in charge of ourselves" is the foundation to connecting—meaningfully, sustainably, and lovingly—within an accountable community.

2   Over time, F.A.R. OUT became formally integrated into the NW Network's approach to direct services and community engagement. For example, "safety planning," a staple of anti-violence advocacy, has now become "safety & support" planning at the NW Network. Part of the task of safety planning was to bring into consciousness all the things a person does to assess vulnerability and decrease exposure to harm, as well as surface new or missed opportunities to increase safety. By bringing a similar focus to "support" planning, folks can consider the effect of isolation on their lives, evaluate how they access friends and family, and make and execute plans to ask for specific types of help. A person might practice how they would explain their situation and ask for assistance, or consider the limits they might want to assert on the assistance they receive. Survivors can also think critically about how they want to reciprocate support to their friends.

In our community organizing work, the principles of F.A.R. OUT and RSC are congruent with our commitment to "engagement before opposition." Whenever we notice that we are complaining about or avoiding or just hating some group or individual, we know we have to reach out and engage with them. We have to try to understand them better, establish some common ground, or simply agree to disagree. We in activist communities can spend all our time ever refining our critiques of one another and ever-fracturing our potential for a cohesive movement. It can be compelling to join in hating someone or some group because they have failed us or a friend, but we have to choose to engage with them instead. It's the difference between eating lentils with brown rice or a Hostess cupcake: the sugar rush might be more fun, but we need complex carbs to sustain us for the long haul.

RESOURCES

COMMUNITY ACCOUNTABILITY WITHIN PEOPLE OF COLOR PROGRESSIVE MOVEMENTS

Selections from the 2004 Report*
by INCITE! Women of Color Against Violence

HOW IS GENDER OPPRESSION WITHIN PROGRESSIVE, RADICAL, AND/OR REVOLUTIONARY MOVEMENT(S) MAINTAINED, SUPPORTED, ENCOURAGED?

PATRIARCHY: THE ROOT OF GENDER OPPRESSION

The system of patriarchy is the root of gender oppression. We all exist within a system of oppression that assumes rigid gender binaries of women and men, female and male; that values males and the male-identified and devalues female and the female-identified; that assumes heterosexual normativity; that delegates men/boys/the male-identified to roles and positions that have higher statuses and involve higher levels of decision-making than are delegated to women/girls/the female-identified; which assume masculine values as universal and given. This system of patriarchy intersects with racism, classism, homophobia/heterosexism, transphobia, ableism, ageism, nativism (anti-immigrants) to oppress women of color/queer people of color. Ultimately, [patriarchy] oppresses us all. Despite our commitment to social justice and liberation, we as activists, organizations and movements are not immune.

Gender oppression is not just an act, it's a state of mind and a way of doing. The patterns of power and control, acts of abuse and violence, and cultures and conditions tolerating, condoning, encouraging, and perpetrating abuse and violence appear to follow certain patterns.

---

* Ad-Hoc Community Accountability Working Group Meeting (February 7-8, 2004, Seattle, WA). Co-sponsored by INCITE! Women of Color Against Violence and Communities Against Rape and Abuse (CARA). Available in its entirety at http://www.incite-national. org/media/docs/2406_cmty-acc-poc.pdf.

Denial, Minimizing, Victim-Blaming, Counter-Organizing

Patriarchy upholds and supports gender oppression. Four primary tools for maintaining gender oppression and for avoiding accountability are: (1) Denial, (2) Minimizing, (3) Victim-Blaming, and (4) Counter-Organizing.

1. DENIAL.

Our progressive, radical, revolutionary people of color as individuals, organizations, and movements (just as the rest of the world) have been pretty good at denying that gender oppression exists.

What can denial look like?
— Silence
— Inability to take any action
— Moving issues, acts, or patterns of gender oppression to the back burner (forever)
— Characterizing issues, acts, or patterns of gender oppression as individual, personal, or private rather than acts of gender oppression requiring public and collective responsibility and solutions
— Writing off sexual harassment or sexual assault e.g., as a "date," "affection," "showing that he likes you," "flirting," or "misunderstandings"
— Viewing any issue of gender oppression (which requires more than abstract discussion) as "bourgeois," "middle class," "white feminist," "dividing our movement," or "playing into the hands of the race/class/nation enemy"

2. MINIMIZING.

Our progressive, radical, revolutionary people of color as individuals, organizations and movements (just as the rest of the world) have been pretty good at minimizing gender oppression as an issue and/or minimizing situations/acts/patterns of gender oppression.

What can minimizing look like?
— Moving issues, acts, or patterns of gender oppression to the back burner (forever)
— Characterizing issues, acts, or patterns of gender oppression as individual, personal, or private rather than acts of gender oppression requiring public and collective responsibility and solutions
— Writing off issues, acts, or patterns of gender oppression as individual or "only a misunderstanding"
— Writing off sexual harassment and/or assault e.g., as "dating" or "asking someone out"
— Writing off domestic or intimate partner violence e.g., as "fighting," "an argument," "they have problems," "they both have problems," or "she should just leave him (or her)"
— Viewing any issue of gender oppression (which requires more than abstract discussion) as taking away from the "real" and/or "important" work
— Hoping that it goes away—or that the people raising or causing the issues go away
— Addressing it very ineffectually (and knowing it)

3. VICTIM-BLAMING.
Our progressive, radical, revolutionary people of color as individuals, organizations and movements (just as the rest of the world) have been pretty good at "blaming the victim," or others who call for accountability when gender oppression as an issue or situation arises. Blaming the victim or allies is often done in combination with denial and/or minimizing.

What can victim-blaming look like?
— Characterizing the people (usually women) raising the issue of gender abuse, oppression, or violence as "bourgeois," "middle class," "white feminist," or "race/class/nation enemy"; accusing them of "dividing the movement," "destroying unity," "lynching," or "taking us away from the 'real' or 'serious' work"
— Characterizing women/girls/trans folk who raise the issue of gender

oppression, abuse, or violence as "deserving it," "flirt," "young," "wanting attention," "must have done something wrong," "slut," "man-hater," "lesbian/dyke," or "making a power play"

— Characterizing women/girls/trans folk who take a stand against gender oppression as "bitches," "controlling," "angry," "man-haters," "lesbians/dykes," or "white feminists"

— Turning abusers into "victims," by characterizing people (usually men) accused of sexist, abusive, or violent attitudes and behavior as "victims," "nice guys," "heroes," or "important to our work" (read: more important than the women/girls/trans folk raising the issue or experiencing the abuse)

4. COUNTER-ORGANIZING.

Our progressive, radical, revolutionary people of color as individuals, organizations and movements (just as the rest of the world) have been pretty good at deploying the skills and tactics better used for fighting real enemies against people (usually women/girls/female-identified) who raise the issue of gender oppression, abuse or violence, or a situation of gender oppression, abuse or violence.

What this means is that our own people (mostly men/boys/male-identified but also women/girls/female-identified) have been involved in counter-organizing. And counter-organizing can involve a higher level of the devaluation, deceit, and manipulation which are all also a part of the dynamics of gender oppression and avoidance of accountability.

What can counter-organizing look like?

— Harassing, demeaning, denouncing, gossiping about, spreading rumors and/or lies about (or threatening to do these things) people who raise the issue of gender oppression either as survivors/victims or as allies

— Demoting, firing, or threatening to demote or fire people who raise the issue of gender oppression either as survivors/victims or as allies

— Isolating or discrediting persons who raise concerns and/or call for accountability

— Questioning the legitimacy of concerns raised to detract from the need to be accountable
— Questioning the legitimacy of the accountability process to detract from the need to be accountable
— Accusing others of abuse to call attention away from one's own accountability
— Denying, minimizing, victim-blaming, and plain-old lying about doing any of these things when called on this behavior

MORE ON COUNTER-ORGANIZING

Or, What Is the Opposite of Accountability?

People who commit acts of gender oppression, abuse, and violence often engage in additional acts of manipulation to (1) make sure the person or persons they abuse don't do anything that might end the violence or otherwise change the terms of the relationship, (2) make sure they don't get caught, or (3) make sure that if they do get caught they can get out of it.

What can the opposite of accountability look like?
— Make sure their victims/survivors don't do anything back:
  * Picking someone they think won't tell or is not in a position to tell, e.g., who is vulnerable, powerless, young, feels guilty or responsible, or is not believed by others
  * Using denial, e.g., silence, "I didn't do anything," or "What did I do?"
  * Minimizing, e.g., "I didn't do anything," "It was nothing," "It didn't mean anything," "I'll never do it again," "It was such a little thing," or "What, that?"
  * Blaming, e.g., "You wanted it," "You asked for it," "You didn't say no," "You should have known," "You liked it," "You made me do it," or "You provoked me"

* Discrediting the survivor/victim's work and/or personality
* Threatening them by saying that they'll out them about something, ruin their reputation, or will make up stories
* Threatening to physically harm them, fire them, call the police and/or INS on them, hurt family or friends or pets

— Make sure they don't get caught:
* Doing things when people aren't looking or in ways that people can't easily see
* Regularly discrediting the survivor/victim's work and/or personality to undermine their credibility
* Recruiting and organizing others to isolate the survivor/victim and any allies
* Tactically acting in heroic, self-sacrificing, or other ways so other people think they could do no wrong or feel indebted to them

— Make sure if they do get caught they can get out of it:
* Making up a story or stories to explain away their behavior
* Silently or not so silently threatening those who try to raise the issue or confront them
* Threatening to sue, call the police, call INS, report to funders
* Claiming that they are being victimized, e.g., by "white feminists" or "the race/class enemy"
* Characterizing the accusations as "personal gripes," "individual issues," or "power-plays"
* Apologizing and thinking that's all they have to do
* Apologizing and then getting mad if they have to do anything else
* Claiming they didn't know and expect this to be all they have to do
* Saying it's a misunderstanding and expect this to be all they have to do
* Saying they didn't mean it and expect this to be all they have to do
* Crying (looks like remorse but can be a way of manipulating people so they feel sorry for them)

* Making excuses for their behavior (not to explain or understand, but to rationalize their behavior and avoid accountability) e.g., a bad childhood, stress, too much work, too much responsibility, or they're so dedicated to the movement
* Trying to meet with the victim/survivor as a good-will gesture or as a way to be direct and honest (but really to interrogate/intimidate them)
* Recruiting leaders, sometimes from outside of the community, to back them up, e.g., white allies with power and a reason to back up a person of color especially when the survivor/victim is someone less powerful
* Mobilizing relationships with respected folks within the movement to back them up, prove that they cannot be abusers, or shield them from accountability
* Quitting or leaving immediately if they think they have to take some accountability (not to ensure the survivor's safety or because it's the right thing to do, but only because they want to avoid accountability)
* Using delaying tactics until everyone gets worn out

and it can get even sneakier and nastier

Some oppressive, abusive, and violent people (typically people who are men/boys/male-identified but also women/girls/female-identified/transgender) go beyond these actions and devote considerable energy toward increasing their opportunities for abuse. Some examples include:

— Chronic abusers, harassers, rapists, and batterers who find one person (usually women/girls/female-identified) after another to oppress and abuse
— Abusive persons who ask others to cover for them or organize others to cover for them
— Abusive persons who mentor other (often less powerful or younger) individuals to exercise power and control over them or to take advantage of them

— Abusive persons who mentor other (often less powerful or younger) individuals to groom them to mimic their attitudes and behaviors and to offer protection

— Abusive persons who use their skills to gain positions of leadership, status, and power within the political movement in part to gain more power and control over others, increasing opportunities for abuse and escape from accountability

NOTES FOR SURVIVORS AND SUPPORTERS

1. It is not your fault. The abuse is the responsibility of the perpetrator and/or the organization allowing the abuse to occur.

2. Think about what you want for safety and healing. Safety and an opportunity to heal from oppression and abuse are your right. Think about what you need from your friends, family, co-workers, comrades, your organization, and the movement for safety and healing. Do you want additional support? Should your organization be providing leave time? Support for counseling? A space for you to be heard?

3. Think about the role of the organization in addressing accountability and reparations. Accountability for oppression/abuse is different for different people, for different situations. Do you want a statement of accountability and apology? Do you want it made public? Do you want it written? Do you want a supportive space for your abuser to hear and understand what you have experienced? Do you want a public statement from your organization?

4. Think about how you want to be involved in the process of accountability. Do you want to be involved in every step? Do you want to be involved in specific aspects of the process? Do you want to stay out of the process but be informed at certain times, regarding certain decisions?

5. Think about how you want to communicate with the perpetrator. Do you want to face the perpetrator in person? Alone? With other support? If you face the perpetrator in person, do you want to that person to remain

silent? Do you want to give them an opportunity to respond? In person? In writing? Will you accept communication only if it is in the form of apology and accountability?

SPECIAL NOTE FOR THOSE SUPPORTING SURVIVORS OF OPPRESSION/ABUSE

1. Remind them that they are not to blame. Survivors often blame themselves for the abuse or for not taking action which could prevent it. Remind them who is responsible: the perpetrator, the organization which allowed abuse to occur, the movement, systems of oppression.
2. Help them explore what they may need for safety or healing. Survivors, especially within the movement, often deny the traumatizing impact of oppression and abuse on themselves. Validate their need for safety and healing. Help them explore what would make this possible.
3. Help them explore what would help with accountability and reparations. Advocate for a process which supports the survivor and leads to accountability of the perpetrator and the organization. Help them explore what they want from the process of accountability and reparations.

SPECIAL NOTE FOR ABUSERS OR THOSE ACCUSED OF ABUSE/OPPRESSION

1. Take accountability. Regardless of intention or motivation, your attitudes and actions have had a negative impact on someone else. You are responsible for the consequences. Not intending to hurt someone (if you feel you did not have this intention) does not excuse you from the impact of your attitudes and/or behavior.
2. Understand the negative impact of your attitudes or actions on the individual(s), organization, community, and movement. Your attitudes and actions have hurt another person within your organization or movement. They have also hurt your organization, community, and movement. Understand the widespread impact of gender oppression and abuse and demonstrate a willingness to be held accountable.

3. Understand that evading accountability has a further cost on the person you have hurt/offended, the organization, its constituents, community, and the movement.

4. Support for you means support for taking accountability, not support for defending yourself from being held accountable. If you have friends, family, co-workers, comrades whom you trust, ask them to help you to take accountability.

5. Take accountability for full reparations. Consider what you might need to do to take accountability e.g., full public apology, offering resources (including money) to the survivor/organization to help with healing/reparations for the abuse, counseling, leaving the organization (whether on a temporary or permanent basis), committing to political education for yourself and others.

6. Understand gender oppression/abuse and accountability as fundamental issues of social justice.

SPECIAL NOTE FOR SUPPORTERS OF ABUSERS OR THOSE ACCUSED OF ABUSE/OPPRESSION

---

1. Support them in their effort to demonstrate accountability. Being held accountable is the right thing to do for the survivor/victim, for the community, for the movement, and for the abuser or person accused of oppression/abuse. The best way to support them is not to enable them to make excuses, but to be held fully accountable.

2. Support their transformation. If you are involved in the process of accountability, advocate for a process which fully educates the abuser on the nature of the oppression/abuse, the consequences for the survivor, the organization, and the movement, and which requires full reparations.

3. Support ongoing political education on patriarchy/gender education/gender oppression for the organization, constituents, and movement.

INCITE! COMMUNITY ACCOUNTABILITY
FACT SHEET

HOW DO WE ADDRESS VIOLENCE WITHIN OUR COMMUNITIES?

We are told to call the police and rely on the criminal justice system to address violence within our communities. However, if police and prisons facilitate or perpetrate violence against us rather than increase our safety, how do we create strategies for addressing violence within our communities, including domestic violence, sexual violence, and child abuse, that don't rely on police or prisons?

Developing community-based responses to violence is one critical option. Community Accountability is a community-based strategy, rather than a police/prison-based strategy, to address violence within our communities. Community Accountability is a process in which a community—a group of friends, a family, a house of worship, a workplace, an apartment complex, a neighborhood, and so on—work together to do the following:

— Create and affirm VALUES & PRACTICES that resist abuse and oppression and encourage safety, support, and accountability
— Develop sustainable strategies to ADDRESS COMMUNITY MEMBERS' ABUSIVE BEHAVIOR, and create a process for them to account for their actions and transform their behavior
— Commit to the ongoing development of all members of the community, and of the community itself, in order to TRANSFORM THE POLITICAL CONDITIONS that reinforce oppression and violence
— Provide SAFETY & SUPPORT to community members who are violently targeted that RESPECTS THEIR SELF-DETERMINATION

BIOGRAPHIES

morgan bassichis is a staff member at Community United Against Violence (http://www.cuav.org), a San Francisco-based organization founded in 1979 that works to build the power of queer and trans people to eliminate intimate, community, and state violence. CUAV's membership supports the healing of LGBTQQ survivors of violence and abuse; uses art and community building to create a vibrant culture of safety; and organizes as a part of the broader racial, gender, and economic justice movement to transform the root causes of violence. Morgan is also a member of the Transgender, Gender Variant, and Intersex Justice Project (TGIJP) and the Transforming Justice Coalition.

A mom of four boys, **connie burk** emphatically agrees that the revolution starts at home. Connie cofounded the first regional LBTG domestic violence survivor services in Kansas nearly twenty years ago. Since 1997, she has directed the Northwest Network of Bisexual, Trans, Lesbian, and Gay Survivors of Abuse in Seattle (http://www.nwnetwork.org). Connie coauthored *Trauma Stewardship: An Everyday Guide to Caring for Self While Caring for Others* (BK Press; http://www.traumastewardship.com) and is an executive producer of the documentary film *A Lot Like You* (http://www.alotlikeyoumovie.com).

ching-in chen is the author of *The Heart's Traffic* (Arktoi Books/Red Hen Press) and a multigenre, border-crossing writer. The daughter of Chinese immigrants, she is a Kundiman, Macondo, and Lambda fellow. A community organizer, she has worked in the Asian American communities of San Francisco, Oakland, Riverside, Milwaukee, and Boston. Her work has been recently published in journals such as *BorderSenses, Rio Grande Review, Poemeleon, Cha, OCHO, Iron Horse Literary Review, Water~Stone Review, Boxcar Poetry Review, Verdad,* and *Chroma.* Ching-In is currently in the process of editing an anthology on gender, militarism, and war from the perspective of women and gender nonconforming people of color. (http://www.chinginchen.com)

the chrysalis collective is a grassroots group of multiracial, multigendered, and multigenerational activists who seek to end sexual assault through transformative justice. Grounded in women of color and Indigenous visions of transformative justice, we are currently in the middle of facilitating a community accountability and healing process. We would love to hear from you and welcome your thoughts, stories, critiques, strategies and dreams. Contact us at chrysalisjustice@gmail.com.

timothy colm grew up in New York City and now lives in Philadelphia. His work has appeared in *Make/shift* magazine, "In the Middle of a Whirlwind," and elsewhere. He writes here about his work as part of Philly's Pissed (http://www.phillyspissed.net), a grassroots group that provided direct support to survivors of sexual assault from 2004 to 2009, as well as education and advocacy promoting the idea of survivor autonomy and perpetrator accountability.

meiver de la cruz is a Dominican dancer and activist. Her anti-violence, feminist work integrates dance as part of community building and political education programs focused on low-income youth and women of color. Meiver has done work with the Boston chapter of INCITE! Women of Color Against Violence, and is currently a board member of MataHari: Eye of the Day, an organization whose work addresses human rights violations, sexual and labor exploitation, and immigrant rights violations in the US. Currently she's a performance studies doctoral student at Northwestern University. She can be contacted at meiver.delacruz@gmail.com.

gina de vries is a queer femme Paisan pervert, writer, performer, cultural worker, and survivor. Her work has appeared dozens of places, including *Coming & Crying, Bound to Struggle: Where Kink & Radical Politics Meet,* and *$pread* magazine. Gina is pursuing her MFA in fiction writing at San Francisco State University. She co-curates "Girl Talk: a cis & trans woman dialogue" with Julia Serano; facilitates "Sex Workers' Writing Workshop" at The Center for Sex & Culture; and tours, teaches, and performs all over the US & beyond. Find out the whole story at http://ginadevries.com.

jai dulani is an MFA candidate in the Integrated Media Arts program at Hunter College. An interdisciplinary storyteller, Dulani has been a Kundiman Asian American Poet Fellow, a member of the Austin Project, and a BCAT/Rotunda Gallery Multi-Media Artist-in-Residence. His work has appeared in SAMAR, bustingbinaries, and the anthology *Experiments in a Jazz Aesthetic: Art, Activism, Academics, and the Austin Project.* Dulani has served as a consultant and provided trainings on LGBTQ Intimate Partner Violence issues. Currently, Dulani is a media educator at Global Action Project, where he works with LGBTQ and immigrant youth.

Born and raised in Brooklyn, **bran fenner** has been involved in community activism and organizing around issues facing poor and low-income trans and queer people of color since age 15. He has worked in leadership development, incorporating tools that address institutional and interpersonal trauma at organizations like FIERCE! and the Audre Lorde Project, both based in New York City. Currently, Bran is pursuing photography, serves as a DJ, and is finishing nursing school.

carol gomez is a relentless community organizer with a knack for jumping into the driver's seat and getting things done. She migrated from her home country of Malaysia, quickly immersing herself in social justice work, strategically choosing the fields of violence against women, public health, mental health care, criminal justice and higher education to gain skills and insider knowledge of each system. She founded MataHari: Eye of the Day (http://www.eyeoftheday.org), winning numerous awards for innovative community work since 2002. A skilled therapist, facilitator and popular education trainer, she currently lives in California. She can be contacted at caroljg@gmail.com.

alan greig (Challenging Male Supremacy Project): Male supremacy has to end for another world to be truly possible. This conviction has only strengthened over the last twenty years, in which I have worked to challenge male privilege and end male violence, as an activist, consultant, writer, trainer, and documentary filmmaker. And I still struggle with what it means to be a white, straight, middle-class cisgender male who is committed to challenging the arrangements of power that privilege me; what it means to really live the personal as political, and the political as profoundly personal.

alexis pauline gumbs is a queer black troublemaker manifesting love as lifeforce! Alexis recently achieved her PhD in English, Africana studies, and women's studies from Duke University, and is the instigator of the Eternal Summer of the Black Feminist Mind community school and multimedia educational movement and the co-creator of the MobileHomecoming Project, a queer black intergenerational experiential archive project. She is a cofounder of UBUNTU and a member of the Harm Free Zone organizing committee.

vanessa huang is a poet, writer, and community organizer whose practice feeds resilience from the margins and draws on a history of collaboration with and teachings from the anti-prison, gender liberation, immigrant rights, anti-violence, disability justice, and reproductive justice movements.

incite! women of color against violence is a national, activist organization of radical feminists of color that is mobilizing to end all forms of violence against women, gender nonconforming, and trans people of color and our communities. By supporting grassroots organizing, we intend to advance a national movement to nurture the health and well-being of communities of color. Through the efforts of INCITE!, women, gender nonconforming, and trans people of color and our communities will move closer toward global peace, justice, and liberation.

gaurav jashnani (Challenging Male Supremacy Project) is a Sindhi from Queens and Missouri, and an educator and organizer around issues of male privilege and violence. He draws resilience from his many loved ones and the music of Jorge Ben, particularly when faced with the gentrification and police occupation of Central Brooklyn. His past ventures have included teaching filmmaking and practicing popular education at Global Action Project; doing community-building and youth education work as a member of the Detroit Summer Collective; organizing around issues of trauma and sexual violence while in Argentina on a Fulbright research grant; and co-editing a slightly embarrassing anarchist newspaper when he was fourteen.

ana-maurine lara is an award-winning novelist, playwright, and Cave Canem poetry fellow. She has been active in the LGBTI movement for 15 years. Currently, she is working on her PhD in African American studies and anthropology at Yale University.

rj maccani's (Challenging Male Supremacy Project) first organizing experience was cofounding a multiracial gang in kindergarten. Women of color feminists, prison abolitionists, his mother and the Zapatistas are largely to blame for moving him to join the struggle for a better world over a decade ago. Whether challenging empire and war in mass direct actions, storytelling through print, film and theater, building transformative justice responses to heteropatriarchal violence, training in the healing justice arts of Generative Somatics and herbalism, learning to care for children, the Earth and himself, or transforming the (white American cisgender) man in the mirror, RJ has been active ever since.

miss major is a black, formerly incarcerated, male-to-female transgender elder. She has been an activist and advocate in her community for over forty years, mentoring and empowering many of today's transgender leaders to stand tall, step into their own power, and defend their human rights, from coast to coast. Currently, Miss Major is the executive director of the TGI Justice Project where she instills hope and a belief in a better future to the girls that are currently incarcerated and those coming home.

gita mehrotra is a former staff member of the Asian Women's Shelter and part of the Organizing Committee for the TSIA project. gita has done anti-violence work since 1995 in Minneapolis and the Bay Area. Now based in Seattle, WA, she is pursuing a PhD in social welfare and is committed to liberatory teaching/research that supports social change and new ways to imagine justice and well-being for queer people of color.

peggy munson is the author of the Project Queerlit–winning, Lambda finalist novel *Origami Striptease*, descried by *Curve* as "a seductive, often raunchy fantasy of the disarming effects of love and trouble." She also wrote the acclaimed poetry collection *Pathogenesis*, praised by Yusef Komunyakaa as "forthright and magical." She is the editor of *Stricken: Voices of the Hidden Epidemic of Chronic Fatigue Syndrome*, and blogs about disability and environmental politics at peggymunson.blogspot.com. More of Peggy's work can be found at http://www.peggymunson.com and http://www.theexitproject.org.

n. is a queer femme living and working in Toronto.

juliet november is a working-class femme, radical sex worker, organizer, writer and fierce femme of French/Irish/Ukrainian descent. She works with Maggie's: The Toronto Sex Workers Action Project and Rittenhouse in Tkaronto (Toronto) on building community power and visioning beyond the prison industrial complex.

mariko passion, educated whore and urban geisha, is a performance artist | activist | educator | whore revolutionary. She sings and rhymes her experiences and reality over beats and produces auto-documentary videos. She educates the community and fights for social justice issues related to sex workers rights in Los Angeles, across the US, and around the world. Presentation topics include her own life experiences as an escort, as a sex worker rights activist, sexual and relationship violence survivor, professional bisexual and Asian sex worker community organizer. Her words and views can also be read in *Yes Means Yes, $pread* magazine, and on her blog http://marikopassion.wordpress.com.

shannon perez-darby is a queer mixed Latina femme living in Seattle, WA. She is passionate about supporting the people in her communities to live fabulous joyful lives. Shannon is the youth program manager at The Northwest Network of Bi, Trans, Lesbian & Gay Survivors of Abuse (http://www.nwnetwork.org), working to create the conditions possible to support loving equitable relationships. For questions, comments, and ideas about creating stronger communities, get in touch with Shannon at perezdarby@gmail.com.

leah lakshmi piepzna-samarasinha is a queer disabled Sri Lankan writer, teacher, and cultural worker. The author of *Consensual Genocide,* her work has been widely anthologized. She cofounded Mangos With Chili, the national queer and trans people of color performance tour, is a lead artist with Sins Invalid, and teaches with June Jordan's Poetry for the People. In 2010, she was named one of the Feminist Press's 40 Feminists Under 40 and nominated for a Pushcart Prize. Her life's work is at the intersection of community accountability, disability justice, queer and trans people of color artistic community, and teaching for liberation.

orchid pusey has been the National Network Coordinator at the Asian Women's Shelter since 2002, and coordinated the Transforming Silence Into Action project and four national gatherings held between 2003 and 2008. Her other areas of focus at AWS include organizational development and transformative organizational structures, multilingual digital storytelling, peer-to-peer training and technical assistance, and Chai Chats—a 10-week workshop series for queer women and trans people of color on nurturing healthy and happy relationships in our families, intimate partnerships, and communities.

cristy c. road (cover art) is a 28-year-old Cuban American illustrator and writer who's been contributing to punk, writing, and activism since 1996. Road published the zine *Greenzine* for ten years and has released three books: *Indestructible, Distance Makes the Heart Grow Sick,* and *Bad Habits.* She's currently working on a Tarot card deck with author Michelle Tea; a graphic memoir entitled *Spit and Passion;* and her band The Homewreckers. She lives in Brooklyn, NY. (http://www.croadcore.org/)

andrea smith is a cofounder of INCITE! Women of Color Against Violence and the Boarding School Healing Project. She is the author of *Conquest: Sexual Violence and American Indian Genocide,* and through INCITE!, co-editor of *Color of Violence: The INCITE! Anthology* and editor of *The Revolution Will Not Be Funded: Beyond the Nonprofit Industrial Complex* (all South End Press). Smith is also the author of *Native Americans and the Christian Right: The Gendered Politics of Unlikely Alliances* (Duke University Press).

the storytelling & organizing project (stop) is a community media project documenting and sharing stories of everyday people who have addressed situations of violence without relying on the police or traditional social service agencies, instead accessing family, community, and organizational networks. STOP helps us know that we are not alone. People are taking action all the time—not only to end violence, but to create self-determined ways of thinking, acting, and living. STOP is a project of Creative Interventions, a resource center dedicated to creating and promoting community-based responses to interpersonal violence. Rachel Herzing was the director of research and organizing for STOP. Isaac Ontiveros was the production coordinator for Creative Interventions and has worked on community-based media projects for the last five years as an archivist, sound editor, videographer, and video editor.

ACKNOWLEDGMENTS

Thank you to bell hooks, Ariel Gore, Pearl Cleage, Roxanne Dunbar-Ortiz, June Jordan, and Elaine Brown for courageously breaking silence about their experiences with violence within activist communities, as well as *The Peak's* special issue on sexual assault within activist communities for opening the door. Thank you to INCITE! Women of Color Against Violence for being instrumental in spreading the word, posting the PDF of the zine for free download, and fearlessly growing the brilliant feminist of color community and movement that is the heart and roots of this book. Thank you to the many organizations and individuals, especially Critical Resistance 10, The Femme Collective, Modern Times Bookstore, Pidge Vera at Reed College, the Allied Media Conference (AMC), Northwest Network, Community United Against Violence (CUAV), and Dexter Mar, who invited us to read and do workshops.

Thank you to *Feminist Review, Bitch, Make/shift,* and *Left Turn* magazines for supporting this project. Thank you to Morgan Bassichis and everyone at CUAV and Safetyfest, the AMC's Creating Safer Communities track, the Transforming Silence Into Action Project, Philly Stands Up, Communities Against Rape and Abuse (CARA), Audre Lorde Project's Safe Outside the System Collective, Chrysalis Collective, Harm Free Zone Durham, ASS, Creative Interventions, Young Women's Empowerment Project (YWEP), UBUNTU, MataHari, Northwest Network, and everyone we forgot to mention for your brilliant vision. Thank you to Sham-e-ali al-Nayeem for being an OG RSAH collective member. Thank you to every writer who courageously shared their stories and polished them til they were brilliant and to those who were only able to walk some of the way with us. To Cristy Road for making two of the absolutely most beautiful pieces of cover artwork we could've dreamed. To each other, for six years of conference calls, nervous breakdowns and uproarious laughter. Thank you to you, the reader, for opening this book. We're going to change the world.

Leah...Thank you to everyone in the queer and feminist of color communities of Toronto who had my back in the long walk to finding safety from my ex-partner. Thank you to my crip, queer, and trans people of color and poetry communities for loving me and allowing me to live. There are so many people who loved me hard over these past six years—thanks to all my giant friend family in Toronto, New York, and Oakland for loving me like crazy, especially Amir Rabiyah, Sham-e-ali al-Nayeem, Juliet November, S. H., Arti Mehta, The Shark Pit, Ejeris Dixon, Victor Tobar, Zavisha Chromicz, and my Sins Invalid, Poetry for the People, Mangos With Chili, and Creating Collective Access folks.

jai dulani...There are so many people who have been an amazing source of support and inspiration these past six years of working on this project. For friendship and family, for lessons on what it means to heal and love, thank you: Myrl Beam, Namita Chad, D'lo, Jeetander Dulani, Tina Dulani, Kate Eubank, Cherry Galette, H. Y. Griffin, Virginia Grise, Margarita Guzman,

Ang Hadwin, Rage Kidvai, Ana Lara, gita mehrotra, Soniya Munshi, Yasmeen Perez, Orchid Pusey, Nadia Qurashi, Avy Skolnik. Chase Strangio, and Amita Swadhin.

ching-in...Thank you to family far and wide who have held me in so many different ways over the last six years and for the communities I belong to for inspiring me daily. Thank you for teaching me about transformative thinking and action—Melissa Roxas, Vanessa Huang, Tamiko Beyer, Marlon Unas Esguerra, Sabeena Shah, Aimee Lee, Rosalind M. Sagara, Porschia L. Baker, Dimple Rana, and to the next generation of activists, Chardae Chou and Kimberly Zarate.

INDEX

aaaa

ableism, 55, 116–119, 124–125, 128–129, 132–134; care and accessibility, lack of, 117–120, 121–126, 127–133; "caregiver privilege," 120; "caregiver stress," 126; sexual violence and simultaneous oppressions, 28–29; social abandonment, 119, 123, 124, 132–133. *See also* activist communities; disability justice and politics

abuse. *See* generationFIVE; violence

accountability, personal: in accountability circles, 218–223; in activist communities, 142–145, 157–159, 254–256, 265–266; "Community Accountability Within People of Color Progressive Movements" (INCITE!), excerpt, 289–290; "Identifying and Unlearning Our Own Violence," 256–257; male supremacy, addressing, 223–229; skills, 107–108, 110–111, 267; survivor strategies, 288–290

Accountable Communities: differences with community accountability, 273–278; Friends Are Reaching Out (F.A.R. OUT), xxv, 275–278, 279n2; inception and process, 273–276; Relationship Skills Class series, 276–279. *See also* community accountability; The Northwest Network activist communities: ableism in, xxxviii, 55, 119, 122–124, 132–134; accountability in, 27–29, 254, 256–259; assumptions about: "intact," xvi; burn-out in, xxxv, 15; "calling out" in, xxi, 26, 147, 157, 181, 224, 245, 248, 250, 252, 254; co-option of, state criminal justice system, 6–7, 10–12, 75–76; counter-organizing within, 195, 265–267, 282, 284–287; criminal legal system, reliance on, xiii–xvi; "exiling" from, xxi, 20, 224; gender violence in, xv–xvi; homophobia in, xvi, 143, 253–254; intimate partner violence in, xx–xxi, 26–29, 109–110, 157–159, 267–269; male entitlement in, 203, 213; oppressive structures, replication of, 23n9, 28–29, 33–38; perpetrators of violence within: impact on, 28–29, 223–224; personal accountability, 142–145, 157–159, 254–256, 265–266; prevalence of intimate violence in, xxvii; racism in, xiv; romanticized notions of, xvi, xxiv, 69; rape culture, 203; sexism in, xvi, 240; sexual violence in, xxvi–xxvii, 25–29, 32–33; social collusion within, 115–116, 157; survivor support, 182. *See also* movements for social change; narratives; organizing documents

alternatives to state approaches to violence. *See* strategies and tools, anti-violence

Americans with Disabilities Act (ADA), 119–120

anti-oppression: community accountability fundamental to, xvi; framework, of Community United Against Violence (CUAV),

10–11; limitations in analysis, 272–273; organizing, 109, 302. *See also* movements for social change; oppression

anti-violence movement. *See* movements for social change

Anzaldúa, Gloria E., xxxi

Asian and Pacific Islander Americans: anti–intimate partner violence activism, 238–239; communities, intimate partner violence in, 238–239, 241–249; and community accountability, 248–255; leadership building, 237; survivors, 252–253. *See also* Transforming Silence Into Action

Asian Women's Shelter (AWS), 238, 260, 262

Audre Lorde Project: National Day of Truth-Telling, 80–81; "Reclaiming Safety," 5–6, 7; Safe OUTside the System Collective (SOS), xxv–xxvi, xxx, 5–6, 227. *See also* movements for social change

bbbb

Bambara, Toni Cade: *The Salt Eaters,* xxxiv–xxxv

Bancroft, Lundy, 117, 121, 122–123

Bassichis, Morgan: Community United Against Violence (CUAV), xxxii

Bierra, Alisa: Communities Against Rape and Abuse (CARA) cofounder, xxii–xxiii

binary: anti-oppression analysis, limitations to, 143, 272; gender, xv, 49, 80, 262; survivor/batterer, 101, 143; "survivor or perpetrator?" dilemma, 242–245. *See also* capitalism; cisgender politics; gay politics; LGBT and gender nonconforming politics; oppression; queer politics; racism; sexism; trans/transgender politics; violence

bisexuality and politics: national gathering on community accountability, xxx–xxxii; "Safety Lab," 6, 18. *See also* Audre Lorde Project; Community United Against Violence (CUAV); LGBT and gender nonconforming politics; queer politics

Bitch, xxix

Black Panthers, xxxii

Brown, Elaine, xxxii

Burk, Connie, xxxiv. *See also* Accountable Communities; The Northwest Network

CCCC

capitalism: exploitation and gender binary roles, 226; gender binary systems, 126–127; gender violence as strategy of, xiv–xvii; as limiting and counter-revolutionary, 75–76; police replicating oppressive structures of, 224; replication of its oppressive structures in activist communities, 23n9; resistance to, 75–76; revolution, and backlash, 9. *See also* movements for social change; oppression

Challenging Male Supremacy Project (CMS): accountability circle: experience and process, 218–223; inception, 217–218, 225; male supremacy, addressing, 223–229; narrative, 219–223, 229–231; Somatics, 225–226; "Study-into-Action" group, 218,

225–231, 233–234. *See also* movements for social change; perpetrators, of violence

Chen, Ching-In: narrative, xix–xx

childcare, 133, 229, 273, 298

childhood abuse. *See* violence, childhood

Chrysalis Collective, The: Accountability Team, 191–201; community accountability process, xxxiv; gathering the team, 190–193; implementation, 195–201; inception of, 189; lessons learned, 202–204, 205n1; plan, 195–196; preparation and approach, 196–198; Survivor Support Team, 190–195, 198–200, 202–203; transformative justice: initiation of plan, 198–202; working with the Accountability Team, 191–194, 198–200, 202–203. *See also* movements for social change; perpetrators of violence

cisgender politics, xxii, 217; cisgender men: holding men accountable, 218, 223–229, 233; narrative, 219–223, 229–231; cisgender women, 87, 218; definitions, 218, 231n1; violence against women: second wave white feminism analysis of, xxvi–xxvii. *See also* activist communities; binary; Challenging Male Supremacy Project; feminisms; LGBT and gender nonconforming politics; male supremacy; queer politics; sexism; trans/transgender politics; violence, gender

class and class politics: ability to leave a dangerous situation, 124; class oppression, xxxi;

class and class politics *(continued):* criminalization, 7–8; disability, 133; gender oppression, 282–283; intimate personal violence, xxvii; poverty, as violence, 69; sex workers, 58, 60, 73–74. *See also* capitalism; classism; disability justice and politics; oppression; sex workers; violence

classism: activism against, xxxi; class, and ability to leave a dangerous situation, 124; court system, narrative, 164; heteropatriarchy, 281; intimate partner violence, 124; masculinities, 234; multiple oppressions, 7–8, 28–29, 71; organizing for justice, 145; relationships, xxvii. *See also* class and class politics; oppression

Colm, Timothy: narrative, 175–184. *See also* Philly's Pissed

Color of Violence: Violence Against Women of Color conference (INCITE!, 2000), xxiv

collusion. *See* activist communities; perpetrators, of violence

Combahee River Collective, xxxi

Communities Against Rape and Abuse (CARA): anti-violence initiatives, xxii–xxiii, xxv; Bierra, Alisa, cofounder, xxii–xxiii. *See also* movements for social change

community accountability: accountability circles, 191–201, 218–223, 229–231; Accountability Team, action (Chrysalis Collective), 191–201; in activist communities: intimate partner violence, 27–29; in Asian and Pacific Islander American communities, 238–239,

241–255; Challenging Male Supremacy Project, 218–223, 229–231; "Community Accountability Within People of Color Progressive Movements" (INCITE!), excerpt, 281–290; "Community Accountability Working Document" (INCITE!), xxiv–xxv; "Creating Community Solutions: A Pull-Out Guide," 51–55; Critical Resistance 10th anniversary, xxix–xxx; definitions, xxiii–xxiv, 248–249; early attempts, organizing, xxiv–xxvi; as fundamental to revolution, xvi; HIV/AIDS, 12; homophobia, 253–254; "Identifying and Unlearning Our Own Violence," 256–257; impact of oppression on, 249–250, 253–254; "INCITE! Community Accountability Fact Sheet," 291; intimate partner violence, xv–xvii, 108, 142–143, 254–256; national gathering on, xxx–xxxii; people of color, xxiv–xxv; perpetrators, failure to hold accountable, 27–28; in queer Asian and Pacific Islander American communities, 238–239, 241–249; restorative justice, xvi; Rock Dove Collective, 221; Story-Telling & Organizing Project (STOP), 209–212; survivor support, steps for, 51–55; Transforming Silence Into Action (TSIA), 248–256. *See also* accountability, personal; Accountable Communities-justice, transformative; movements for social change; The Northwest Network

community organizing. *See* movements for social change

Community United Against Violence (CUAV): Bassichis, Morgan, xxxii; in coalition with other groups, 17; funding, 15, 19; "gradients of agreement" decision-making tool, 13; members and membership, 17; organizational transformation of, xxxii, 6–7, 10, 12–13, 15–20; programmatic vision, 13–15; queer awareness raising, 9–10; "Reclaiming Safety," 5–7; resolutions/actions, 16–19; Safetyfest, 19; Safety Lab, 6, 18; Speakers Bureau, 10; stakeholders, identifying and communicating with, 15–16; state, the, critique of, 7–12; strategic planning, 12, 16, 23n10; TransAction, 10; transformative justice, 5–7; violence, alternatives to state approaches to, 9–10, 14–15, 17–18, 19–20, 22n7. *See also* bisexuality and politics; gay politics; gender nonconforming politics; lesbian politics; movements for social change; queer politics; trans/transgender politics

Compton's Cafeteria Riot, 9

Creative Interventions: anti-violence initiative and community accountability, xxv; community accountability, 209–212, 248–249; mission, 208; national anti-violence gathering, xxx. *See also* movements for social change; StoryTelling & Organizing Project

criminal justice system. *See* criminal legal system

criminal legal system: alternatives to, xvi–

xvii; immigrants, 54; reliance on, antiviolence movement and, xiii–xvi; state oppression, xiv–xvii, 7–12. *See also* movements for social change; police violence; prison industrial complex, and abolition

Critical Resistance: Beyond the Prison Industrial Complex, xxv, xxix: in coalition, 6–7; community accountability, 219; conferences, xiv, xxix–xxx, 72; "Gender Violence and the Prison Industrial Complex," 224; Harm Free Zone anti-violence project, xxv, 81, 88; impact on anti-violence movement, xiii–xiv; prison industrial complex abolition, xiv, 6; state violence, 232n4. *See also* movements for social change; prison industrial complex, and abolition

Cruz, Meiver De la: MataHari, xxxiii

dddd

Day to End Violence Against Sex Workers, 66

Desiree Alliance, 74

disability justice and politics: abandonment of by activist communities, 116, 118–119, 123–124, 132–133; abuse, what qualifies as, 117, 127–129, 130; advocacy organizations, critiques of: 126–127 (West Virginia Coalition Against Domestic Violence), 120 (Wisconsin Coalition Against Domestic Violence), 120 (Wisconsin Council on Developmental Disabilities); Americans with Disabilities Act (ADA), 119–120; care and accessibility, lack of, 117–120, 121–133; caregivers, violence by, 115, 117–130, 134;

disability justice and politics *(continued):*

> class politics, 120, 124, 127; critique and solutions, 119, 124, 127–134; Domestic Violence and Developmental Disabilities Committee, 120; intimate partner violence, 119–120, 122–134; narrative, 115–122, 126; "Power and Control Wheel," 120; survivors, 132; violence against minimized, 125. *See also* ableism; movements for social change; oppression; survivors

Duke University rape case, 79–81, 89n2; UBUNTU, xxxiii, 79, 88

Dulani, Jai: narrative, xxi

Durham Harm Free Zone, xxv, 81, 88

eeee

Ella Baker Center for Human Rights, 10, 88

ffff

Factora-Burcher, Lisa, 88

feminisms: cisgender violence against women, analysis, xxvi–xxvii; community accountability, xxx; feminists of color: analyses of violence, xxvi; Indigenous: critiques of the settler-state, xvi–xvii; intimate violence within activist communities, xxvi–xxvii; second wave white, xxvi–xxvii, 75; sex work, 60; Smith, Andrea, xxiv; women of color, xxvii–xxviii, 75; Yee, Jessica, xxxii, 63, 66–67, 69–70, 72–73, 75–76. *See also* Kitchen Table: Women of Color Press; movements for social change; oppression

Feminist Review, xxix

Fenner, Bran, xxxiii; narrative, 155–161

Few, Robyn, 71

Forum Against Police Violence and Impunity, 72

Frederici, Silvia: *Caliban and the Witch,* 227

Friends Are Reaching Out (F.A.R. OUT), xxv, 275–278, 279n2. *See also* The Northwest Network

gggg

gay politics: capitalism, 126–127, 226; concept of, xv; deconstructing, 240; gender binary system, 262n3; narrative: N., 163–166; national gathering on community accountability, xxx–xxxii; rights and trans/transgender rights, 75; system of oppression, 281; violence against trans sex workers, 58. *See also* Audre Lorde Project; Community United Against Violence (CUAV); LGBT and gender nonconforming politics; movements for social change; oppression; queer politics

gender nonconforming politics: Duke University, multiple sex worker rapes at, 79–80; national gathering on community accountability, xxx–xxxii; police violence against, 10. *See also* Audre Lorde Project; Community United Against Violence (CUAV); LGBT and gender nonconforming politics; movements for social change; queer politics

generationFIVE: anti-violence initiative, xxvi,

217, 219, 228, 231n3; preventing and healing from childhood sexual abuse, 204,
217, 228; Staci Haines, cofounder, 226;
transformative justice, xxiii, 6; Transformative Justice Collaborative, 225. *See also*
movements for social change; violence,
childhood

Gomez, Carol, xxxiii. *See also* MataHari: Eye
of the Day

Griffin, Susan, 122

Gumbs, Alexis Pauline, xxxiii, 79; interview,
81–88. *See also* UBUNTU

hhhh

Haines, Staci, 226

harassment by police. *See* police harassment

harassment, sexual: minimization, 36–38;
narrative, 33–38. *See also* violence, intimate partner; violence, sexual

Harm Free Zone, xxv, 81, 88

hate crimes bill, federal, 5, 21n1

heteropatriarchy. *See under* oppression

heterosexism. *See under* oppression

heterosexuality and politics, 106, 109, 118,
244, 267; compulsive, 139, 176, 281;
oppression, xxxi. *See also* binary; cisgender politics; LGBT and gender nonconforming politics; male supremacy;
oppression; queer politics; violence

HIV/AIDS, 12, 65, 67–68, 130

homophobia. *See under* oppression

Huang, Vanessa, xxxiii; poem, 153

iiii

immigration and immigrant politics: justice
activism, xxxiii, 27; San Francisco Immigrant Rights Coalition, 17; sexual assault,
undocumented immigrants and, 30–33;
state oppression, 7–12, 86–87; Sun-hi,
38–41; vulnerability within legal system,
30–33, 39–41, 43–44, 54, 208, 249–250. *See
also* MataHari: Eye of the Day; narratives;
Transforming Silence Into Action (TSIA)

INCITE! Women of Color Against Violence: in coalition, 227; "Community
Accountability Within People of Color
Progressive Movements:" 285–288
(counter-organizing), 281–285 (gender
oppression), 288–290 (survivor strategies); "Community Accountability
Working Document," xxiv–xxv; formation
of, xxiv; gender violence and systems of
oppression, xiv–xv; "Gender Violence
and the Prison Industrial Complex," 224;
"INCITE! Community Accountability
Fact Sheet," 291; revolution, xiv–xv; Smith,
Andrea, cofounder, xxiv; transformative
justice, activism, 6–7; zine, "The Revolution Starts at Home," xxvi, xxviii, xxix–xxx.
See also feminisms; movements for social
change; people of color and politics

Indigenous people: and restorative justice,
69–70; racism, 66–67; sex work, 58–60.
See also feminisms; movements for
social change; oppression; settler
colonialism *under* the state

internalized oppression. *See* oppression, internalized

internalized supremacy. *See* binary; cisgender politics; Challenging Male Supremacy Project; male supremacy; oppression; white supremacy

intimate partner violence (IPV). *See* violence, intimate partner

jjjj

justice, restorative: communities of accountability, xvi; critique, xv–xvii, xxiii–xxiv; definition and process, xv–xvi, xxiii–xxiv; Indigenous forms of, 69–70; sexual violence, xv–xvi; victim-blaming, xvi; women of color, violence against, xxiv. *See also* justice, transformative; movements for social change

justice, transformative: Community United Against Violence (CUAV), 5–7; definition, xxiii; and male supremacy, 223–228; "Toward Transformative Justice," 231n3; Transformative Justice Collaborative, 225; women of color: and intimate partner violence, failure of, xxiv. *See also* community accountability; justice, restorative; *see also under* Chrysalis Collective

kkkk

King, Jr., Martin Luther: "Loving Your Enemies," 20

Kitchen Table: Women of Color Press, xxxi.

See also feminisms; movements for social change; people of color and politics

llll

Lara, Ana-Maurine, xxxiii, 141–148. *See also* rights and responsibilities *under* survivors

legislation: Americans with Disabilities Act (ADA), 120; hate crimes bill, federal, 5, 21n1; Proposition K (San Francisco), 71; Violence Against Women Act, xiii

lesbian politics: national gathering on community accountability, xxx–xxxii; rape, vulnerability to as undocumented immigrant, narrative, 30–33; rights, and trans/transgender and gay rights, 75; "Safety Lab," 6, 18. *See also* Audre Lorde Project; Community United Against Violence (CUAV); LGBT and gender nonconforming politics

LGBT and gender nonconforming politics: in Asian and Pacific Islander American communities, 238–239, 241–249; community accountability, 111–113, 143–144, 164–165; Community United Against Violence (CUAV), community activism and, 17–19; Friends Are Reaching Out (F.A.R. OUT), activism, x; homophobia, 28, 54, 106, 239, 253–254, 281; intimate partner violence, xxvii, 106–110, 267–269; marginalized identities, 7–8, 108–110, 249–251, 267–269; national agenda: complicity and co-option with state violence,

7–8; and neoliberalism, 11–12; Relationship Skills Class, 276–279; sex workers, 58–59, 70–71; "Stonewalled: Police Abuse and Misconduct...," 21n3–22n3; UBUNTU, activism, 79–80, 82–83; violence against, 5–11. *See also* Audre Lorde Project; bisexuality and politics; disability justice and politics; gay politics; gender nonconforming politics; lesbian politics; movements for social change; narratives; queer politics; Transforming Silence Into Action (TSIA); trans/transgender politics

Liberation Tigers of Tamil Eelam, xxxii

Lorde, Audre: "A Litany for Survival," 80

mmmm

Major, Miss: interview, 60–62, 64–65, 67–68, 70–71, 73–74; TGI Justice Project founder, xxxii

male supremacy: addressing, in activist communities, 223–229; challenging, 226–228; classism, 164; heteropatriarchy, xv, 14, 224; male privilege, 109–110, 203, 213, 239–240; perpetrators of violence, 223–224. *See also* feminisms; oppression; sexism; violence

Masaki, Beckie, 260

MataHari: Eye of the Day: "Creating Community Solutions: A Pull-Out Guide," 51–55; Cruz, Meiver De la, xxxiii; Gomez, Carol, xxxiii; immigrant harassment/abuse case: the legal system, 39–41, 43–44; immigrant (Sun-hi), narrative,

38–41; and immigration justice activism, xxxiii, 27; intimate partner violence: in activist communities, 27–29, 48–49; oppression and activists of color, 28–29; sexual assault, vulnerable populations: undocumented immigrant, narrative, 30–33; sexual harassment, narrative, 33–38; simultaneous oppressions, 28–30; Solidarity Team: objectives, organizing, structure, 42–48, 51–52; as strategy, 41–48. *See also* immigration and immigrant politics; movements for social change; oppression; racism; sexism

Matthew Shepard and James Byrd, Jr. Hate Crimes Prevention Act, 5, 21n1

Mattison, Jason, 5, 6

mehrotra, gita, xxxiv. *See also* Transforming Silence Into Action (TSIA)

Mercado, Jorge Steven Lopez, 5, 6

militarization, xiii–xiv, 7–11, 19–20, 72–73

Milk, Harvey, 9

Montgomery Bus Boycott, 20

Moraga, Cherríe, xxxi; *This Bridge Called My Back: Writings by Radical Women of Color,* foreword, co-editor, xxix, xxxi

Morales, Iris, xxxii

movements for social change: organizations and projects: Accountability Team, 191–201; Asian Women's Shelter, 238, 260, 262; Audre Lorde Project, xxv, xxx, 5, 21, 227, 232; Challenging Male Supremacy Project (CMS), 217–225, 229–231; Chrysalis Collective, xxxiv, 189–190, 203–205;

movements for social change *(continued):*

Color of Violence: Violence Against
Women of Color conference (INCITE!,
2000), xxiv; Combahee River Collective,
xxxi; Communities Against Rape and
Abuse (CARA), xxii–xxiii, xxv; Critical
Resistance, xiv, xxv, xxix, 6–7, 72, 219, 224;
Day to End Violence Against Sex Work-
ers, 66; Desiree Alliance, 74; Durham
Harm Free Zone, xxv, 81, 88; Ella Baker
Center for Human Rights, 10, 88; Forum
Against Police Violence and Impunity, 72;
Friends Are Reaching OUT (F.A.R. OUT),
xxv, 275–278, 279n2; INCITE! Women of
Color Against Violence, xiv–xv, xxiv, xxvi,
xxviii, xxix–xxx, 6–7, 224, 227, 281–291;
National Coalition of Anti-Violence Pro-
grams, 10; National Day of Truth-Telling,
80, 86; Native Youth Sexual Health Net-
work, xxxii, 304; North Carolina Coalition
Against Sexual Assault, 86; People's
Justice Coalition, 232n4; Philly's Pissed/
Philly Stands Up, xxv–xxvi, xxxiii, 179–184;
Queers for Economic Justice (QEJ), 227,
232n6; Reclaiming Safety, 5–7; Relation-
ship Skills Class, 276–279; Revolution
Starts at Home collective, xiii–xvii, xxiv,
xxvii–xxxv; Rock Dove Collective, 219,
221, 227; Safe Outside the System (SOS)
collective, xxv–xxvi, xxx, 5–6, 227; Safety
Lab, 6, 18; Sex Work Outreach Project
of LA (SWOP-LA), 66, 71; Sista II Sista's
Liberated Ground project, xxv, xxxvi-n4;
Solidarity Teams, 41–49; Southerners
on New Ground (SONG), 87; Speaker's
Bureau, 10; SpiritHouse, 87; Stonewall
Rebellions, 9; StoryTelling & Organizing
Project (STOP), 17, 208–215, 229; Study-
Into-Action, 218, 225–234; Support New
York, 230, 231n4, 232; Survivor Support
Team, 190–196, 198–200; Sylvia Rivera
Law Project (SRLP), 21n3–22n3; TGI
Justice Project, xxxii; TransAction, 10;
Trans Health Conference, 175; Welfare
Warriors Project, 227, 232n6; and women
of color, xiii–xiv. *See also* accountability,
personal; activist communities; Audre
Lorde Project; Black Panthers; Chal-
lenging Male Supremacy Project (CMS);
Chrysalis Collective; community ac-
countability; Community United Against
Violence (CUAV); Creative Interventions;
disability justice and politics; generation-
FIVE; INCITE! Women of Color Against
Violence; justice, restorative; justice,
transformative; Kitchen Table: Women
of Color Press; MataHari: Eye of the Day;
narratives; The Northwest Network;
organizing documents; Poorani House;
sex workers; South End Press; strategies
and tools, anti-violence; Transforming
Silence Into Action (TSIA); UBUNTU;
Young Lords

Munson, Peggy, xxxiii; disability and intimate
partner violence, 119–120, 122–134; narrative, 115–122, 126

nnnn

N., xxxiii–xxxiv; intimate partner violence: and gender, 163–166

narratives: accountability circles, 219–223, 229–231; Chen, Ching-In, xix–xx; Chrysalis Collective, action, 189–203; Colm, Timothy, 175–184; Dulani, Jai, xxi; Fenner, Bran, 155–161; Mr. X, 219–223, 229–230; Munson, Peggy, 115–122, 126; N., 163–166; Perez-Darby, Shannon, 101–105, 111–113; Piepzna-Samarasinha, Leah Lakshmi, xxi–xxii; Sun-hi, 38–41; police harassment, xxi–xxii; sexual assault, undocumented immigrants, 30–32, 189–190; sexual harassment, immigrant, 33–38; StoryTelling & Organizing Project (STOP), action, 212–215; survivors, 102–106, 141–143, 155–157. *See also* movements for social change

National Coalition of Anti-Violence Programs, 10

Native Youth Sexual Health Network, xxxii, 304

North Carolina Coalition Against Sexual Assault, 86

Northwest Network, The: accountability skills, 107–108, 110–112; Accountable Communities framework, 273–278; anti-violence initiative, xxv, xxxiv, 22n7; Burk, Connie, xxxiv; community accountability, 107–108, 110–112, 265–273; critique, 265–273; Friends Are Reaching Out (F.A.R. OUT), xxv, 275–278, 279n2; intimate partner violence: narrative, 101–105; in queer and trans communities, 106–107, 108–110; Relationship Skills Class series, 276–279; survivors, 102, 266–267. *See also* movements for social change; Perez-Darby, Shannon

November, Juliet: interview, xxxii–xxxiii

oooo

oppression: in Asian and Pacific Islander American communities: and intimate partner violence, 247–248; classism, 7–8, 71; co-option, unintentional, 72–73; counter-organizing, 284–286; criminal legal system: anti-violence movement reliance on, xiii–xvi; gender violence as strategy of, xv–xvii; heteropatriarchy, xv–xvi, 226, 281–284; heterosexism, 9–10, 27, 29, 281; homophobia, 28, 54, 106, 239, 253–254, 281; and immigration, 28–30; impact on ability to respond, 28–29; oppressive structures replicated in helping organizations, 23n9; resistance, forms of, 144–145; simultaneous, 28–29; social services: as survival not solution, xiv; state responses to violence, xiv, 7; systems of, and gender binary system, 281; systems of, and gender violence, xiv–xv. *See also* anti-oppression; movements for social change

Orange County Rape Crisis Center, 86

organizing documents: "Community Accountability Within People of Color Progressive Movements" (INCITE!), organizing documents *(continued):* "Community Accountability Within People of Color Progressive Movements" (INCITE!) excerpts, 281–290; "Community Accountability Working Document" (INCITE!), xxiv–xxv; "Creating Community Solutions: A Pull-Out Guide," 51–55; "Gender Violence and the Prison Industrial Complex," 224; "Identifying and Unlearning Our Own Violence," 256–257; "INCITE! Community Accountability Fact Sheet," 291; "It's War in Here," 21–22n3; "Power and Control Wheel," 120; "Raising Our Voices," 260n1; "Stonewalled: Police Abuse and Misconduct...," 21n3; "Toward Transformative Justice," 231n3. *See also* movements for social change; strategies and tools, anti-violence

pppp

Passion, Mariko, xxxii–xxxiii; interview, 62–63, 65–66, 68–69, 71–72, 74–75
patriarchy. *See* oppression
people of color and politics: anti-violence organizations, xiv; Color of Violence: Violence Against Women of Color conference (INCITE!, 2000), xxiv; "Community Accountability Within People of Color Progressive Movements" (INCITE!), excerpt, 281–290; community responses to violence, xxiv–xxvii, xxx–xxxii, xxxv, 27–29, 109–110, 143–144; criminalization and militarization of, 9–12; criminal legal systems impact on, xii–xiv, 7–12, 139; Friends Are Reaching Out (F.A.R. OUT), 277; intimate partner violence, xxi–xxii, xxvi–xxvii, 5, 28–29; intimate partner violence and transformative justice, xxiv; justice in the Jim Crow South, xxxi; mainstream feminism, xxvi–xxvii, 75; male-dominated political organizations, xxxii; marginalized identities, 7–8, 109–110, 249–251, 267–269; movement gathering, xxx–xxxi; national gathering on community accountability, xxx–xxxii; oppression of activists, 28–29; restorative justice, xxiv–xxvi; second wave white feminism, xxvii–xxviii; sex workers, 58–59; state oppression, xiv, xxxi, 7–12, 86–87, 139–140; "Stonewalled: Police Abuse and Misconduct...," 21n3; survivors, 54; *This Bridge Called My Back,* xxix; trans/transgender: Chrysalis Collective, 190; violence against, xxiv, 5–7; violence against, strategies to intervene, xviv–xxv; violence against and community accountability, xxv; women: activists, and sexual violence, 27–29, 80. *See also* Chrysalis Collective; Community United Against Violence (CUAV); Friends Are Reaching Out (F.A.R. OUT); INCITE! Women of Color Against Violence; Kitchen Table: Women of Color Press; MataHari: Eye of the Day; movements for social change; UBUNTU

People's Justice Coalition, 232n4

Perez-Darby, Shannon, xxxiii; on intimate partner violence, 105–111; narrative, 101–105, 111–113

perpetrators, of violence: and activist communities: 115–116 (collusion with), 33–38 (harassment in, narrative), 28–29 (impact on), xxvii (prevalence of in); cisgender men, holding accountable, 218; community accountability, failure, 27–28; Duke University, multiple sex worker rapes at: community collusion with, 79–81; holding accountable, xxxiv; social collusion with, 115–116, 250–251, 282–288; "survivor/perpetrator dilemma," 241–246; victim-blaming, 251; within people of color movements: collusion with, xxv. *See also* Accountable Communities; activist communities; Challenging Male Supremacy Project (CMS); Chrysalis Collective; community accountability; survivors; "survivor/perpetrator dilemma" *under* binary; victim-blaming; violence

Persephone Press, xxxi

Philly's Pissed, xxv, xxxiii, 179–183

Philly Stands Up, xxv–xxvi, xxx, 5, 21, 227, 232. *See also* movements for social change

Piepzna-Samarasinha, Leah Lakshmi: interview, of Gumbs, Alexis Pauline, xxxiii; narrative, xxi–xxii; "when your parents made you," xxxiv, 169–172

police harassment: narrative, xxi–xxii; against sex workers, 58–60

police violence: against African American communities in the Jim Crow South, xxxi; Forum Against Police Violence and Impunity, 72; People's Justice Coalition, 232n4; against queer, LGBT and gender nonconforming people, 10–11, 21n3–22n3; riots, 9; against sex workers, 57–60, 64; "Stonewalled: Police Abuse and Misconduct...," 21n3; TransAction, 10. *See also* Audre Lorde Project; criminal legal system; prison industrial complex, and abolition; the state; violence

Poorani House, xxxii. *See also* movements for social change

prison industrial complex, and abolition, xiv, 6; "Gender Violence and the Prison Industrial Complex," 224; "Reclaiming Safety," 5–7; War on Drugs, impact, 11. *See also* criminal legal system; Critical Resistance: Beyond the Prison Industrial Complex; police violence

Proposition K (San Francisco), 71; racism and, 71–72

Pusey, Orchid, xxxiv. *See also* Transforming Silence Into Action (TSIA)

qqqq

queer politics: awareness raising, 9–10; Community United Against Violence (CUAV), 9–10; Duke University, multiple sex worker rapes at, 79–80; intimate partner violence, xxxiv, 27–28; N.'s narrative, queer politics *(continued):* N.'s narrative, 163–166; people of color: gathering in response to violence against, 5–6; and resistance, 139; Queers for Economic Justice (QEJ), 227, 232n6; "Reclaiming Safety," 5–7; relationships, narrative, 93–98; Safetyfest, 19; "Safety Lab," 6, 18; state violence, 21; survivors of intimate partner violence: marginalized identities, 109; violence against queer people, 5–6. *See also* Audre Lorde Project; bisexuality and politics; cisgender politics; Community United Against Violence (CUAV); heterosexuality and politics; lesbian politics; LGBT and gender nonconforming politics; movements for social change; oppression; trans/transgender politics; violence

Queers for Economic Justice (QEJ), 227, 232n6

rrrr

racial politics and justice: racialized masculinities, 225, 233–234; racial justice, struggle for, xxxi, 10, 12, 17, 190; racial violence, 66–67. *See also* movements for social change; oppression; racism; whiteness; white supremacy

racism: in the anti-violence movement, xiv; court system, narrative, 164; Duke University, multiple sex worker rapes at: racist backlash against, 79–81, 89n2; Indigenous women, 66–67; institutional, 39, 43, 55, 139; MataHari: Eye of the

Day, 27; Proposition K, 71–72; sexual violence, 28–29; sex workers, 73. *See also* MataHari: Eye of the Day; movements for social change; oppression; the state; violence; white supremacy

rape culture: in activist communities, 203; Communities Against Rape and Abuse (CARA), xxii–xxiii, xxv; Duke University, multiple sex worker rapes at, 79–81, 89n2; Orange County Rape Crisis Center, 86; sexism, xxvi–xxvii, 159–161, 201–204, 239–241; sex workers, 70; victim-blaming, xxxix; vulnerability to, undocumented immigrants, 30–33. *See also* male supremacy; sexism; violence

revolution: community accountability as fundamental to, xvi; dismantling of heteropatriarchy as fundamental to, xv–xvii; liberatory movements, and oppression of, 9–12. *See also* movements for social change; oppression

Revolution Starts at Home collective: anti-violence movement and the criminal legal system, xiii–xvii, xxiv–xxvi; book introduction, xxxii–xxxvi; community accountability, national gathering on, xxx–xxxii; gender violence, xiv–xv, xxiv; prison abolition, xiv; project collective, xxvii–xxx, xxxiv–xxxv; zine, xxvi, xxvii, xxix–xxx. *See also* movements for social change

Rock Dove Collective, 219, 221

Rukeyser, Muriel, xxvii

SSSS

settler-state. *See* settler colonialism *under*
the state

sexism: activist communities: 25–26 (dating
a "conscious" man within, narrative),
33–38 (harassment, narrative), 203, 213
(male entitlement in), 284–288 (tactics
of oppression within); challenging, 240;
class, 164; court system, narrative, 164;
Duke University, multiple sex worker
rapes at: sexist backlash against, 79–81,
89n2; as form of violence, 58–60;
heteropatriarchy, xv, 226, 281–284; male
privilege, 109–110, 239–240; MataHari:
Eye of the Day, 27; sexual violence:
simultaneous oppressions, 28–29. *See
also* activist communities; binary;
male supremacy; MataHari: Eye of the
Day; movements for social change;
oppression; violence

Sex Worker Outreach Project of LA (SWOP-
LA), 66, 71

sex workers: activism, xxxii–xxxiii; class
politics, 58, 60, 73–74; client violence,
emphasized over experiences of intimate
violence, 58; communities of support,
67, 73–74; criminalization, 57–60, 63–64,
70–73; Day to End Violence Against
Sex Workers, 66; decriminalization/
legalization, action, 70–72, 74; Duke
University, multiple sex worker rapes at,
79–81; Forum Against Police Violence
and Impunity, 72; Indigenous women,

58–60; legal and social barriers to
justice, 63; National Day of Truth-
Telling, 80–81; and police violence,
57–60, 64; prison industrial complex,
59–60; racism, 73; rape and sexual
assault, 70; rights and rights movements,
74–75; risks, on-the-job, compared with
other workers, 57–58; second wave white
feminism, 60; self-defense, 61–62, 65–66,
68–69; Sex Worker Outreach Project of
LA (SWOP-LA), 66, 71; stigmatization,
59–60, 71; stranger violence, 58;
survivors, 58–61, 65–66; and trans
women, 60–62; whorephobia, 89n2;
workers, recognition as, 57–58. *See also*
movements for social change; violence

Sista II Sista Liberated Ground, xxv, xxxvin4

Smith, Andrea: INCITE! Women of Color
Against Violence cofounder, xxiv

social services: as survival, not solution, xiv

Solidarity Teams, 41–48, 51–52

Somatics, 225–226

South End Press, xxix

Southerners on New Ground (SONG), 87

SpiritHouse, 87

the state: co-optation, 6–8, 10–12, 75–76;
gender violence as primary strategy
of, xv–xvii; hierarchies, replication
of in activist communities, 33–38;
Indigenous forms of justice, 69–70;
liberating movements, backlash,
9–12; as main perpetrator of violence,
217–218; oppression by, xiv–xvii, 7–12;

the state *(continued):* oppressive structures, replication of in nonprofit and
foundation structures, 23n9; settler
colonialism, xvii, 58–60, 69–70, 75–76;
systems of justice: failure to deal with
male violence, 224; as violent force in
people's lives, 9–12. *See also* criminal
legal system; movements for social
change; oppression; police violence;
prison industrial complex; violence
Stonewall Rebellions, 9
StoryTelling & Organizing Project (STOP):
community organizing, 209–212; mission
and process, 17, 208–212, 229; narrative,
212–215. *See also* Creative Interventions;
movements for social change
strategies and tools, anti-violence, 9–10, 12–20,
22n7; accountability initiatives: 218–223,
229, 231 (Challenging Male Supremacy,
narrative), 191–201 (Chrysalis Collective,
initiative), 6, 18 (Safety Lab), 41–52
(Solidarity Teams), 10 (Speakers Bureau),
190–195, 198–200, 202–203 (Survivor
Support Teams), 248–256 (Transforming
Silence into Action [TSIA]); anti-prison
industrial complex initiatives: 5–7
(Reclaiming Safety), 6, 18 (Safety Lab), 10
(TransAction); anti-violence initiatives
in intimate relationships: xxv, 275–278,
279n2 (Friends Are Reaching Out [F.A.R.
OUT]), 276–279 (Relationship Skills
Class), 225–226 (Somatics), 17, 208–215,
229 (StoryTelling and Organizing Project

[STOP]); disability rights critique and
solutions, 119, 124, 127–128, 129–131,
132–134. *See also* organizing documents;
movements for social change
Study-Into-Action, 218, 225–234
Support New York, 230, 231n4, 232
survivors: accountability, 157–161, 266–267,
288–290; agency, 101–102, 144–145; anti-
violence movement, leaders in, 14–15;
in Asian and Pacific Islander American
communities, 252–253; community,
impact on healing, 29–30; "Community
Accountability Within People of Color
Progressive Movements" (INCITE!),
excerpt, 288–290; complexity of, 101–102;
"Creating Community Solutions: A Pull-
Out Guide," 51–55; disability, 132; Duke
University, multiple sex worker rapes at:
support of survivors, 79–81; effects of
abuse, personal and community, 139–
140, 143–144, 145–148, 177–178; healing,
140, 179–184; narratives, 102–106, 141–143,
155–157; rights and responsibilities,
137–138; "Risk-Assessment Checklist," 55;
sex workers, 58–59, 60–63, 65–66, 79–81;
social and legal barriers to justice, 54–55;
social transformation, 85–86; support:
in activist communities, 182; "survivor/
perpetrator dilemma," 241–246; Survivor
Support Team, action, 190–196, 198–200;
UBUNTU, action, 83–85; vulnerability
factors, 53–54, 155–156, 177–178. *See also*
Accountable Communities; activist

communities; binary; community accountability; perpetrators, of violence; rape culture; victim-blaming; movements for social change; violence

Sylvia Rivera Law Project, 21–22n3

tttt

TGI (Transgender, Gender Variant and Intersex) Justice Project, xxxii

This Bridge Called My Back: Writings by Radical Women of Color, xxxi

Tochecha, 275–276

To Wong Foo, Thanks for Everything! Julie Newmar, 62

TransAction, 10

Transformative Justice Collaborative, 225

Transforming Silence Into Action (TSIA): community accountability, 248–256; "Identifying and Unlearning Our Own Violence," 256–257; inception and organizational goals, 237–239, 257–260; intimate partner violence in queer API relationships, 238–239, 241–249; "Raising Our Voices," 260n1; violence against women, 239–241. *See also* immigration and immigrant politics

trans/transgender politics: Chrysalis Collective, 190; gathering on community accountability, xxx–xxxii; gathering in response to violence, 5–6; intimate partner violence, xii, 106–107, 175–178, 182–184; leadership building, 237; narratives, 106–110; national

organizations holding perpetrators accountable, 218; police violence, 10; racism, 58; rights, and gay rights movement, 75; Safetyfest, 19; "Safety Lab," 6, 18; sex workers, violence against, 58; state violence, 21; "Stonewalled: Police Abuse and Misconduct…," 21n3; survivors of intimate partner violence: marginalized identities, 109–110; violence against, 10, 61. *See also* LGBT and gender nonconforming politics; movements for social change; queer politics

Trans Health Conference, 175

Tshuvah, 275–276

uuuu

UBUNTU: community, as resource, 81–87; Duke University rape case, xxxiii, 79–80, 88, 89n2; Durham Harm Free Zone project, xxv, 81, 88; intimate partner violence survivor support, 83–85; love letters to survivors, strategy, 88; National Day of Truth-Telling, 80–81; origin, structure and membership, 79–80, 86–88. *See also* Gumbs, Alexis Pauline; movements for social change

vvvv

victim-blaming: domestic violence movement, 101; Duke University, multiple sex worker rapes at, 79–81; perpetrators of violence, 251, 268; rape, xxix;

victim-blaming *(continued):* restorative justice, xvi; sexism, 282–284. See also binary; perpetrators, of violence; rape culture; violence

violence. *See* community accountability; movements for social change; oppression; police violence; violence, caregivers and; violence, childhood; violence, gender; violence, intimate partner; violence, male; violence, sexual; violence, state

violence, caregivers and. *See* ableism; disability justice and politics; violence, intimate partner

violence, childhood: abuse, xiii, 38, 171–172, 287, 291; protective services, xxiii; sexual violence, 155, 159, 220. *See also* generationFIVE

violence, community-based responses to. *See* community accountability

violence, gender: class politics, 282–283; colonialism, capitalism, white supremacy, strategy for, xxvi–xxvii; oppression, systems of, xiv–xv; in progressive movements, xv–xvi; strategy of oppression, xv–xvii; trans men/transgender men, 61. *See also* binary; cisgender politics; LGBT and gender nonconforming politics

violence, intimate partner: accountability: analysis of, 246–247; in activist communities, xx–xxi, 157–159, 267–268, 267–269; in Asian and Pacific Islander American communities, 238–239, 241–255; choice/agency, 144–145; classism,

124; class politics, xxvii, 124; community accountability, xv–xvii, 108, 142–143, 254–256; community organizing, impact, 28–29; determination of responsibility, 268–269; failure of restorative justice models, xv–xvi; feminist activism, xxx; gender-based analysis of, 239–240, 267–268; "Gender Violence and the Prison Industrial Complex," 224; homophobia, 106; interventions checklist, 51–55; in LGBT and gender nonconforming communities, xxvii, 106–110, 267–269; marginalized identities, 7–8, 108–110, 249–251, 267–269; "No Excuse for Domestic Violence," 62; people of color, xxi–xxii, xxiv, xxvi–xxvii, 28–29; perpetrators, failure to hold accountable, 27–28; power, 105–109; prevalence, 27; in queer Asian and Pacific Islander American communities, 238–239, 241–249; queer relationships, 27–28; rape culture and sexism, 201–204, 239–241; as replicated state violence, xiii–xv; risk-assessment checklist, 55; against trans/transgender people, 175–178, 182–184; trans/transgender survivors, 106–107; West Virginia Coalition Against Domestic Violence, 126–127; Wisconsin Coalition Against Domestic Violence, 120; zine on, in activist communities, xxvi, xxvii, xxix–xxx. *See also* ableism; activist communities; Accountable Communities; community accountability; disability justice and politics; harassment, sexual; sex workers; survivors; trans/transgender politics; violence, male; violence, sexual; violence, state; *see also under* narratives

violence, male: heteropatriarchy, xv, 14, 224; male supremacy, 223–229; power relationships, 105–109; rape culture and sexism, xxvi–xxvii, 201–204, 239–241; replication of state logics, 228–229. *See also* activist communities; binary; male supremacy; violence, gender; violence, intimate partner; violence, sexual

violence, police. *See* police violence

violence, sexual: in activist communities, 27–28; activist groups, responses to, 32–33; Communities Against Rape and Abuse (CARA), xv, xxii–xxiii; North Carolina Coalition Against Sexual Assault, 86; Orange County Rape Crisis Center, 86; restorative justice, xv–xvi; sex work, 65, 70; survivors, 177–183; against undocumented immigrant workers, 30–33. *See also* Chrysalis Collective; Community United Against Violence (CUAV); Duke University rape case; harassment, sexual; Philly's Pissed; Philly Stands Up; survivors; violence, intimate partner; violence, male; violence, state

violence, state: against queer people of color, 21; replicated in interpersonal relationships, xiii–xv; state responses to violence, xiv, 7; "Stonewalled: Police

Abuse and Misconduct...," 21n3; structured on oppression, xvii; against trans/transgender people of color, 21. *See also* oppression; the state

Violence Against Women Act, xiii–xiv

Vries, Gina de, xxxiii; narrative, 93–98

WWWW

Wallerstein, Judith, 118

War on Drugs, 11

War on Terror, 11

Welfare Warriors Project, 227, 232n6

"when your parents made you," xxxiv, 169–172

White, Dan, 9

whiteness. *See* cisgender politics; feminisms; people of color and politics; racism; violence

White Night Riots, 9

white supremacy. *See* racial politics and justice; racism; the state; violence

whorephobia. *See* sex workers

YYYY

Young Lords, xxxii

Young Women's Empowerment Project, xxx

ZZZZ

zine. *See* activist communities; Revolution Starts at Home collective

AK Press is small, in terms of staff and resources, but we also manage to be one of the world's most productive anarchist publishing houses. We publish close to twenty books every year, and distribute thousands of other titles published by like-minded independent presses and projects from around the globe. We're entirely worker-run and democratically managed. We operate without a corporate structure—no boss, no managers, no bullshit.

The Friends of AK program is a way you can directly contribute to the continued existence of AK Press, and ensure that we're able to keep publishing books like this one! Friends pay $25 a month directly into our publishing account ($30 for Canada, $35 for international), and receive a copy of every book AK Press publishes for the duration of their membership! Friends also receive a discount on anything they order from our website or buy at a table: 50% on AK titles, and 20% on everything else. We have a Friends of AK ebook program as well: $15 a month gets you an electronic copy of every book we publish for the duration of your membership. You can even sponsor a very discounted membership for someone in prison.

Email friendsofak@akpress.org for more info, or visit the Friends of AK Press website: https://www.akpress.org/friends.html

There are always great book projects in the works—so sign up now to become a Friend of AK Press, and let the presses roll!